Prophets in the Qur'ān and the Bible

Prophets in the Qur'ān and the Bible

Edited by
Daniel S. Baeq
and Sam Kim

WIPF & STOCK · Eugene, Oregon

PROPHETS IN THE QUR'ĀN AND THE BIBLE

Copyright © 2022 Wipf and Stock Publishers. All rights reserved. Except for brief quotations in critical publications or reviews, no part of this book may be reproduced in any manner without prior written permission from the publisher. Write: Permissions, Wipf and Stock Publishers, 199 W. 8th Ave., Suite 3, Eugene, OR 97401.

Wipf & Stock
An Imprint of Wipf and Stock Publishers
199 W. 8th Ave., Suite 3
Eugene, OR 97401

www.wipfandstock.com

PAPERBACK ISBN: 978-1-6667-3261-0
HARDCOVER ISBN: 978-1-6667-2651-0
EBOOK ISBN: 978-1-6667-2652-7

05/20/22

All Scripture quotations, unless otherwise indicated, are taken from the Holy Bible, New International Version®, NIV®. Copyright ©1973, 1978, 1984, 2011 by Biblica, Inc.™ Used by permission of Zondervan. All rights reserved worldwide.

Contents

Contributors | vii
Preface | xi

1. Rasūlology: Qurʾānic Messengers and Biblical Prophets | 1
   MARK DURIE

2. Intertextuality of Adamic Narratives in
   the Qurʾān and the Bible | 28
   DANIEL SHINJONG BAEQ

3. Prophet Nuh: The Proclaimer of Islamic Holism | 56
   SAM KIM

4. Textual and Contextual Reading of Biblical
   Abraham and the Qurʾānic ʾIbrāhīm | 75
   IL JOO KONG

5. The Joseph Narrative in the Bible and Qurʾān | 92
   PETER G. RIDDELL

6. Variant Versions of the Moses Story in the Qurʾān | 114
   GORDON D. NICKEL

7. Dawud | 135
   MARK DURIE

8. The Prophet Ezekiel: Constancy and Patience | 146
   DAVID W. SHENK

9 A Comparative Study of Zakariya/Zachariah and Yahya/John
   the Baptist in the Islamic and the Biblical Narratives | 161
      WONJOO HWANG

10 Mary/Maryam as a Prophet in the Islamic
   and Christian Traditions | 181
      JACQUELINE HOOVER

Contributors

Daniel Shinjong Baeq is a PCA pastor and the founding director of Center for Ishmael Blessings (CIB) since 2012. He graduated Fuller Seminary (ThM), Chong-Shin Graduate School of Theology (MDiv), and Choong-Ang University (BA) and currently enrolled as PhD Candidate at Trinity Evangelical Divinity School (TEDS), Deerfield, Illinois. He taught cultural studies at Cambodian University for Specialties (2006–9), cultural anthropology at Trinity International University (2012–14), and church and culture at Denver Seminary (2021–present). He has worked in missiology related fields for about twenty-two years (1993–2015) in various contexts. In 2011, he established Paul G. Hiebert Global Center for Intercultural Studies at TEDS and served as director until being called to serve as a senior pastor at Bethel Korean Presbyterian Church, Ellicott City, Maryland in 2015. He published *Short-Term Mission Manual* (1998), *Joining God's Mission: A Perspective on Short-Term Missions* (2008), and twenty-eight articles in various journals and books in Korean and English.

Mark Durie is an Anglican pastor and an Adjunct Research Fellow at the Arthur Jeffery Centre for the Study of Islam, at Melbourne School of Theology. He has doctorates in linguistics and theology, and has published many articles and books on linguistics, Christian-Muslim relations, and religious freedom. He has held visiting appointments at the University of Leiden, MIT, UCLA, and Stanford. He was elected a Fellow of the Australian Academy of the Humanities in 1992. His most recent book is *The Qur'ān and Its Biblical Reflexes* (2018, Lexington Books).

Wonjoo Hwang is a professor of the Bible at Petrescue Bible Institute in North Africa since 2015. After having served in one Islamic country for ten years, he studied the biblical-theological foundation for ministries to Muslim nations. After the completion of his doctoral work, he returned to the region for equipping national leaders from North Africa and Middle East. He is the author of *Toward a Healthier Contextualization among Muslims: A Biblical Theological Evaluation of the Insider Movement and Its Lessons* (Pickwick, 2019). He is also a coeditor for *Journal of Arab and Islamic World Studies*, and a regular contributor to *Korea Missions Quarterly* and *Muslim-Christian Encounter*.

Jacqueline Hoover is a freelance lecturer in Islamic Studies. She is a member of the Sessional Faculty at Anabaptist Mennonite Theological Seminary in Elkhart, Indiana. She has also taught in Egypt, Lebanon, Nigeria, Sudan, Kenya, Tanzania, Germany, and the United Kingdom. She lived for almost twenty years in the Arab world. Originally from Switzerland, she is a minister in the Mennonite Church and currently lives in the United Kingdom.

Sam Kim is Assistant Professor of the E. Stanley Jones School of World Mission at Asbury Theological Seminary. She received a BA from Sungkyunkwan University (pharmacology), a Master's from Seoul Theological University, a ThM from Asian Center for Theological Studies (missiology), a PhD from Asbury Theological Seminary (intercultural studies), and studied cultural anthropology in Yarmuk University (MA pending). Before coming to Asbury Seminary, she served as a missionary in Jordan for fifteen years with her family. She was involved in sharing the gospel and discipling converts from Muslim background. She is an ordained pastor and is married to Jaehyung Yoon and has two sons (David and Daniel). Sam has written several books and articles, including *Identity Crisis: Standing Between Two Identities of Women Believers from Muslim Backgrounds in Jordan* (Wipf & Stock, 2015)

Contributors

I. J. Kong. Upon graduating with a PhD in linguistics from Omdurman Islamic University in Sudan, Dr. I. J. Kong taught Arabic language at the Hankuk University of Foreign Studies for nine years. He also taught (Arabic-Korean) Interpretation in the Graduate School of Interpretation and Translation (HUFS), as well as teaching Islamic studies at the graduate school of ACTS and the Juan International University, Korea. In 1998 he joined the Jordan Evangelical Theological Seminary as a professor. In 2002 he transferred to the University of Jordan. He was a coeditor of the journal Korean Studies in the Middle East and North Africa from 2005 to 2008. He established the Institute for Middle Eastern and African Studies in 2014 and worked as an editor of the *Journal of Arab and Islamic World Studies* since then. His published works in Korean and Arabic include twenty-six books on Islamic studies, Qur'ānic exegesis, Arabic linguistics, and the sounds of Korean language.

Gordon Nickel is a professor of Islamic Studies and an author on Islam, especially academic study of the Qur'ān and its commentaries. He began his study of Islam at the School of Oriental and African Studies (MA in South Asian religious studies, 1987) and completed his PhD in Qur'ānic studies under Dr. Andrew Rippin at the University of Calgary in 2004. He has taught on Islam and the Qur'ān at Associated Canadian Theological Schools, the University of Calgary, Trinity Evangelical Divinity School, and the University of British Columbia. For much of the last thirty-three years Gordon has worked as a missionary supported by the Mennonite Brethren churches, teaching at national church seminaries in South Asia. This year is completing a five-year assignment as director of the Centre for Islamic Studies at the South Asia Institute of Advanced Christian Studies in Bangalore. Gordon is the author of *Peaceable Witness among Muslims* (Herald, 1999); *Narratives of Tampering among the Earliest Commentaries on the Qur'ān* (Brill, 2011); and *The Gentle Answer to the Muslim Accusation of Biblical Falsification* (Bruton Gate, 2015). He is currently completing a book for Zondervan/HarperCollins titled *The Qur'ān with Christian Commentary*.

Peter G. Riddell took his PhD at the Australian National University, focusing on Islam in Southeast Asia. He studied Qur'ānic exegesis at the Sorbonne (Paris) and was post-doctoral fellow at the Hebrew

University of Jerusalem. He has taught at the Australian National University, the Institut Pertanian Bogor (Indonesia), the London School of Oriental and African Studies, and served as Professor of Islamic Studies at the London School of Theology, where from 1996 to 2007 he was the founding Director of the Centre for Islamic Studies and Muslim-Christian Relations. He is currently Vice Principal Academic at Melbourne School of Theology and is also a Professorial Research Associate in the Department of History, SOAS University of London. Peter has published widely on Southeast Asia, Islam and Christian-Muslim relations. His books include *Transferring a Tradition* (Berkeley, 1990); *Islam and the Malay-Indonesian World: Transmission and Responses* (London, 2001); *Islam in Context* (with Peter Cotterell, Grand Rapids, 2003); and *Christians and Muslims: pressures and potential in a post-9/11 world* (Leicester, 2004). His edited volumes include *Islam: Essays in Scripture, Thought and Society* (with Tony Street, Leiden, 1997); *Angels and Demons* (with Beverly Smith Riddell, Leicester, 2007); *Islam and Christianity on the Edge: Talking Points in Christian-Muslim Relations into the twenty-first Century* (with John Azumah, Melbourne, 2013); and *The Qur'ān in the Malay-Indonesian World: Context and Interpretation* (with Majid Daneshgar and Andrew Rippin, London, 2016).

David Shenk is an internationalist. He was born in Tanzania and has served in Somalia, Kenya, Lithuania, and the USA. He has authored or coauthored some twenty books related to faithful witness in a pluralist world. A special focus has been Christian Muslim peacemaking. Noteworthy is *A Muslim and a Christian in Dialogue* wherein David and a Muslim dialogue in regards to the core Muslim and Christian beliefs. David has taught and lectured in over a hundred countries on themes related to the religions and peacemaking. He and his wife Grace are blessed with four children and seven grandchildren.

Preface

THE GENESIS OF MY study into the Qur'ānic prophets goes back to when I was serving as a missionary in the Southeast Asia. As a missionary among a Muslim minority community in the Southeast Asia, I was intrigued to read and learn of the Qur'ānic prophets with the help of my language informant, who himself was equally fascinated with the prophets in the Holy Bible. In 2010, while I was conducting research on Islamic studies at TEDS, Deerfield, Illinois, God gave me an opportunity to initiate a project on the prophets that overlap from the Qur'ān and the Bible, beginning with Adam.

With my multiple responsibilities, however, I found the task to be overwhelming for one person, as I was also serving as a regional director and project manager of mission agency, teaching college courses, and working to establish the Paul G. Hiebert Global Center for Intercultural Studies at TEDS. Then in 2015, I was called to serve as a senior pastor at Bethel Korean Presbyterian Church, Ellicott City, Maryland, at which time all research came to a full stop.

Nearly a decade has passed since my first paper on Adam. Since then, on the academic front more evangelical Christian scholars have researched and published on the Qur'ānic prophets. I was especially excited to receive Dr. Durie's article on Rasūlology. His article will provide foundational information for scholars and practitioners to anchor their research. Missiologically, a greater number of Christian seminaries have initiated Islamic studies programs. Churches have also hosted seminars on Islam to deepen their understanding so as to find a way to win them over to Christ.

As for the part I was to play, God was faithful by providing the funding that was needed to start such a project. God also brought Dr. Sam Kim, a professor of Islamic studies at Ashbury Theological Seminary, to get this project to lift off. I firmly believe that God has brought all of scholars contributed significant chapters together for the Prophet Consultation according to his sovereign timing.

As Christians we know that all prophets testify about Jesus (Luke 24:27; John 5:39). And even though the Qur'ān itself also encourages Muslims to read and learn of the biblical stories (وَاذْكُرْ فِى الْكِتٰبِ Q19:51, 54, 56) to learn more about prophets, this has been suppressed. It is my hope that this compendium of the Prophet Consultation will provide tools for those who want to use prophets to engage the Muslims to read and study about the biblical narratives of prophets whom they know only through their books, traditions, and teachings. May the Holy Spirit use our works to open their eyes to see who Jesus really is!

In this compendium of the Prophet Consultation, I expect that readers will encounter various perspectives, thoughts, and opinions on the selected Qur'ānic prophets. Not all of us may be comfortable with every research presented and the attitudes toward how the Qur'ānic prophets should be approached. It is my prayer, however, that despite our differences, we will not lose the sight of our purpose for which we have come together. May God bless our works on the prophets of the Qur'ān help to illuminate the pathway to discover that Jesus is indeed the Messiah!

Daniel S. Baeq, General Editor
President of Bethel Theological Seminary
Senior Pastor of Bethel Korean Presbyterian Church

1

Rasūlology

Qur'ānic Messengers and Biblical Prophets[1]

Mark Durie

ONE OF THE MOST obvious *prima facie* points of similarity between the Qur'ān and the Bible is the existence in each scripture of a category of persons who mediate revelation from God: in biblical Hebrew these are *navī'*, "prophet" (Greek *prophetes*), and in Qur'ānic Arabic *rasūl*, "messenger."[2] Some Qur'ānic messengers are also referred to as *nabī*, "prophet" (pl. *nabīyuna*).

Similarities between these two categories of people are clear enough, and there is some overlap between the list of Qur'ānic messengers and figures identified in the Bible as prophets. However differences are also readily apparent: for example, some messengers of the Qur'ān, such as Hud, Salih, and Shu'ayb, are not biblical figures, and the Qur'ān describes some figures as messengers (or prophets) who have biblical counterparts,

---

1. This paper is a revision of chapter 5 of *The Qur'ān and Its Biblical Reflexes* by Mark Durie, used by permission.

2. Some authors translate *rasūl* as "apostle" (e.g., Penrice, *Dictionary and Glossary*, 57), because the original meaning of Greek *apostolos* is "someone sent, emissary." However this translation can be confusing, because a New Testament *apostolos* plays a very different role from the Qur'ānic *rasūl*.

e.g., Lut (Lot), Nuh (Noah), and Sulayman (Solomon) yet in the Bible these individuals are not called prophets, nor do they function as such.

Messengers loom large in the Qur'ān, playing a central role in its whole theological system. Indeed the category of messenger is of such rich importance to the Qur'ān that its study deserves its own title, and for this we prefer the term *Rasūlology*, by analogy with *Christology*. This is preferable to "prophetology"[3] since in the Qur'ān *nabī*, "prophet," is a subcategory of *rasūl*. Here we shall give a detailed account of the role and characteristics of Qur'ānic messengers and consider what affinity, if any, the Qur'ānic office of *rasūl* shows with biblical prophets. However, we will first consider the closely connected Qur'ānic term *nabī*, "prophet," arguing that *nabī* is a subcategory of *rasūl*.

Qur'ānic Prophets

Although the distinction between *rasūl*, "messenger," and *nabī*, "prophet,"[4] has been much discussed in Islamic tradition as well as in the secondary literature,[5] and although the two terms are used in somewhat different contexts in the Qur'ān, there seems nevertheless to be no denotative semantic difference between them, except that a *nabī* must always be human, while a *rasūl* can be an angel.[6] Jeffery concluded that Muhammad "made no special distinction between the two names *rasūl* and *nabī*"[7] and Wansbrough came to the same conclusion: "rigorous and consistent distinction between the designations *nabī* and *rasūl* is not justified by Qur'ānic usage."[8]

---

3. Griffith, "Sunna of Our Messengers," 215; Neuwirth, "Qur'ānic Studies and Philology," 195; Wansbrough, *Quranic Studies*, xxi.

4. *Nabī* is a borrowing from Jewish or Christian sources, probably via Syriac, see Jeffery, *Foreign Vocabulary of the Qur'ān*, 276.

5. See Jeffery, "Qur'an as Scripture," 115–16; Bijlefeld, *Prophet and More Than a Prophet*, 19, 27; Wansbrough, *Quranic Studies*, 54–55; Brinner, "Prophets and Prophecy"; Bobzin, "'Seal of the Prophets'"; Griffith, "'Sunna of our Messengers.'"

6. When used in reference to angels, the term *rasū l* appears to be used, not as a title for an office, but as a description of an action taken, i.e., an angel who happens to be delivering a message. For example, when Gabriel tells Maryam that he is "only a *rasūl* from your Lord" (Q19:19; see also Q81:19), he appears to be giving an account of what he is doing at that moment, not making a generic statement about his status or title.

7. Jeffery, *Qur'ān as Scripture*, 115.

8. Wansbrough, *Quranic Studies*, 54.

Nevertheless, the terminological difference does have some semantic content, which is however not denotative but indexical, pointing to a difference in context: past messengers are called *nabī* in stories connected to Israel (e.g., Q19:30–58). The only exception to this rule is the Qur'ānic Messenger[9] himself, who is often referred to as *an-nabī* after the migration from "Mecca" to "Medina"[10] (e.g., Q8:64; Q33:1; Q66:8): none of the other non-biblical figures identified as messengers are referred to as *nabī*. The term *nabī* becomes more frequent and salient in the so-called Medinan surahs. For example, all but one of the references to Nuh (biblical Noah) as a *nabī* occur after the *hijrah*, the migration from Meccan to Medina.[11]

The Qur'ān specifically associates the prophetic office, which it calls *an-nubuwat* 'the prophethood' (Q3:79; Q6:89) with the children of Israel, stating that establishing prophets and kings was a blessing unique to Israel (Q5:20), and it was the descendants of Ibrahim—the "sons of Israel"—who were favored with the institution of prophethood and a scripture (Q29:27; see also Q19:58; Q45:16; Q57:26). The Qur'ān also considers that the prophethood involved genealogical descent lines, saying, "some of them are descendants of others" (Q3:34).[12] Using the repeated formula, "the Book, the judgment and the prophethood," the Qur'ān states that the prophethood has been taken away from those who "disbelieve in it" (i.e., the Jews) and "entrusted it to a people who do not disbelieve in it" (Q6:89). These honors, it is implied, including the title *nabī*, were reassigned to the Messenger (Q3:79) and his followers, so he can be considered to be the first non-Israelite *nabī*, to whom genealogical prophethood has been transferred, even if it ended with him.[13]

---

9. Here, to refer to the principal human protagonist of the Qur'ān, traditionally identified as Muhammad, we shall for the most part simply call him "the Messenger" (*ar-rasūl*), as this is by far and away the most frequent way the Qur'ān refers to him.

10. Meccan and Medinan are placed in quotes because of concerns about the validity of the conventional Qur'ān origin story: see Durie, *Qur'ān and Its Biblical Reflexes*, 11–20. Further references to the Meccan/Medinan contrast are to be read as if in quotes.

11. See, e.g., Q4:163; Q33:7; Q57:26; the exception is Q19:58. See Neuwirth's discussion of the prophetic lineage of Nuh (Neuwirth, *Der Koran als Text der Spätantike*, 631–32).

12. This connected the qur'ānic conception of prophethood with the Arab idea that identity is "determined by one's genealogy" (Hoyland, *Arabia and the Arabs*, 116).

13. For an extended discussion of this notion of genealogical prophethood and its cessation with Muhammad, see Powers, *Muhammad Is Not the Father*.

Having made these observations, and noting the distinctives of the term *nabī*, nevertheless it remains true that the role of "prophets" in the Qur'ān is simply that of messengers with a few bells and whistles added, namely the association with Israel and a genealogical line. At this point it is necessary to acknowledge a prophetic bias in Western scholarship, which has preferred to speak of Muhammad as a prophet—or even *the* Prophet—rather than as a messenger, even though the title *rasūl* is mentioned much more frequently than *nabī*, and the earliest surahs only use the title *rasūl* (e.g., Q69:10; Q77:11; Q81:19; Q91:13). The use of *prophet* rather than *messenger* suggests a cultural bias which prefers to contemplate Islam through a biblical frame. In contrast, here, as in the Qur'ān, our focus is on the more prominent concept of messenger. The phrase "Allah and the *nabī*" (Q5:81) is only used once in the Qur'ān, in contrast to the expression "Allah and the/his *rasūl*," which appears almost one hundred times. Furthermore the Islamic *shahadah*, the confession of faith, declares that Muhammad is the *rasūl* of Allah, not his *nabī*.

The Western preference for *prophet* is despite the fact that *nabī* is the secondary category in the Qur'ān, more restricted in its application, which piggybacks off the primary category of *rasūl* and is but a subtopic of Rasūlology.

Messengers

In the Qur'ān messengers are men[14] (or angels) chosen and sent by Allah to humankind down through history. Messengers have a characteristic biography, which includes being sent to a particular people. Marshall has distilled a generic messenger biography from the Qur'ān's stories as follows:

> The messenger will typically criticize his people for not worshipping God alone, and perhaps for certain moral failings as well. However, he is rejected by most of his contemporaries, although he does have some obedient followers. The messenger also warns his people that, if they do not repent, they will suffer a great punishment from God. The story ends with a dramatic act of divine intervention: the unbelievers, as warned, are destroyed by God in a variety of ways. . . . The completeness of the

---

14. In contrast to biblical prophets, no female messengers are reported in the Qur'ān.

destruction of the unbelievers is often emphasized. The messenger and his followers are saved and vindicated.[15]

Stories which report the biographies of past messengers using this frame have come to be known as *punishment stories*,[16] although they might better be called *messenger stories*.

The central human protagonist of the Qur'ān is most frequently referred to as *ar-rasūl*, "the Messenger," and much of the discussion of messengers (and prophets) in the Qur'ān functions to present and validate the claims and identity of the Qur'ānic Messenger.

Guidance and Signs

Qur'ānic messengers are, above all, presented as instruments of guidance (*huda*), which is the essential core of the Qur'ān's message to humankind.[17] This is reflected, for example, in the first surah of the Qur'ān, *al-Fatihah*, "the opening." This is a simple prayer, which neatly frames the message of the Qur'ān as an invitation to Allah for the supplicant to be rightly guided:

> Guide us to the straight path: the path of those You have blessed, not of those on whom anger falls, nor of those who are astray. (Q1:6–7)

The Qur'ān sees human beings as created weak (Q4:28) and needing help to stay on *as-sirat al-mustaqim*, "the straight path." The special task of a messenger is to provide the needed guidance by calling people to the right path (Q3:101; Q7:43; Q11:112; Q16:125; Q23:73). This involves a call to repentance, a process by which a person *turns* off their wrong path, and *returns* (*raja'a*) onto the right path.

There are very many passages which advocate "returning" to Allah in response to a word brought by a messenger. For example in Q43:26–28, it is explained that a word from Allah was given to Ibrahim so that his descendants after him would hear it and thus be moved to return to Allah for themselves: "He made it a lasting word among his descendants,

---

15. Marshall, *God, Muhammad and the Unbelievers*, viii–ix.

16. See Watt and Bell, *Introduction to the Qur'ān*, 127–35 for a list of such stories in the Qur'ān, and Welch, "Formulaic Features of the Punishment Stories," for an exploration of some of their features.

17. Wansbrough, *Quranic Studies*, 101.

so that they might return." The concept of *'ayat*, "signs," is another key element in the message of the Qur'ān. The concept of a sign can be considered an extension of the metaphor of the path. Just as travelers look out for signs along their journey to guide them on their way, so the spiritual pilgrim must pay attention to Allah's signs if they wish to stay on the rightly guided path. It is the unique role of messengers to "bring signs" (Q2:129, 151; Q3:164; Q13:38; Q21:5; Q40:78) to the attention of humankind. However the characteristic response of disbelievers to hearing the signs recited by messengers is to reject them by "calling them a lie" (Q2:39; Q4:140; Q17:59, 98; Q18:56, 106; Q43:47).

Attributes of Messengers

We will now consider the attributes of messengers. Messengers are frequently called *nudhur*, "warners" (sg., *nadhir*) because they call people to Allah's path, and warn those who refuse to attend to the signs. Messengers are models of piety. They fear Allah (Q21:28) and are themselves rightly-guided on Allah's path (Q6:84, 87).[18] Other pious attributes of messengers are that they do not ask people to serve them, but only to serve Allah (Q3:79); they give their message without charge (Q6:90; Q3:161); and they intercede only for those of whom Allah approves (Q21:28).

Messengers are associated with a specific group of people, "their people." The Qur'ān makes clear that each messenger is called to go to this particular group (Q13:30; Q23:44). Messengers usually also come from the people they are sent to, speaking their language, just like the Qur'ānic Messenger (Q14:4). Even messengers whose people remain unnamed are nevertheless still linked to a group; for example, the Qur'ān refers to the "people of Nuh" (Q11:89), and the unnamed people Lut was sent to are called his brothers (Q50:13). There are also references to peoples whose messengers are implied to exist, but not identified, including ar-Rass, Tubba' the "companions of the grove," and the "companions of the town" (Q50:12-14; Q36:13).

Musa (Moses) is an interesting exception to the principle that a messenger is sent to his own people. Although Musa comes from the Israelites (Q5:20; Q61:5), the Qur'ān speaks of him as being sent to the people of Fir'awn (Pharaoh), i.e., to the Egyptians (Q7:103, see also 105). In all other respects a typical pattern of messengers is played out between

---

18. The doctrine of the moral infallibility of messengers is known as *'ismah*.

Musa and the people he is sent to, in which he brings a message to the Egyptians, calls their attention to Allah's signs, is rejected, and they are punished while he is rescued.

The named figures explicitly referred to as *rusul* (or *mursalin*) in the Qur'ān, and the peoples they are sent to, are set out in the following table. To this list could be added certain biblical figures, like Dawud (Q17:55), who are called *nabī* and can therefore be considered messengers as well.

Name of Messenger	Sent To Which People
Nuh	the people of Nuh (Q7:69; 9:70)
Lut	the people of Lut (Q26:162)
Isma'il (Q19:54)	Unnamed
Musa (Q7:104)	the people of Fir'awn (Q7:103, 105)
'Isa	the sons of Israel (Q61:6)
Shu'ayb	Madyan (Q7:85)
Salih	Thamud (Q7:73)
Hud	'Ad (Q7:65)
Ilyas (Q37:123)	Unnamed

Table 1.1. The Named Messengers of the Qur'ān

Although Ibrahim (Abraham) is not explicitly referred to as a messenger in the Qur'ān, he is treated like one. This is apparent from the inclusion of the "people of Ibrahim" in a list of peoples to whom *rusul* have been sent (Q9:70). Yunus (Jonah) could also be included in this list although he too is not explicitly referred to as a messenger: he was sent to a group called "the people of Yunus" (Q10:98), who, in what was an exception to the general pattern, heeded "the signs" (Q10:95), believed, and were saved.

Messenger Uniformitarianism

The Qur'ān uses many different means to assert continuity in the way Allah acts when he sends messengers. This is the doctrine of *Messenger Uniformitarianism*.[19] The principle of Uniformitarianism was introduced to geology by James Hutton in the eighteenth century, and promoted by Charles Lyell in the nineteenth. It postulates that past geological processes are the same as those acting in the present, so "the present is the key to the past."[20] In the Qur'ān, the principle of Messenger Uniformitarianism is used in a reverse way, deploying accounts of past messengers to make sense of and validate the present circumstances of the Qur'ānic Messenger. In the Qur'ān, the past is used as a key to unlock the present.

Messenger Uniformitarianism is one of the most persistent and salient themes of the Qur'ān.[21] It is essentially a claim about the unchanging nature of Allah's dealings with the world. Many aspects of the stories of past messengers are devoted to affirming this principle, giving numerous examples of its application.

The *Sunnah* of Allah

In the Qur'ān Allah is said to have a *sunnah*, "precedent," or "customary way" of acting,[22] which is particularly emphasized in relation to his messengers. The word *sunnah* is also used to refer to the ways or customs of former peoples who have passed away from the land (Q3:137; Q4:26; Q18:55).[23]

The *sunnah* of Allah is said to be fixed (Q33:38); there can be no change in it (Q33:62; Q35:43; Q48:23). The formula *wa-lan tajida*

---

19. See Durie, *Qur'ān and Its Biblical Reflexes*, 135–42.

20. Allaby, *Dictionary of Geology*, 611.

21. Many previous scholars have noted that qur'ānic accounts of earlier messengers reflect Muhammad's concerns, e.g., Horovitz, *Koranische Untersuchungen*, 18; Bell, *Commentary on the Qur'ān*, commentary on Q7:80; Paret, "Der Koran als Geschichtsquelle"; Watt, *Muhammad's Mecca*, 100; Tottoli, *Biblical Prophets in the Qur'ān*, 4–7. However, to see this simply as a biographical observation is to overlook the significance and explanatory power of the theological principle of Messenger Uniformitarianism. To my knowledge, only Marshall has attempted to provide a systematic account of this insight.

22. Al-Azmeh, *Emergence of Islam in Late Antiquity*, 320.

23. Gwynne, *Logic, Rhetoric, and Legal Reasoning*, 41–58; Morony, *Iraq After the Muslim Conquest*, 434; and Bravmann, *Spiritual Background of Early Islam*, 123.

li-sunnati l-lahi tabdilan/tahwilan, "you will find no change in the customary way of Allah" (Q17:77; Q33:62; Q35:43; Q48:23), is repeatedly used to assert this principle. The focus of these assertions is always on Allah's dealings with messengers, their communities (Q17:77; Q33:38, 62), and disbelievers (Q35:43; Q40:85; Q48:23). According to the doctrine of Messenger Uniformitarianism, Allah's procedure with messengers has always been the same in the past, so the Messenger's current experiences simply repeat those of earlier messengers, including some which might seem frustrating or difficult. References to past messengers and their mission are used to validate the Messenger and his mission, often converting apparent negatives into positives. For example, in an incident which is commented on in Q17:73–77, the Messenger was reportedly tempted to fabricate a revelation in order to win the friendship of disbelievers, but he stood firm. The Qur'ān then reports that this pattern of allowing messengers to be tempted and strengthening them to hold their ground was Allah's *sunnah* for messengers sent in the past, "and you will find no change in Our *sunnah*" (Q17:73–77; see also Q6:112, Q35:43). In this instance the potential shame of wavering while being tempted is turned into an authenticating mark, as the experience of temptation turns out to be a sign of the Messenger's authenticity, since Allah has always acted in this way with his messengers in the past. This illustrates the Qur'ān's use of the past as the key to the present.

It is standard rhetorical device in the Qur'ān that passages which first comment on rejection of the Messenger are followed up with an assertion that messengers have been rejected in the same way before, but they persevered and Allah helped them, for example:

> Indeed We know that what they say grieves you (i.e. the Messenger).... Surely messengers were rejected ("called liars") before you, yet they patiently endured being rejected, suffering harm until Our help came to them. (Q6:33–34; see also Q3:184; Q34:43–45; Q35:4)

The Messenger's experiences are validated by accounts of other messengers in various ways. One way is through a report about a specific messenger from the past. This happens in Q7, in the story of Musa and Fir'awn. Most of Q7 consists of a litany of stories about past messengers, in which they were all accused by rejectors of being liars: for example, Q7:72 (about 'Ad and Hud); Q7:92 (about Musa and Shu'ayb); Q7:101 (about the messengers to "the towns"); and Q7:177 (about parables, or stories of past messengers). In the story of Musa and Fir'awn it is related that Allah took retribution against those who had rejected the signs brought by Musa: "we drowned them in the sea, *because they called Our signs a lie* and did not heed them" (Q7:136). Then in the concluding section of the whole surah, the homiletic application is brought home to the present by applying it to the Messenger himself, who is described as "their companion" who speaks the truth, just like previous messengers, and that those who reject him and call the signs he brings lies will share the fate of previous rejectors, being led, oblivious, to their punishment, just as in all the stories from the past which the surah has rehearsed (Q7:182, 184).

The impact of the principle of Messenger Uniformitarianism on how the Qur'ān is to be read is far-reaching. It shapes the accounts of past messengers—including biblical reflexes—so that histories of past messengers are fashioned to serve as commentaries on the current experiences of the Messenger. In this way, the Messenger becomes the hero of every messenger story.

Manifestations of Messenger Uniformitarianism

There are many and diverse manifestations of Messenger Uniformitarianism, which link the speech, actions, circumstances, and characteristics of the Messenger with the example of past messengers. Here are some examples:

- The often-repeated phrase describing the Messenger's calling—that he was a "bringer of good news and a warner"—is also used of previous messengers (Q2:213; see also Q2:119; Q5:19). The Qur'ān also asserts that the Messenger, who is "not the first of the messengers" (Q46:9), is one of a long line of messengers: "He is a warner, of the warners of old." (Q53:56)

- Previous messengers are said to have faced the same kinds of opposition the Messenger is facing. People also mocked them— "messengers have been mocked before you" (Q13:32), rejected their signs, and called them liars (Q2:87; Q6:34; Q7:36, 64, 92, 101, 136; Q15:10–11; Q16:113; Q21:36, 41; Q22:42–44; Q23:24–26, 33, 38, 44; Q25:36; Q26:176, 189; Q35:4, 25; Q38:14; Q43:7; Q91:14). Previous messengers have also been challenged to bring on the threatened punishment (Q26:187; Q29:29). They too have been called possessed, magicians, bewitched, and forgers (Q5:110; Q7:35–37, 109;

Q11:35, 54; Q15:15; Q17:101; Q23:25; Q26:27, 153, 185; Q43:30; Q51:39, 52; Q54:9). Like the Messenger, previous messengers have also been dismissed as ordinary human beings (Q11:27; Q14:10; Q23:33–34, 38; Q25:20; Q26:186; see also Q21:7–8). When people mock the Messenger as being a mere human being who "eats food and walks about in the markets" (Q25:7–8; see also Q21:3; Q23:33), the Messenger is to reply that 'Isa was "only a messenger," who "ate food," just like the Messenger (Q5:75).[24] Moreover, Musa brought a Book and he was a human being too (Q6:91).

- Not only in the present, but also in the past people preferred the ways of their fathers (Q14:10; Q34:43; Q43:22–23), and they wished to expel messengers sent to them (Q14:13; Q26:167; see also Q2:191; Q9:13). The Messenger's personal experience of enmity from rejectors is nothing new, because Allah has "assigned to every prophet an enemy" (Q25:31). As in the present, wealthy people also rejected previous messengers in the past (Q34:34). In the past people have became divided, a party of them becoming rejectors (Q10:19; see also Q10:93; Q30:31–35). Previous messengers have also despaired until Allah's help came to them (Q2:214; Q12:110).

- In a case of linguistic uniformitarianism Qur'ān puts the same formulae into the mouths of past messengers as are being found in the Messenger's mouth, using Qur'ānic terminology. For example, when 'Isa refers to his message as "This is a straight path" (Q19:36), he is deploying the Messenger's own expression (Q43:61). The same charge "Guard yourselves against Allah" was delivered by messengers to previous generations (Q4:131) as the Messenger is delivering in the present (Q2:189). The phrase *innani /inni bariun mimma tushrikuna*, "surely I am free of what you associate," is attributed both to the Messenger (Q6:19) and Musa (Q6:78). Yet another example is that the Messenger is told to say *wama ana mina al-mushrikina*, "I am not one of the associators" (Q12:108; cf. the similar phrase of Q6:14), which also happens to be the exact words of Ibrahim (Q6:79; see also Q3:67, 95; Q16:123). In a summary of Allah's past covenant with the Jews, the Qur'ān gives a list of key ethical points using phrases taken directly from the Messenger's own preaching

---

24. This is one reason why the Qur'ān emphasizes the humanity of 'Isa: this is not merely an anti-Christian polemic, but a way to validate the Messenger by countering the charge that he is only human.

(Q2:83; Q5:12; see also Q4:36). From this we may conclude that the Qur'ān's understanding of the Mosaic covenant is that it was essentially the same as what was being sent down via the Messenger.

- It is explicitly asserted that messengers bring the same message: "nothing is said to you but what has already been said to messengers before you" (Q41:43; Q22:78): past messengers preached the same *din* 'commandment' or 'religion' (Q42:13; see also Q3:84; Q4:150), which is the "religion of Ibrahim" (Q2:130; Q4:125; Q16:121–23). This idea of the same message is further reinforced when the Qur'ān repeatedly states that the Messenger was only sent to confirm what was sent down by previous messengers (Q2:91, 97; Q3:3, 50; Q5:48; Q12:111; Q16:43–44; Q35:31), just as previous messengers had done for messengers who preceded them. For example 'Isa "confirmed" the *Tawrah* of Musa (Q5:46) just as Qur'ān confirms the book (s) sent by previous prophets (Q4:47).
- Previous messengers were rightly guided (Q6:84, 87) and the Messenger was rightly guided too (Q6:161).
- Like the Messenger, previous messengers have been given a scripture: "for every time there is a written decree" (Q13:38; see also Q5:44; Q6:154; Q42:15).
- As with past messengers, sent to their own peoples (Q14:4; Q16:36, 113; Q30:47), the Messenger has been sent to his own people (Q2:151; Q10:2; Q50:2), among whom he had been living (Q10:16), and speaking their own Arabic language clearly (Q16:103; Q44:58).
- Warnings are issued via the Messenger to the wealthy (e.g. Q68:14; Q89:17–20; Q92:11; Q100:8; Q104:2–3; Q111:2) and parallel warnings given by previous messengers and all "warners" have been rejected by rich people (Q17:16; see also Q15:4) in the past: "We never sent a warner to a town without its wealthy ones saying, 'Surely we disbelieve what you have been sent'" (Q34:34).
- The Messenger and his people are the inheritors of Allah's dispensation to Israel. In the past Allah entrusted "the Book, the judgment, and the prophetic office" to the people of Israel. However, "If these (people) disbelieve in it"—and the implication is that they have already disbelieved (Q6:91)—"We will entrust it to a people who do not disbelieve in it" (Q6:89; see also Q2:129). In this way the

dispensation of the past for Israel is perpetuated in the present for the Messenger and his followers.

- Just as 'Isa is reported to have brought new legislation to amend the *Tawrah* for the Jews (Q3:49–50), so too the Qur'ān declares that the Messenger's commands replace those of Musa and 'Isa for Jews and Christians (Q7:157; see also Q2:286).

- When people ask questions of the Messenger and they do not like his answer, he warns them that people in the past had asked such questions and became disbelievers as a result (Q5:101–2).

- Paralleling the Messenger's own experiences (Q3:176; Q5:41, 58; Q7:93; Q15:88; Q26:3) the previous messenger Nuh is told not to be upset by disbelievers: "do not be distressed by what they have done" (Q11:36; see also Q5:68).

- The Messenger is not to ask for any reward, just like previous messengers (compare Q25:57–58 concerning the Messenger with Q11:29 concerning Nuh).

- At some point, all previous messengers or prophets were led astray by ash-Shaytan (Q22:52–53) and the Qur'ān implies that the same kind of objection has been made against the Messenger.[25]

- 'Isa was strengthened by a *ruh* from Allah (Q2:87, 253; Q5:110); the Messenger and his community are also being strengthened by a *ruh* from Allah (Q16:102; Q58:22) in the present.

- Ibrahim is called a "beautiful example" for those with him (Q60:4, 6) and the Messenger is also called a "beautiful example" to the believers (Q33:21).

- Repeated references to migration of believers (e.g., Q16:41, 110; Q59:8) are paralleled by a passage in which the past messenger Lut (Q26:162) declares his readiness to migrate (Q29:26) for Allah's sake.

---

25. Islamic tradition supplies an explanation for this verse by connecting it to the story of the "Satanic verses," in which Muhammad was given false verses that he later repudiated (see Guillaume, *Life of Muhammad*, 166).

After the "Mecca-Medina" Transition

The doctrine of Messenger Uniformitarianism notwithstanding, there is in the Qur'ān a marked internal development in the understanding of the Messenger and of messengers in general. The watershed point of change is the transition from "Meccan" to "Medinan" surahs. Many earlier (Meccan) verses state that the Messenger is "only a warner" (Q7:184, 188) or "only a reminder" (Q88:21), who has no responsibility, power or guardianship (Q17:54; Q6:66) over people: "I am not a watcher over you" (Q6:104, 107). His job is not to force others to do what is right (Q72:21). However, and despite many previous statements that the *sunnah* of Allah with messengers never changes, after the Mecca-Medina transition, the Messenger takes on a distinctly new role of leadership and command. From this point on, believers are to "Obey Allah and the Messenger" (Q3:31–32), a characteristic Medinan formula. After the transition, it is said that the Messenger takes up the power of "judgment" over others (Q3:79; see also Q4:105), and a litmus test of true believers is that they are those who look to the Messenger for adjudication (*h-k-m*) of their disputes (Q3:23; Q4:59–61, 65; Q5:41–50; Q24:48).[26] There are also numerous repeated calls to "obey Allah and obey the Messenger" (Q4:13–14, 59, 69; Q8:20, 24, 27), for "whoever obeys the Messenger has obeyed Allah" (Q4:80; see also Q48:10). Zahniser reports that "the phrase 'God and his messenger' occurs at least eighty-five times, all but one (Q72:23) in Medinan passages" and the phrase is associated with the theme of obedience twenty-eight times.[27]

This shift in the role of the Messenger alters the way previous messengers are described: thus Q4:64 states the messengers were always sent to be obeyed, invoking the principle of Messenger Uniformitarianism. In line with these changes, certain expressions of Messenger Uniformitarianism are only introduced in the Medinan surahs, reflecting the changed understanding of messengers; as the Messenger's role changes, the role of past messengers are brought into line with the new conditions:

- Like the Messenger and many commands to obey him after the transition (e.g., Q3:32; Q26:108–79), past messengers also had to be obeyed: "We have not sent any messenger, but to be obeyed, by the

---

26. Sinai, "Unknown Known," 5.
27. Zahniser, "Messenger," 382.

will of Allah" (Q4:64; see also Q3:50 and Q43:63 referring to 'Isa; Q20:90 referring to Harun; and Q71:3 referring to Nuh).

- The Messenger now renders judgment (*hakama*: Q24:48, 51); past messengers have rendered judgment also (Q2:213; Q5:44).
- In the past the people became divided after true knowledge reached them (Q3:19) and these divisions led to fighting (Q2:253; see also Q3:13). Likewise in the present people are divided by the Messenger's preaching, which leads to transgression by some (Q5:68) and to fighting (Q2:244; Q3:167).
- Fighting in the "way of Allah," which the Messenger calls believers to, is no different from what took place with past messengers (Q48:22–23), specifically Musa and 'Isa (Q9:111). It is said that after the time of Musa people were "fighting in the way of Allah." This is described using the same phrases and concepts as used for the Messenger and his people, such as "fighting is prescribed for you" and "expelled from our homes and our children" (Q2:246; see also Q2:216; Q4:77; Q22:40). The Messenger is fighting (Q8:64–71) and previous messengers fought too (Q3:146; see also Q8:67). It is now the "customary way" of Allah that disbelievers will turn and flee in battle before believers (Q48:22–23). The killing of hypocrites is also Allah's "customary way" (Q33:60–62).
- Marks on the faces of believers from prostrating themselves[28] are the same for followers of the Messenger as they were for the followers of Musa and 'Isa (Q48:29).
- Followers of the Messenger are warned against attachments to disbelieving family members: "Neither your family ties nor your children will benefit you on the Day of Resurrection" (Q60:3; see also Q4:135). Likewise, in the accounts of past messengers believers are dissociated from unrighteous, disbelieving family members; for example, Ibrahim breaks with his idolatrous father (Q6:74, 79; Q19:42–46; Q60:4); Musa's adopted father, Fir'awn, becomes his enemy (Q26:10–22; Q28:8); Nuh parts ways with his son (Q11:40; 45–46) and he has an unbelieving wife (Q66:10); and Lut has an unbelieving wife (Q66:10; Q7:83) who was destroyed.

---

28. In Islam a prayer bump on the forehead is known as a *zabibah*, "raisin."

It is surely a great internal inconsistency in the Qur'ān that the supposedly unchanging way of Allah changes so dramatically after the Mecca-Medina shift. It is also very striking that when the Messenger's function shifts, the Qur'ān rescues the principle of Messenger Uniformitarianism by adapting the actions, speech, and roles of past messengers to the new "Medinan" realities. While the Qur'ān had been insisting that the past is the key to the present, in fact what this shift reveals is that the present is driving the narratives of the past, which are reshaped and repurposed as present realities demand.

This concludes our discussion of the Qur'ānic doctrine of Rasūlology, including an investigation of the internal development of the doctrine within the Qur'ān. We will now consider the biblical theology of prophets and prophecy, to facility our inquiry into the relationship between Qur'ānic Rasūlology and biblical prophetology.

Prophecy and Prophets in the Bible

We will now shift gear and lay out an outline of a biblical theology of prophecy and prophets,[29] to provide a basis for a comparative consideration of Qur'ānic Rasūlology. Prophecy and prophets are important in both the Hebrew Bible and the New Testament, but since the Qur'ān does not interact in any way with distinctive conceptions of prophecy from the apostolic writings, and references to prophecy and prophets in the Gospels do not add significantly to the understandings in the Hebrew Bible, our focus here will be on prophecy in the Hebrew Bible.

The expression "theology of *prophecy*" points to a distinctive of the Bible, namely that alongside the office of prophet, there is a speech act[30] of prophesying, a social process[31] referred to in Hebrew by the verb *nibbā'*,[32] "to prophesy," and by the noun *nəvū'āh* , "prophecy." In most cases an act of prophesying is not a communication of universal truth,

---

29. Prophecy, like monotheism, is a topic in biblical studies with a vast literature. It encompasses very diverse aspects, including psychological, anthropological, comparative, social, historical, literary, and theological dimensions. Some key studies have been Hölscher, *Die Propheten*; Mowinckel, *Psalmentstudien III*; Johnson, *Cultic Prophet in Ancient Israel*; Heschel, *Prophets*; and Wilson, *Prophecy and Society in Ancient Israel*.

30. Austin, *How to Do Things with Words*.

31. Overholt, *Channels of Prophecy*.

32. This is the Niph'al; the verb also appears in the Hithpaël with a similar meaning.

but is speech addressed to a specific intended audience, individual, or group, "to a particular time, place and circumstance."[33]

In the Bible an act of prophesying involves speaking the words from God, with the prophet acting as God's mouthpiece (Deut 18:18). This understanding is reflected in Exod 4:15–16, where Aaron is described as functioning as Moses' mouth: "he [Aaron] shall serve as a mouth for you, and you shall serve as God for him." Later Aaron is referred to as Moses' "prophet" (Exod 7:1).

It is clear from the Hebrew Bible that the phenomenon of prophecy was not restricted to the Israelite religion. Other deities beside God had their prophets, including the Canaanite deities Baal and Asherah (1 Kgs 18:19; Jer 23:13), and there are "false prophets" who had a recognized social function of prophesying in the name of God, even if their words were not reliably from God (Isa 44:25), and prophets could also be led astray by a "lying spirit" (1 Kgs 22:19–23). In the context of this breadth of references, it is hardly surprising that there is a possibility of error or deception, and prophecies are to be tested (Deut 13:1–5; 18:21–22).[34]

The communication of God's words via a prophecy is often described as a two-stage process: first there is reception of the word of God by the prophet, and then the speaking out of that word. The reception process itself is spoken of as "the word of the LORD came to" the prophet (e.g., 1 Sam 15:10). In Ezek 2–3, words are imparted to Ezekiel, accompanied by a graphic vision of the prophet eating a scroll with God's words inscribed upon them. These consumed words Ezekiel is to subsequently take to the nation of Israel, as if regurgitating them: "Mortal, all my words that I shall speak to you receive in your heart and hear with your ears; then go to the exiles, to your people, and speak to them" (Ezek 3:10–11).

The reception of the word of God can take place by a variety of means,[35] including verbal impressions, dreams (Num 12:6), and visions (Gen 15:1; Ezek 2:9–10), *rō'eh*, "seer," or *hōzeh*, "seer," being synonyms for *navi'*, "prophet" (1 Sam 9:9; Isa 29:10; Amos 7:12). The process of reception is sometimes described as a personal communication in which the prophet stands in God's presence (Jer 15:1; 23:22; Isa 6; Jer 23:18; Amos 3:7), in the divine council.[36] The reception is also sometimes described

---

33. Brueggemann, *Theology of the Old Testament*, 624; Blenkinsopp, *History of Prophecy in Israel*.

34. Paul and Sperling, "Prophets and Prophecy."

35. Lindblom, *Prophecy in Ancient Israel*.

36. Paul and Sperling, "Prophets and Prophecy," 567.

in terms of a visitation of a spirit or the Spirit (Num 11:25, 29; 1 Sam 10:10; Ezek 23:2) or the "hand" (i.e. power) of God (2 Kgs 3:15) upon the prophet, and an act of prophecy may be described as the Spirit of the LORD speaking through the prophet (2 Sam 23:2).

There can sometimes be a simultaneous reception by the prophet of words as they are being spoken out or sung (e.g., 2 Kgs 3:15–16). This can be described as God "putting" words in the mouth of the prophet during the process of utterance (e.g., Num 23:5, 12, 16; see Deut 18:18; Jer 1:9). The medium of communicating the word of God may be direct speech, or a written message dictated by a scribe (e.g., Jer 36:1–8), to be read later to or by the intended recipient. A prophecy may also be communicated with the aid of a symbolic prophetic act,[37] as when Ezekiel lies on his left side for 390 days, and on his right side for a further forty days, and cooks food using human excrement for fuel (Ezek 4; see further examples in Jer 28:10–14, Isa 20, and 2 Chr 18:10).

The form of language used in a prophetic act may be varied in style, encompassing plain speech, or poetry (e.g., 2 Sam 23:1–7), sometimes with musical accompaniment, prayer, parables, hymns, sermons, laments or direct speech. Nevertheless, in some instances the *manner* of an utterance is distinctive enough to identify it as prophecy, as for example when Saul, coming under the influence of the Spirit of God, spends some time prophesying, apparently involuntarily in company with a band of prophets (1 Sam 10:10; see also Num 11:25–26). The function of a prophetic message can be varied. There can be very specific words of guidance about the future (1 Kgs 11:29–39), or counsel towards a course of action (e.g., 2 Sam 24:11). Sometimes there is rebuke or warning (2 Sam 12:1ff; Ezek 3:17–21), including warnings about breaking covenant with God (Hos 8:1; Mal 2:10).

Biblical prophecy is not limited to those having a recognized social function as prophets. David, for example, is not described as a prophet in the biblical books that recount his life (1 and 2 Samuel, 1 Kings)—indeed he seeks out and consults others to prophesy for him when he needs guidance, particularly the court prophet Nathan (1 Chron 17:1) and his personal prophet Gad (2 Sam 24:11)—but there is also a report of a prophetic song, given through David by the Spirit of God (2 Sam 23:2–7). Other examples of a non-prophet prophesying is an incident when Saul prophesies in company with a band of prophets (1 Sam 10:11–12; see

---

37. Paul and Sperling, *Prophets and Prophecy*, 572–73.

also 1 Sam 19:20–24), and a time when the elders of Israel prophesy at their consecration, under the influence of the Spirit of the LORD, "but did not do so again" (Num 11:25). The phenomenon of non-prophets prophesying highlights the distinction between the office of prophet and the function of prophesying.

In the Hebrew Scriptures people styled *navî'* are those who habitually hear the word of the Lord and speak it out in an act of prophesying. They are recognized for this status, and exercise a socially defined function as a prophet,[38] to the extent that people might approach such a person with the expectation of receiving a word from God (2 Kgs 22:14–20; Jer 38:14–28; 1 Kgs 22:5–23).

Biblical prophecy can come, not only through men, but also through women (2 Kgs 22:14–20), several women being identified as prophetesses in the Hebrew Bible (including Miriam, Moses' sister, Deborah the judge and Huldah), and there is even an instance of a child prophesying (1 Sam 3). In the Bible only human beings prophesy: angels never do. Angels can act as messengers for God, but they do so in the normal way, as emissaries passing on a message they have received, not by something described as a prophetic process (e.g., Gen 16:7–12; Num 22:31–35; Judg 6:12).

In the evolution of the kingdoms of Israel and Judah, a pattern of three distinct but complementary anointed roles[39] is reported,[40] in which the king (with their officials), priests and prophets function together, and are repeatedly referred to as a collective (2 Kgs 23:2; Neh 9:32; Jer 2:26; 4:9; 13:13).[41] In the context of these distinct roles, although he or she may exercise political influence, the prophet is not a political office.

Another characteristic of certain biblical prophets is a calling by God.[42] The calling of prophets is a literary trope in the accounts of several prophets, including Moses (Exod 3:10), Elisha (1 Kgs 19:16–21), Jeremiah (Jer 1:5–10), Ezekiel (Ezek 2:1–10), Isaiah (Isa 6:1–8), and Amos (Amos 7:14–15). Although one title for biblical prophets is "man of God," there is no suggestion that prophets are morally perfect or even exemplary figures whose mode of life should be emulated. Prophets

---

38. Petersen, *Roles of Israel's Prophets*.

39. For examples of anointing of priests see Exod 30:30 and Lev 8:12; for kings see 1 Sam 10:1; 16:13; and for prophets see 1 Kgs 19:16 and 1 Chr 16:22.

40. Heschel, *Prophets*, 606–17.

41. Sometimes royal officials are added as a fourth office in this list (Jer 4:9).

42. Brueggemann, *Theology of the Old Testament*, 630; Paul and Sperling, *Prophets and Prophecy*, 574–75.

sometimes disobey God (e.g., Num 20:10–12; 1 Kgs 13:11–22), and some give false oracles, as we have seen. Furthermore, God does not always rescue his prophets (1 Kgs 13:24–26, 18:4). The Bible's focus in relation to a prophet's ministry is not on the special character or personal attributes of the person of the prophet, but on their role as mediators of specific acts of divine utterance.

In this overview of the nature and function of prophecy and prophets in the Bible, we can note a number of systemic theological connections which link prophecy and prophethood into other aspects of biblical theology. Two important theological associations are the role of the Spirit of God in prophecy, and the prophet's encounter with the presence of God in the process of apprehending prophetic utterance. Another theological interaction is the status of a prophet, shared with priests and kings, in an office which is set apart and *consecrated* by God, a status which can, like priests and kings, be marked by a physical anointing. These three offices work together to help sustain the Israelites as a covenant people, under God's guidance and care. Indeed the role of prophets as mediators of revelation is crucial in the establishment and maintaining of covenant relationship between God and his people.[43] This role is reflected in Amos 3:7: "Surely the sovereign LORD does nothing [i.e., in dealing with his covenantal people] without revealing his plan to his servants the prophets." The Mosaic covenant was also initially wholly mediated to Israel through Moses as God's prophet, and later prophets provided the means through which God would comment on the covenantal faithfulness of his people, or the lack of it (e.g., Jer 11:1–5), which acted as a spur or compass to redirect the nation, calling it back to the covenant's true north of faithfulness.

The relationship between biblical prophecy, divine speech, and Scripture is complex, and there is no one fixed pattern in which prophecy comes to be written down; indeed it need not be written down at all.[44]

---

43. Soloveitchik, *Lonely Man of Faith*, 40 maintains that the formation of covenant community between God and humanity is a precondition to genuine "prophecy awareness," the "face-to-face" colloquy between God and humanity, so covenant and prophecy are intimately connected.

44. Firestone, *Problematic of Prophecy*, 20 has sought to discern a common core of "prophecy" in Judaism, Christianity, and Islam. Some of his conclusions seem questionable, for example the idea that biblical prophecies are normally written down. This conflicts with many instances in the Hebrew Bible and New Testament where prophecies are reported to have taken place without being written down (e.g., Num 11:25; 1 Sam 10:8; Acts 21:9; 1 Cor 12:28, 14:29–33). Another questionable proposal is that

Biblical prophecy is not the same thing as scripture. Only some of those who are referred to by the title *navī'* have a book of scripture associated with them, and it is clear, from many examples, that only some prophetic acts ended up being recorded in scripture. Some books of the Hebrew Bible consist entirely of divine speech, after an introductory framing verse declaring that what follows is the word of God to a particular prophet, e.g., Joel, Zephaniah and Malachi. Other prophetic books are third- or first-person narratives, a kind of history of a particular prophet's activities, with oracles interspersed. The books of Haggai and Daniel are examples of narratives of this kind delivered in the third person, as if by someone other than the prophet, while Ezekiel is an example of first-person prophetic narrative, which includes some passages of divine speech, but also extensive reports by the prophet of his visions. The book of Jeremiah is mainly in the first person, but includes third-person passages, perhaps reflecting the role of a scribe in its creation (Jer 36:4). The book of Deuteronomy is presented as an extended address or sermon in the first person by Moses to the people of Israel as part of a covenant renewal ceremony, and which includes some reports of prophetic speech, but which mostly consists of extended retelling by Moses of the conditions of the covenant previously received by him from God. The books known as *Former Prophets* in the Hebrew Bible, including Samuel and Kings, include reports of prophecies by a variety of prophets, some of which purport to be verbatim God's words, but they are not focused on just one prophetic figure, and are not primarily comprised of prophetic oracles. There is no conception at all in the Hebrew Bible that a prophetic calling involves receipt of "scripture" from God, and where there is reference to writing, this is only as a means of conveying the word of God to others.

In the Hebrew Bible some prophets are associated with the performing of miraculous signs or an ability to intercede for others (e.g., Moses, Elijah and Elisha: e.g., Gen 20:7; 1 Kgs 13:4–6; 2 Kgs 5:8–14; Isa 38:8), but an ability to perform signs is by no means a necessary or universal characteristic of a prophet.

---

after canonization, new claims for prophecy are rejected as false. This overlooks a long Christian tradition of unenscriptured prophecy, which is not only referred to in the New Testament, (e.g., 1 Cor 12, 14), but also in early Apostolic writings, e.g., *Didache*'s instructions concerning itinerant prophets: see O'Loughlin, *Didache*, 168–69.

Comparison and Conclusion

We are now in a position to consider to what extent the Qurʾānic text builds upon a biblical theology of prophets and prophecy. The question we are considering is whether the Qurʾānic Theology of messengers shows evidence of theological inheritance from the Bible. What Qurʾānic Rasūlology has in common with biblical prophetology is a conception of a person who acts as an intermediary to convey messages from God to others. However, judging from a Late Sabaic royal monumental inscription, which uses the title *rsl* to refer to emissaries to Abraha, viceroy of Saba,[45] in a non-religious context, it seems that the idea of a *rasūl* as an emissary was already established in the cultural milieu at the time, quite apart from any biblical influence. Furthermore, in the Qurʾān both *rasūl* and *mursal* are used in non-religious contexts to refer to emissaries sent by a ruler (e.g., Q12:50; Q27:35), which implies that the basic concept of a *rasūl* may not have been religious when it was first put to use in the Qurʾān.

When we compare the prophetology of the Bible with the Rasūlology of the Qurʾān, there are notable differences, with non-transference of biblical theological content, and distinctive theological context which is unique to the Qurʾān. Under the heading of non-transference of systemic theological connections, we can note that in the Qurʾān there is no prophetic speech act—no act of *prophecy* as such—and no conception of prophetic speech as words being placed in the mouth of a messenger as Allah's mouthpiece. Indeed it seems significant that there is no verb in Qurʾānic Arabic with the meaning "to prophesy." Perhaps the most characteristic speech act performed by messengers is *talā*, "reciting" (Q2:129), i.e., the performance of the Qurʾānic recitation itself, "sent down" from Allah.[46] However, this act is not unique to messengers, since others who are not messengers also recite passages which they have received from a messenger (Q3:113; Q35:29), and Allah himself "recites" the "verses" (or "signs") to the Messenger, for him to pass on to others (Q2:252; Q3:58; Q45:6).[47] This is like a human act of sending a message by an emissary,

---

45. The Corpus of South Arabian Inscriptions, inscription CIH 541, dated 658 Him. http://dasi.cnr.it/. See also discussion in Smith, "Events in Arabia."

46. Wild, "We Have Sent," 141.

47. Elsewhere the Qurʾan speaks of the reception of the revelation as a "sending down" (*anzala*; Q17:105) of a verbal message in clear Arabic (Q26:195) to the heart (Q26:194) of the messenger, apparently involving an angelic intermediary, a *ruh* from Allah: see discussions of *ruh* and *wahy* in Durie, *Qurʾān and Its Biblical Reflexes*, 166–71, and Rezvan, "Qurʾān and Its World," 13–15.

who first hears the message, and then later passes it on. There is in the Qur'ān also no theology of an act of prophecy being a manifestation of a visitation or impartation of the Spirit of God.

Another difference is the awareness of the separation between heaven and earth which pervades the Qur'ān's descriptions of revelation, which is by a process of "sending down" (v. *anzala*, n. *tanzil*). In the biblical understanding, the prophet enters the divine council, coming into the presence of God, where a meeting of human and divine takes place, after which God speaks through the mouth of the prophet, as mediated divine speech. However in the Qur'ān a portion of a preexisting "scripture" (Q32:2) is "sent down" to the messenger, after which it can be recited by him repeatedly to others. Allah does not speak it through the mouth of a human being in an act of prophecy. In the Qur'ānic understanding, there is an inviolable separation, not a physical mediation, or, as Wild put it, "there is an above and a below."[48]

Also not transferred into the Qur'ānic context is a biblical understanding of a multiplicity of religious roles. In the Bible the social function of prophets exists alongside and in contrast to other kinds of leaders, notably priests and kings, who together play a religious function in maintaining the national covenant with God. In contrast Qur'ānic messengers are unique spiritual community leaders, especially after the transition to "Medina." One effect of the Qur'ān's concentration of spiritual functions onto one office is that a range of biblical leaders, who are not described prophets in the Bible, for example Aaron, David, and Solomon, are shoehorned into a messenger role in the Qur'ān, seemingly because there is no other divinely given office for them to be fitted into. There is only the office of *rasūl*.

Also untransferred is the covenantal framework in which biblical prophets function, including the idea that their role is to maintain an ongoing covenantal relationship between a people and God. The Qur'ānic messenger is sent as a unique solo figure to recite warnings from Allah to the *messenger's* (not Allah's) people. What could be considered a theological retention is the idea of the *rasūl* as a warner of future judgment, although in the Bible this is not so much a systemic theological function of the prophetic office as a characteristic of particular prophecies.

Alongside the non-transference of biblical prophetology we can identify numerous characteristics of Qur'ānic Rasūlology which are

---

48. Wild, "We Have Sent," 141.

distinctive in that they do not reflect the influence of a biblical frame.[49] These distinctives include the idea that messengers are models of piety, who Allah always rescues. Another distinctive is the idea that a messenger's role is to "recite the signs" to guide people along the "straight path." Also distinctive is the idea that Scripture—the Qur'ān—consists solely of prophetic recitation: in the Bible the relationship between scripture and prophecy is, as we have seen, far more complex. Also distinctive to the Qur'ān is virtually the whole stereotypical messenger biography: a man, sent to a people, warning of destruction, who is rejected, after which the people are destroyed and the messenger rescued. Is it possible to find some biblical accounts which resemble this pattern in part, such as the story of Jonah—yet even Jonah is an imperfect match because Nineveh repents and is not destroyed—but there is no such universal pattern for prophets in the Bible. Their stories are highly diverse, and at times there can be plurality of prophetic actors involved simultaneously. The connected concept of the unchanging *sunnah* of Allah in dealing with messengers and the people he sends them to, including the doctrine of Messenger Uniformitarianism, is unique to the Qur'ān, and without biblical precedent. To be sure, the Bible does emphasize the unchanging character of God (Ps 55:19; Mal 3:6), but there is no dogma that God always deals with peoples and prophets following an unwavering, unvarying pattern. Indeed, if anything the situation is quite the opposite: in the Bible God engages with prophets in very diverse ways. All that the biblical prophets have in common is the act of prophecy, not a stereotypical prophetic biography.

Down the centuries Christians have made the mistake of looking at the Qur'ān as some kind of Christian heresy, a deviation from biblical truth. The point of the reflections in this chapter is not to portray the Qur'ānic messenger as some kind of imperfect or misunderstood biblical prophet. That would be an imposition, arising from an irrelevant value judgment. The issue to hand is to ask whether the theological character of the biblical prophet, and a prophet's role within the *system* of biblical theology, is carried over into the Qur'ān, and if so, to what extent.

Messengers play a central role in the whole theological system of the Qur'ān. Because of this centrality, and because of a *prima facie* but

---

49. This observation is not intended to preclude the possibility that certain Qur'ānic distinctives, such as the idea that messengers are models of piety, could have been influenced by Christian or Jewish sources. Our point is just that these cannot be attributed to a biblical influence.

superficial similarity with the biblical prophets, we have given a detailed account of Rasūlology, and inquired into whether the theological attributes of Qur'ānic messengers show a pattern of inheritance from biblical Theology. After considering the two theological constructs of Qur'ānic Rasūlology and biblical prophetology in some detail, we have found striking differences, and little that could be considered inherited by the Qur'ān from the Bible. We conclude that the idea of a Qur'ānic messenger, whatever kernel it may owe to the Bible, was thoroughly repurposed by the Qur'ān, and in a way which meshes with the Qur'ān's own distinctive theology. The similarities are superficial but the differences run deep.

It should also be clear from all the above that a comparison of biblical figures, such as Moses or Jesus, with their Qur'ānic counterparts, needs to take into account the systematic differences between Qur'ānic Rasūlology and biblical prophetology, including the internal developments within the Qur'ān.

Bibliography

Al-Azmeh, Aziz. *The Emergence of Islam in Late Antiquity: Allah and His People.* Cambridge: Cambridge University Press, 2014.

Allaby, Michael. *A Dictionary of Geology and Earth Sciences.* Oxford: Oxford University Press, 2013.

Austin, John Langshaw. *How to Do Things with Words.* Cambridge, MA: Harvard University Press, 1962.

Bell, Richard. *A Commentary on the Qur'ān.* Edited by C. E. Bosworth and M. E. J. Richardson. Manchester: Manchester University Press, 1991.

Bijlefeld, Willem A. "A Prophet and More than a Prophet?" *The Muslim World* 59 (1969) 1–28.

Blenkinsopp, Joseph. *A History of Prophecy in Israel: From the Settlement in the Land to the Hellenistic Period.* 3rd ed. Louisville, KY: Westminster John Knox, 1999.

Bobzin, Hartmut "The 'Seal of the Prophets': Towards an Understanding of Muhammad's Prophethood." In *The Qur'ān in Context: Historical and Literary Investigations into the Qur'ānic Milieu,* edited by Angelika Neuwirth et al., 563–83. Leiden, Netherlands: Brill, 2011.

Bravmann, M. M. *The Spiritual Background of Early Islam.* Leiden: Brill, 1972.

Brinner, William M. "Prophets and Prophecy in the Islamic and Jewish Traditions." In *Studies in Islamic and Judaic Traditions II,* edited by William M. Brinner and Stephen D. Ricks, 63–82. Atlanta: Scholars, 1989.

Brueggemann, Walter. *Theology of the Old Testament: Testimony, Dispute and Advocacy.* Minneapolis, MN: Fortress, 1997.

Durie, Mark. *The Qur'ān and Its Biblical Reflexes: Investigations into the Genesis of a Religion.* Lanham, MD: Lexington, 2018.

Firestone, Reuven. "The Problematic of Prophecy: 2015 IQSA Presidential Address." *Journal of the International Qur'ānic Studies Association* 1 (2016) 11–22.

Griffith, Sidney H. "The 'Sunna of our Messengers': the Qur'ān's Paradigm for Messengers and Prophets; a Reading of Sūrat ash-Shuʿara." In *Qurʾānic Studies Today*, edited by Angelika Neuwirth and Michael A. Sells, 207-27. London: Routledge, 2016.

Guillaume, A. *The Life of Muhammad: A Translation of Ibn Ishaq's Sirat Rasūl Allah*. Karachi: Oxford University Press, 1955.

Gwynne, Rosalind Ward. *Logic, Rhetoric, and Legal Reasoning in the Qurʾān*. London: Routledge, 2004.

Heschel, Abraham Joshua. *The Prophets*. New York: Harper & Row, 1962.

Hölscher, Gustav. *Die Propheten*. Leipzig: Hinrichs, 1914.

Hopkins, Jasper. *Nicholas of Cusa's De Pace Fidei and Cribatio Alkorani*. 2nd rev. ed. Minneapolis, MN: Banning, 1994.

Horovitz, Josef. *Koranische Untersuchungen*. Berlin: Gruyter, 1926.

Hoyland, Robert G. *Arabia and the Arabs: From the Bronze Age to the Coming of Islam*. London: Routledge, 2001.

Jeffery, Arthur. *The Foreign Vocabulary of the Qurʾān*. Baroda: Oriental, 1938.

———. "The Qur'ān as Scripture." *The Muslim World* 40 (1950) 41-55, 106-34, 185-206, 257-75.

Johnson, Aubrey R. *The Cultic Prophet in Ancient Israel*. 2nd ed. Cardiff: University of Wales Press, 1962.

Lindblom, Johannes. *Prophecy in Ancient Israel*. Oxford: Blackwell, 1962.

Marshall, David. *God, Muhammad and the Unbelievers: A Qurʾānic Study*. London: Routledge, 2014.

Morony, Michael. *Iraq After the Muslim Conquest*. Princeton: Princeton University Press, 1984.

Mowinckel, S. *Psalmentstudien III: Kultprophetie und prophetische Psalmen*. Oslo: Dybwad, 1923.

Neuwirth, Angelika. *Der Koran als Text der Spätantike: ein Europäischer Zugang*. Berlin: Weltreligionen, 2013.

———. "Qur'ānic Studies and Philology: Qur'ānic Textual Politics of Staging, Penetrating, and Finally Eclipsing Biblical Tradition." In *Qurʾānic Studies Today*, edited by Angelika Neuwirth and Michael A. Sells, 178-206. London: Routledge, 2016.

O'Loughlin, Thomas. *The Didache: A Window on the Earliest Christians*. Grand Rapids: Baker, 2010.

Overholt, Thomas W. *Channels of Prophecy*. Eugene, OR: Wipf & Stock, 1989.

Paret, Rudi. "Der Koran als Geschichtsquelle." *Der Islam* 37 (1961) 24-42.

Paul, Shalom M., and S. David Sperling. "Prophets and Prophecy." In *Encyclopaedia Judaica*, edited by Fred Skolnik and Michael Berenbaum, 16:566-680. Detroit, MI: Macmillan, 2007.

Penrice, John. *A Dictionary and Glossary of the Ḳor-ân with Copious Grammatical References and Explanations of the Text*. London: King, 1878.

Petersen, David L. *The Roles of Israel's Prophets*. Sheffield: JSOT, 1981.

Powers, David S. *Muhammad Is Not the Father of Any of Your Men: The Making of the Last Prophet*. Philadelphia: University of Pennsylvania Press, 2009.

Reynolds, Gabriel Said. "Biblical Background." In *The Wiley Blackwell Companion to the Qurʾān*, edited by Andrew Rippin and Jawid Mojaddedi, 303-19. 2nd ed. Hoboken, NJ: Wiley, 2017.

Rezvan, E. A. "The Qurʾān and Its World: III. 'Echoings of Universal Harmonies' (Prophetic Revelation, Religious Inspiration, Occult Practice)." *Manuscripta Orientalia* 3.3 (1997) 11–21.
Sinai, Nicolai. "The Unknown Known: Some Groundwork for Interpreting the Medinan Qurʾān." *Mélanges de l'Université Saint-Joseph* 66 (2015–16) 47–96.
Smith, Sydney. "Events in Arabia in the 6th Century A.D." *Bulletin of the School of Oriental and African Studies* 16.3 (1954) 425–68.
Soloveitchik, Joseph B. *The Lonely Man of Faith*. New Milford, CT: Maggid, 2012.
Tottoli, Roberto. *Biblical Prophets in the Qurʾān and Muslim Literature*. Translated by Michael Robertson. London: Routledge, 2002.
Wansbrough, John. *Quranic Studies: Sources and Methods of Scriptural Interpretation*. Oxford: Oxford University Press, 1977.
Watt, W. Montgomery. *Muhammad's Mecca: History in the Qurʾān*. Edinburgh: Edinburgh University Press, 1988.
Watt, W. Montgomery, and Richard Bell. *Introduction to the Qurʾān*. Edinburgh: Edinburgh University Press, 1970.
Welch, Alford T. "Formulaic Features of the Punishment Stories." In *Literary Structures of Religious Meaning in the Qurʾān*, edited by Issa J. Boullata, 77–116. London: Routledge, 2000.
Wild, Stefan. "'We Have Sent Down to Thee the Book with the Truth . . . ': Spatial and Temporal Implications of the Qurʾānic Concepts of *nuzul, tanzil* and *'inzal*." In *The Qurʾān as Text*, edited by Stefan Wild, 137–53. Leiden, Netherlands: Brill, 1996.
Wilson, Robert R. *Prophecy and Society in Ancient Israel*. Philadelphia: Fortress, 1980.
Zahniser, A. H. Mathias. "Messenger." In *Encyclopaedia of the Qurʾān*, edited by Jane Dammen McAuliffe, 3:380–82. Leiden, Netherlands: Brill, 2003.

2

Intertextuality of Adamic Narratives in the Qur'ān and the Bible

Daniel Shinjong Baeq

Introduction

During my work in a South Asian country, I often heard my language informant refer to Adam as *nabī Adam* (prophet Adam). When I asked why Adam was a prophet, he could not offer me a clear answer but insisted that Adam was the first prophet. In Christian circles, Adam has never been considered as one and it puzzled me how the Muslims had come to a different conclusion. This led me to search the Qur'ān for clues about Adam's prophethood but was unsuccessful in finding any direct evidence.

Similar to my initial findings, a professor at the *Universita degli Studi di Napoli L'Orientale*, Roberto Tottoli, also attests that Adam "is not directly referred to as a prophet or a messenger (in the Qur'ān), nor does his name appear in those [Qur'ānic] verses that contain lists of the prophets."[1] However, in an important extra-Qur'ānic source, Adam was

1. Tottoli, *Biblical Prophets in the Qur'ān*, 18.

referred to as the first prophet. In the Hadīth of Ibn Hibbān (d. 965 CE), a conversation between Muhammad and Abū Dharr is recorded in reference to Adam's prophethood.

> I [Abū Dharr] said, "Apostle of God, who was the first of them [prophets]?" He said, "Adam." I said, "Apostle of God, was he a prophet sent as a messenger?" He said, "Yes, God created him with His hand, breathed into him from His spirit, and spoke with him face to face."[2]

If Hadīth records that Adam is a prophet,[3] it is most probably that clues about Adam's prophethood would be hidden in the Qur'ān and other books recognized by the Qur'ān.

The Legitimacy of the Books of Divine Revelations

The four books of revelation recognized by the Qur'ān are *Suhuf*, *Tawrāt*, *Zabūr*, and *Injīl*.[4] Because these revelations overlap with the biblical texts and the historically ongoing friction between Judaism, Christianity, and Islam, some antagonism towards these texts exist among the Muslim

---

2. Wheeler, "Arab Prophets of the Qur'ān," 25. Original text is taken from cAlī ibn Balaban al-Farsī, *Ihsān bi-tartīb Sahīh Ibn Hibbān* vol. 1, 207–8, hadāth 363.

3. A contradicting narrative is found in another version of Hadīth, collected by Sahih al-Bukhari. The narrative records that when all the people come and ask Adam for intercession on the Day of Resurrection, Adam will reply, "You'd better go to Noah as he was the *first Apostle* sent by Allah to the people of the Earth" (Vol. 9, Book 93, No. 507, italic is mine). Online Collections of Sunnah Hadīth. Bukhari, "Hadith of Sahih Bukhari."

4. The Arabic word *Suhuf* means "sheet, scroll, or book" that earlier prophets like Ibrahim (Abraham) received (Q87:18,19). *Suhufi* (pl.) are regarded as written forms of revelation like the other scriptures, which have since disappeared and are currently nonexistent. *Tawrāt* (the Law) is the revelation that Moses received from God for the Jewish people. *Zabūr* (the Psalms) is the revelation that David received and *Injīl* (the Gospel) is the revealed word of God by *Isa al-Masi* (Jesus the Messiah).

Beside the four scriptures, which are traditionally regarded as major revelations, Gordon Nickel provides additional classifications of other Arabic terms such as *al-alwāh* (tablets), *nuskha* (inscription), and *bayyināt* (the clear signs) that were mentioned in the Qur'ān. Nickel, *Narratives of Tampering*, 45–46.

scholars.[5] However, it is clear that the Qur'ān "confirms" them as revelations for the people.[6]

Concerning these four books of divine revelations, Qur'ān instructs Muslims "to study them as they should be studied" (Q2:121). A Muslim scholar, Badru Kateregga, also asserts that all Muslims need "to accept and believe in them completely."[7] The Qur'ān mentions the importance of these "earlier revelations" several times.[8]

Islamic scholars allege that the Jewish and the Christian scriptures have been corrupted (*tahrīf*, Q 2:73) and have, in reaction, formed the doctrine of corruption (*tabdīl*, Q 4:48; 5:16,45,52).[9] Abdullah Saeed, acknowledges, however, that conflicting verses in the Qur'ān which express reverence for these scriptures exists. He concludes that the accusation of the Islamic scholars on the Jewish and the Christian scriptures were aimed to point out "false interpretations" rather than major alterations made to them (Q15:9).[10] In conclusion, Saeed states, "Even if there is textual corruption associated with interpretation, the actual scriptures can still be relied upon and considered as 'Books of God.'"[11] Having briefly discussed the legitimacy of the four scriptures, they need to be studied

---

5. Nickel and Rippin says that there are "polemical passages" in the Qur'ān in which materials are antagonistic against the "Jews and Christians (*Nasārā*)." It is well argued that these verses need to be interpreted with careful investigations on the historical backgrounds. Nickel and Rippin, "Qur'ān," 144.

6. Nickel and Rippin, "Qur'ān," 144.

7. Kateregga and Shenk, *Muslim and a Christian in Dialogue*, 53; Shenk, *Journeys of the Muslim Nation*, 105.

8. Lumbard, "Prophets and Messengers of God," 108.

9. Nickel, *Narratives of Tampering*, 15–26.

10. In Ali's translation, this verse is read, "We have without doubt sent down the Message; and *We will assuredly guard it [from corruption]*." Ali, *Holy Qur'ān*. This verse is commonly used to confirm the fact that the Qur'ān has not corrupted nor altered. Asad, *Message of the Qur'ān*, 383. It is, therefore, illogical that the unchanging attribution of God allowed any corruption or alteration of the previous scriptures. The former advisor on Interfaith Affairs to King Abdulla II of Jordan, professor Joseph Lumbard, also takes the tamper of messages as an "err in their interpretation of the message." But he insists that the true meaning of revelation is not accessible until the end of time. Lumbard, "Prophets and Messengers of God," 102. It is, however, irrational that God bestowed incomprehensible revelation of which meaning is kept secret until the end of time.

11. Saeed, "Charge of Distortion." Nickel investigated this issue of the "Islamic accusation of scriptural falsification" in a single volume of his recent publication. For more academic and historic investigation on this subject refer to Nickel, *Narratives of Tampering*.

along with the Qur'ān for the "completion of belief."[12] In this sense, the biblical narrative of the Adam saga should be included for a complete understanding of what the Qur'ān attempts to teach.

Thesis and Research Questions

The thesis of this research is to compare the Qur'ānic narratives of Adam with the biblical narratives in order to uncover in what manner Adam is considered as a prophet in Islam and to create a bridge for an interfaith dialogue. In this paper, the qualifications for a prophet will be reviewed from both the Qur'ān and the Bible. Then the Adamic narratives from the Qur'ān and the book of Genesis will be examined for content analysis. Next, using the guidelines for a prophet, the narratives in the Qur'ān and the Bible will be examined to uncover how Adam satisfies the criteria for prophethood. Finally, the nature of Adam's prophecy will be discussed along with possible findings that may be used to encourage the Christian and Muslim interfaith dialogue. Thus this paper will be written in a manner that is not biased against Islam or side with Christian beliefs, but rather, unguarded observations will be made on the concerned texts.

The following questions will be addressed to guide the investigation. What is the definition and qualifications for a prophet (*rasūl* and *nabī*) in Islam and in Christianity? What accounts of Adam as the first prophet exist in the Qur'ān and the Bible? What qualities of Adam qualify him as a prophet? Finally, what is the nature of Adam's prophecy?

The Concept of Prophethood

The Qur'ān uses two different words, *nabī* (prophet) and *rasūl* (messenger or apostle),[13] to refer to prophets in Islam. The Qur'ān itself does not make a clear distinction between *rasūl* and *nabī* but uses them interchangeably.[14] Generally, however, they are distinguished into two classes of prophets "according to their missions."[15]

---

12. Kateregga and Shenk, *Muslim and a Christian in Dialogue*, 53.

13. In the Arabic Qur'ān, *Nabī* (including plural forms of *nabīyun* and *'anbiya'a*) is used seventy-five times, and *rasūl* (and a plural form *rasūl*) is used 333 times. Kassis, *Concordance of the Qur'ān*, 1023–29. Cf. Tottoli, *Biblical Prophets in the Qur'ān*, 73.

14. Esposito, *Oxford Dictionary of Islam*, 225, 262.

15. Glassé, *New Encyclopedia of Islam*, 417.

The term *nabī*[16] is a general term for prophets used to refer to all the prophets in the Qur'ān, including the prophet Muhammad (Q6:83–90).[17] *Rasūl*, which means a messenger[18] or an apostle,[19] however, is used to refer to only a select group of prophets. The messenger is the one who is sent with the Book[20] of divine message (Q3:3; 6:89) to "guide and reform humankind" whereas a prophet simply carries the message of God to the people.[21] Thus, it is generally accepted that a *rasūl* has greater responsibilities than a *nabī*.

Conditions of Prophethood in the Qur'ān

Adam is widely accepted as the first prophet among the modern Islamic scholars. In *Jesus: Prophet of Islam* (2002, 1977), Muhammad 'Ata Ur-Rahim states that the prophets began from Adam.[22] Similarly, Ziaul

---

16. The Arabic word *nabī* was derived from *naba'* which is translated "news, tiding, story, and tale." Kassis, *Concordance of the Qur'ān*, 806–7. Al-Ashqar explains the etymology of *nabī* as follows: "It is said that the word *nubuwwah* (prophethood) is derived from the word *nabwah*, which means a raised portion of land. The Arabs used the word *nabī* to refer to landmarks which could be used for navigation. This semantic denotation befits the word *nabī*, because a Prophet is the one who has a high status in this world and in the Hereafter, and the Prophet are the most noble of creation, the signposts by whom people are guided and reformed in this world and in the Hereafter." Al-Ashqar, *Messengers and the Messages*, 30.

17. The Prophetic characters associated with the term are Noah, Abraham, Ishmael, Isaac, Jacob, Joseph, Moses, Aaron, David, Solomon, Idris, Job, Jonah, Zechariah, John the Baptist, Jesus, Elijah, Elisha, and Lot. Tottoli, *Biblical Prophets in the Qur'ān*, 73. Although not explicitly stated in the Qur'ān, Adam is considered as a *nabī* in Islam as well.

18. A verbal form of *rasūl* is *arsala*, which means "to send (or to loose)." Kassis, *Concordance of the Qur'ān*, 1029.

19. This term appear in an important doctrinal confession in Islam (*shahāda*); *Lā Ilāha illā'llāh wa Muhammad rasūl Allāh* (There is no god but God and Muhammad is the Messenger of God). Rippin, *Muslims*, 104.

20. A messenger is the one who is sent with the book of divine messages in the form of a "written revelation." Esposito, *Oxford Dictionary of Islam*, 262.

21. Kateregga and Shenk, *Muslim and a Christian in Dialogue*, 63. Al-Ashqar explains the difference between the two as follows; "The Messenger is the one to whom laws (*shari'ah*) are revealed and he is commanded to convey them, whereas a Prophet is the one who receives revelation but he is not commanded to convey it. On this basis, every Messenger is a Prophet, but every Prophet is not a Messenger." Al-Ashqar, *Messengers and the Messages*, 32. *Rasūls* are also believed to have brought "a new religion or a major new revelation." Glassé, *New Encyclopedia of Islam*, 417.

22. Ur-Rahim and Thomson, *Jesus: Prophet of Islam*, 158.

Haque who earned a PhD in Islamic studies from Chicago University also repeatedly identifies Adam as "the first and original" prophet without presenting any Qur'ānic evidences.[23] With the clear majority already having accepted Adam as a prophet, it is difficult to trace where the original rational or explanation for Adam's prophethood began. It would be possible, however, to investigate what conditions need to be met in order to be considered as a prophet in the Qur'ān and examine the Adamic narratives in the Qur'ān to see whether Adam met those conditions.

What then are the qualifications of a prophet? Hammudah Abd al-Ati, the director of the Canadian Islamic Center of Alberta and associate professor of Syracuse University, in his statement about prophets sheds light on this matter.

> They were *chosen by God* to teach mankind and deliver His *Divine Message* . . . their message, their religion, was basically the same and was called ISLAM, because it came from One and the Same Source, namely, God, to serve one and the same purpose, and that is to *guide humanity* to the Straight Path of God. All the messengers with no exception whatsoever were mortals, human beings, endowed with Divine Revelations and appointed by God to perform certain tasks.[24]

His statement implies that certain conditions need to be met in order to be considered as a prophet. What are the criteria that the Qur'ān sets for a prophet? The first criterion is the origin of their prophethood. Prophets are those who were elected by God (Q6:87, 57:25). Their appointment was confirmed by the message that they delivered and the signs (*ayāh*) which accompanied them (Q3:4; 21:5; 57:17, 25).[25] The divine selection of the prophets in the Qur'ān is explicitly documented; Abraham (Q16:121), Moses (Q7:134), and other prophets (Q6:87).

The second criterion is that they received the message of God to proclaim; they were the recipients of "the Book, Authority, and

---

23. They include Noah, Ishmael, Moses, Lot, Jesus, Muhammad, and three other Arabian messengers Hūd, Sālih, and Shuʿayb. Haque, *Prophets and Progress in Islam*, 81; Haque, *Revelation And Revolution in Islam*, 101.

24. Al-ʿĀtī, *Islam in Focus*, 27–28. Italics are mine.

25. *Ayāh*, in most cases, has used in connection with the message of God. But there are other verses that connect *ayāh* with the judgment of God (Q27:51–52), the salvation of God (Q29:15), and miracles (Q43:46–48). Al-Hilali and Khan, *Interpretation of the Meanings of the Noble Qur'ān: In the English Language with Arabic Text*. Cf. *Ayāh* also indicates "verse" of the Qur'ān.

Prophethood" (Q6:89). Qur'ān 33:7 lists the five messengers of God, which are Noah, Abraham, Moses, Jesus, and you (Muhammad).[26] In the Qur'ān, Abraham (Q87:19), Moses (Q2:87, 6:154, 11:110, 17:2, 23:49, 87:19) and Jesus (Q2:87) received the message (the Book). Unlike the others, Noah received only inspirations (Q4:163) and guidance (Q6:84). Their message proved their "Prophethood" (Q2:136; 29:27; 57:26a). These prophets who received revelations are regarded to be more privileged than other prophets.

The third criterion is the duty to guide the people to God. The prophets of God are sent to their community in order to "reestablish the relationship" between God and the people.[27] It is written in the Qur'ān, "We assuredly sent amongst *every People* an apostle (with the Command)" (Q16:36).[28] Tottoli states that since a prophet "receives revelations from God," he has "the obligation to communicate them to his people."[29] The following Figure 2.1. shows a few examples of known prophets who satisfy the condition for prophethood.

God	Called/Sent . . .	with (reveled) messages	to guide his people.
Noah	3:33; 7:59; 11:25; 29:14; 57:26	11:36, 48	7:59; 11:25; 23:23; 29:14; 71:7
Abraham	2:124; 3:33; 4:125; 57:26	2:136; 3:84; 4:163; 87:19	2:124; 29:16; 60:4
Moses	7:103, 143, 144; 10:75; 26:10	2:53, 87, 136; 3:84; 6:154; 11:110; 17:2; 23:49; 28:43; 32:23;	2:54, 67; 7:128; 17:2; 40:53; 61:5

Figure 2.1. The Qur'ānic Qualifications of a Prophet

26. Al-Hilali and Khan, *Interpretation of the Meanings of the Noble Qur'ān: In the English Language with Arabic Text*, 616. The same Sūra, however, is also used as an evidence of Adam's prophethood along with Noah, Abraham, Moses, and Jesus "as prophets from whom God took a covenant." Wheeler, "Adam," 11.

27. Lumbard, "Prophets and Messengers of God," 102.

28. God "gave Abraham against his people" (Q6:83) and "sent Noah to his people" (Q11:25). In regard to the prophets and their message, a clear command is also given to the people to follow in the teachings, "Those were the (prophets) who received Allah's guidance: *copy [follow]* the guidance they received." (Q6:90)

29. Tottoli, *Biblical Prophets in the Qur'ān*, 72.

Conditions of Prophethood in the Bible

The Tawrāt (Pentateuch), like the Qur'ān, does not label Adam with a prophetic title nor does it explicitly state what Adam's prophecy may have been. In Deut 18:18 (NIV), God sets the criteria for prophethood,[30] when God said, "I will raise up for them a prophet [*nabī*] like you from among their brothers; I will put my words in his mouth, and he will tell them everything I command him." Given with strict warnings against the practices of pagan prophets (Deut 18:9–22), the above verse clearly spells out what the prophetic role is to be.[31]

The first condition is that a prophet has to be "raised" or called by God from among the people. Willem A. VanGemeren, an Old Testament scholar at Trinity International University, lists a "calling from God" as one of the qualifications for a prophet.[32]

Second condition is that a prophet received God's words. It is described, "I will put my words in his mouth." This phrase implies that the words are from God and that it is God who enables the prophet to speak those words. Prophets received God's revelation through various means including hearing voices (Isa 5:9; 22:14) and visions (Ezek 1–3). Often God's revelations through the prophets were recorded as scriptures. Prophets could not choose or change a message that he was to deliver. Instead, the message in its entirety had to be delivered. Norman Gottwald remarks that, "The pitch of Hebrew prophecy is not prediction or social reform but the declaration of divine will."[33] A prophet is, therefore, a spokesperson[34] for God.

The last condition for a prophet is that the prophet was sent to the people to become a spokesperson for God. Prophets were responsible to

---

30. Young, *My Servants, the Prophets*, 13–37.

31. Merrill, *Deuteronomy*, 273.

32. VanGemeren, *Interpreting the Prophetic Word*, 33. He provides seven qualifications of a prophet of God. First, the prophet should be an Israelite. Second, he received *a call from God*. Third, the empowerment of the Holy Spirit will enable him to speak the word of God. Fourth, the prophet declares God's word as his spokesperson. Fifth, authority of the prophet is the privilege of speaking in the name of the Lord. Sixth, the prophet is a good shepherd like Moses. Seventh, the prophet is verified with a given sign from God. VanGemeren, *Interpreting the Prophetic Word: An Introduction to the Prophetic Literature of the Old Testament*, 32–33.

33. Gottwald, *Light to the Nations*, 277.

34. Based on Exod 7:1b, Leon Wood also summarizes the meaning of *nabī* as the "one who spoke in the place of another." Wood, *Prophets of Israel*, 61.

"tell them everything" that God commanded. They conveyed God's message through spoken words and actions.

It is not surprising that the conditions for prophethood are mostly the same in the Qur'ān as they are in the Bible. Both texts agree that a prophet is chosen by God, is given God's words, and is commanded to declare them to the people. Having demarcated the qualifications for a prophet in the Qur'ān and the Tawrāt, the Adamic narratives from both texts will be reviewed. Then, the narratives will be sifted through to find evidences for Adam's prophethood.

Qur'ānic Account of the Adamic Narrative

The name "Adam" is mentioned twenty-five times in the English translation of the Qur'ān.[35] The Qur'ānic narratives of Adam do not appear in one specific Sura (chapter) of the Qur'ān nor are they arranged chronologically.[36] For example, chronologically, the first Qur'ān that contains the Adamic narrative is Sura 20, which is placed after Suras 2 or 7, in turn containing narratives that were written later. The Adamic narratives in the Qur'ān were written at different times and at different locations and thus emphasize different aspects of the story.[37] Therefore, to gain a comprehensive understanding of the Adam saga, each narrative found in the Qur'ān regarding Adam needs to be investigated.[38]

The longer narratives of Adam are found in five chapters: Suras 2, 7, 15, 17, and 20. Among them Suras 2, 7, and 20 are regarded as the "*major*

---

35. Reeves, *Bible and Qur'ān*, 36. There is a strong Qur'ānic tendency to compare Adam with Jesus (Q3:33–59). "Jesus" is mentioned the same number of times as "Adam" in the Qu'rān. The creation of Jesus and Adam shows great similarity (Q3:59). Reeves lists twenty-five verses that refer to Adam. Sura 5:27, however, reflects the versification of the Cairo edition of the Qur'ān. In most English translations, this part follows the Fluegel's edition in which the name of Adam found in Q 5:30. According to the Ali's translation of the Holy Qur'ān, twenty-five verses that refer the name of Adam are as follows; Q2:31, 33, 34, 35, 37; 3:33, 59; 5:30; 7:11, 19, 26, 27, 31, 35, 172; 17:61, 70; 18:50; 19:58; 20:115, 116, 117, 120, 121; 36:60. Cf. it is reported that the Arabic name of *Adam* appears eighteen times in the Qur'ān. Nickel, "Adam (Person)," 321. According to Kassis, however, the Arabic name ADM appears in twenty-five different verses where he shows the different versifications between the Cairo and the Fluegel edition. Kassis, *Concordance of the Qur'ān*, 108.

36. Haleem, *Understanding the Qur'ān*, 126–30.

37. Mawdūdī, *Towards Understanding the Qur'ān*, 232.

38. Mawdūdī, *Towards Understanding the Qur'ān*, 232.

Adamic texts"[39] because they contain the backbone of the Adamic narrative. The other two passages found in Suras 15 and 17 are the *"minor* Adamic texts" and contain the supporting details of the Adamic narrative as well as correlating theological implications. Beside the five major passages, "additional texts" which mention Adam in Qur'ān 3:59; 5:30; 7:26–58, 172; 18:50; 19:58; 36:60; and 38:71–85 will also be briefly examined.[40]

Three Major Adamic Texts

The Qur'ān was revealed to Prophet Mohammad spanning the latter twenty-two years of his lifetime.[41] Traditional Arab scholars divide the revelation into the Meccan[42] and the Medina sūras[43] depending on where the Prophet Muhammad was when he received the revelations.[44] The majority of sūras, however, were revealed in Mecca.[45] For the interest of the academic research, the Meccan sūras are subdivided into three periods; the first, second, and third Meccan period.[46]

According to Bell and Watt's analysis which was based on the classification of a German scholar, Theodor Nöldeke's *Geschichte des Qorāns (History of the Qur'ān, 1860)*, Sura 20 was written first and dates to the

---

39. Steenbrink, *Adam Redivivus*, 8. The major texts are determined by the intratextual correlations of the Qur'ānic narratives and the intertextuality to the Bible.

40. Although Q38:71–85 is not directly related with the Adam saga, the account of Iblis provides a supplementary explanation of the temptation and the fall, through the evil scheme of Iblis.

41. Mir, "Qur'ān, the Word of God," 47.

42. The Meccan sūras date from 610 to 622 CE and are considered to have been composed in Mecca before Muhammad's migration (*hijra*) to Medina in 622 CE. The Medinan sūras are thought to have been written between 622 and 630 CE when the Muslims controlled the city of Medina.

43. Mir, "Qur'ān, the Word of God," 49. Mir said about the characteristics of these two periods that "the Meccan revelations deal with matters of faith, such as the fundamentals of Islamic dogma and the principles of ethics . . . the Medinan revelations deal with the political, social, and economic aspects of Muslim life." Mir, "Qur'ān, the Word of God," 49.

44. The European Islamic scholars, however, divided the Meccan period into three sub-periods: the first, the second, and the third Meccan periods. Bell and Watt, *Bell's Introduction to the Qur'ān*, 108–12.

45. Al-A'zamī, *History of the Qur'ānic Text*, 59.

46. Bell and Watt, *Bell's Introduction to the Qur'ān*, 110, 111.

second Meccan period, Sura 7 to the third Meccan period, and, Sura 2 to the Medinan period.⁴⁷

The Second Meccan Period		The Third Meccan Period		The Medinan Period	
20:115–23	**Maj Text**				
15:26–42	Minor Text				
19:58	Additional T	7:26–58	Add *Text*	2:30–39	**Maj Text**
38:71–85	Additional T	7:172	Add Text	3:59	Add Text
36:60	Additional T	7:11–25	**Maj Text**	5:30	Add Text
17:60–77	Minor Text				
18:50	Additional T				

Figure 2.2. Chronological Order of Adamic Texts

The chronological order of the complete Adamic narratives based on Nöldeke's classification, including the major, minor, and additional texts, is provided in Figure 2.2 above. In the following examination of the three major texts, the content of each passage will be briefly surveyed. The minor and additional texts will also be succinctly examined.

*Major Text 1 (Qur'ān 20:115–23)*⁴⁸

According to Bell and Watt, a total of twenty-one sūras are dated to the second Meccan period and are characterized by "lengthy" and "stylish doctrinal writings."⁴⁹ Sura 20, classified as a text of the second Meccan period, begins by recalling what had happened with Adam previously but does not divulge what that was. The text describes that there was an understanding between God and Adam, but Adam forgot and was

---

47. Bell and Watt, *Bell's Introduction to the Qur'ān*, 110, 111.

48. See Appendix 1 for the Qur'ānic text.

49. Bell and Watt, *Bell's Introduction to the Qur'ān*, 110. It is likely that during the second Meccan period the early Muslim community deepens their theological thoughts to account more doctrinal discourse with the Jewish and the Christian community. The analysis and the comparison of the Creation discourse between the first and the second Meccan Sūras also indicates this analysis. The second Meccan Sūras said that man is created from clay not from sperm, of which the first Meccan Sūras originates the creation of man (Adam). O'Shaughnessy, *Creation and the Teaching of the Qur'ān*, 14–15.

irresolute about keeping the covenant (Q20:115). God warns Adam not to go hungry and thirsty lest Iblis, who had refused to prostrate himself to Adam, evict him from the Paradise by deceiving him into eating the fruit of the Tree of Eternity (Q20:116–20).

Adam does not follow the instruction or heed God's warnings. Consequentially, his nakedness appears before him and he sews leaves as a cover (Q20:121). Then God turns to Adam and gives him guidance (Q20:122). Continuing on, God promises that those who follow God's guidance will not go astray nor fall into misery (Q20:123). This new promise given to Adam and his wife is an extension to all of their descendants.[50] The exact nature of the "guidance" that Adam received from God and the rest of humankind is to receive is also unclear.

Major Text 2 (Qur'ān 7:11–25)[51]

The second major text is dated to the third Meccan period. This period is characterized by "the prophetic stories" that are "repeated with slight variations of emphasis."[52] This text adds greater detail to Adam's temptation and disobedience narrative in Sura 20. Compared to Sura 20, where a total of eight verses are dedicated to the Adamic narrative, Sura 7 contains the most number verses dedicated to Adam: fifteen verses.

This passage begins with the creation of Adam. When God commanded all the angels to bow down to Adam, Iblis refused (Q7:11). The next few verses describe why Iblis disobeyed God's command to fall prostrate, why he considered himself to be better than Adam (Q7:12), and how with his debasement and granted respite, Iblis decides to lure Adam to go astray, and how God passes judgment to send Iblis and his followers to hell (Q7:12–18).

God warns Adam and his wife not to approach "this tree" which is not explicitly named in this text (Q7:19). Iblis tempts Adam and his wife by saying that "this tree" would lead them to be like angels and the immortals and swears that he is giving a sincere advice (Q7:20–21). When they are deceived by Iblis and taste the fruit of "this tree," God calls them

---

50. Steenbrink, *Adam Redivivus*, 10. In the last verse of the first major text, it is recorded that "*whosoever* follows My guidance will not lose his way nor fall into misery" (Q20:123). Steenbrink interprets this as an universal promise of God which is extended to all humanity.

51. See Appendix 2 for the Qur'ānic text.

52. Bell and Watt, *Bell's Introduction to the Qur'ān*, 110.

and judges their wrongdoings (Q7:22). Although Adam and his wife repent and asked for God's mercy, they are expelled from the paradise to earth and become enemies of Iblis (Q7:23, 24). The earth is given to them as a temporary dwelling place until they die and are taken out (Q7:25).

Major Text 3 (Qur'ān 2:30–39)[53]

The last major passage, dated to the Medinan period, was written and reflects the attitude of a time when there were increased polemics against the large Jewish and the Christian community surrounding the new institution of Islam in Medina.[54] A total of nine verses are dedicated to the Adamic narrative in Sura 2.

This passage begins with God's plan to create humankind on earth and the angel's forewarning of human beings who "will make mischief and will shed blood" (Q2:30). God's plan, however, was based on the divine knowledge to judge the arrogant and rebellious angel, Iblis. The uniqueness of this passage can be found in following verses where it tells how Adam had come to know the names of God's creation because God had previously told them to Adam. Then all the angels in the paradise are commanded to prostrate themselves before Adam but Iblis refuses, however, to bow down (Q2:31–34). Next, God warns about "this tree" (Q2:35) but Adam is duped by Iblis and ends up being evicted from the paradise (Q2:36).

The nature of how Iblis deceives Adam and how the eviction came about is not repeated in this text, however. Verse 37 is unique to the Adamic narrative in two ways. First, Adam receives words from his Lord. It is, however, not clear what words Adam receives from God. Arberry translates it as "certain words" (Q3:35).[55] Second, God turns toward (forgives) Adam. The account of repentance, which is recorded in Qur'ān 7:23, is omitted. Al-Hilali's translation assumes that the reader has foreknowledge of the repentance account, "And his Lord pardons him (accepted his repentance). Verily, He is the One Who forgives (accepts repentance), the Most Merciful" (Q2:37).[56]

---

53. See Appendix 3 for the Qur'ānic text.
54. Steenbrink, *Adam Redivivus*, 14; Waardenburg, *Muslims and Others*, 180.
55. Arberry, *Koran: Interpreted*, 6.
56. Al-Hilali and Khan, *Interpretation of the Meanings*, 9.

Textual Analysis of the Three Major Texts

A total of thirty-five different story elements exist in the Adamic narrative. The content analysis of the Adamic narrative in Figure 2.3 shows an interesting development of the Qur'ānic revelations. Although there is some overlap between the accountings, there is a developmental progression from the previous narratives so that yet unknown detail is told in the latter. Subsequent sūras seem to add untold details to each previous revelation while not repeating the old information. Later sūras record seemingly more dramatic and paranormal elements to the previous accountings. For example, concerning Iblis's role in the temptation of Adam, the first major accounting, Sura 20, records only that Iblis tempts humankind (Q20:116). In the next major accounting, Sura 7, the details of how Iblis disobeys God's command to fall prostrate before Adam and how Iblis becomes a fallen angel is recorded. Lastly, in Sura 2, yet-unknown spiritual accounting of the heavenly events reveal on what basis Iblis decides to disobey God; that Adam's status above the angels was ungrounded since God had already told Adam the names of his creation and was not realized on his own. The pre-creation discourse between God and the angels recorded in these sūras explains why the arrogant Iblis become envious of Adam and disobeyed God after the naming incident.

A brief view of the chart will show that there are three elements of the Adamic narrative that is repeated in all three major sūras. By repeating certain elements, the Qur'ān implicitly (if not explicitly) emphasizes the significance of the emergence of enmity between Iblis and the human kind. The three overlapping elements are 1) God's command to angels to prostrate themselves to Adam (Q20:116; 7:11; 2:34), 2) Iblis's disobedience and decision to lure Adam and his wife (Q20:120; 7:20; 2:36), and 3) the enmity between Iblis and Adam and his wife as they settle down on earth (Q20:123; 7:24; 2:36).

	Chronology of Adamic narratives	**Q 20:115-23**	**Q 7:11-25**	**Q 2:30-39**
Pre-Creation	God's plan to create humankind			2:30
	Objection of the angels			2:30
	God knows what the angels do not know			2:30

	Chronology of Adamic narratives	Q 20:115–23	Q 7:11–25	Q 2:30–39
Creation	God created a man (Adam)		7:11	
Creation	God gave Adam shape (clay)		7:11 (12)	
Creation	God made a covenant with Adam	20:115		
Naming Incident	God taught names of his creation to Adam			2:31
Naming Incident	God asked names of his creation to angels			2:31
Naming Incident	Angels confessed that God only has the perfect knowledge and wisdom			2:32
Naming Incident	Adam answered the names			2:33
Naming Incident	God commanded angels to prostrate to Adam	20:116	7:11	2:34
Iblis Narrative	Iblis rejected God's command to prostrate		7:11	2:34
Iblis Narrative	God's question and answer of Iblis		7:12	
Iblis Narrative	God punished Iblis (as meanest of creatures)		7:13, 14	
Iblis Narrative	Petition of Iblis and God's grant		7:14, 15	
Iblis Narrative	Iblis decided to lure humankind	20:116	7:16, 17	
Iblis Narrative	God expelled Iblis from the paradise		7:13	
Warning	God warns about Iblis	20:117		
Warning	God commanded Adam not to taste "the tree"		7:19	2:35
Warning	Not to be hungry or be naked to avoid thirst and heat	20:118, 119		

	Chronology of Adamic narratives	Q 20:115–23	Q 7:11–25	Q 2:30–39
Disobedience	Iblis (Satan) deceived Adam and his wife	20:120	7:20	2:36
	The Tree of Eternity and a permanent kingdom/eternity	20:120	7:20	
	Iblis swore that he was a sincere adviser		7:21	
	Adam disobeyed God	20:121	7:22	
	Nakedness appeared	20:121		
	They sew leaves together for covering	20:121	7:22	
Forgiveness	God found (chose) Adam and his wife	20:122	7:22	
	Adam repented and asked for mercy		7:23	2:37
	God gave Adam his words			2:37
	God gave Adam his guidance	20:122		
Aftermaths	Adam expelled from Paradise to earth	20:123		
	Adam and his wife settled on earth with enmity	20:123	7:24	2:36
	God asks to follow his guidance not to fall into misery	20:123		2:38
	Warnings to those who reject Faith and Signs			2:39
	Earthly livelihood		7:24, 25	2:36

Figure 2.3. Major-Texts Comparison Chart of Adamic Narrative in the Qurʾān

Minor and Additional Sūras of the Adamic Narrative

The minor texts in Qur'ān 15:26–42 and 17:60–77 do not provide a direct accounting of the Adamic narrative. In fact, Adam's name does not appear in Qur'ān 15:26–42. The text, however, provides details about the Iblis incident, similar to the Adamic narrative in Qur'ān 7:11–25. Another minor text of Adamic narrative is Qur'ān 17:60–77. This text records the divine narrative of the judgment of Iblis and of the sons of Adam given during the "Journey by night" (Night Journey, Q 17:1).

Other relevant details about the Adamic narrative are recorded in other Sūras: the creation of Adam is compared with Jesus in Qur'ān 3:59, the story of Adam's two sons is recorded in Qur'ān 5:30, the creation of the children of Adam is mentioned in Qur'ān 7:172, and a series of warnings to the children of Adam are recorded in Qur'ān 7:26–58. Qur'ān 19:58 also records the grace that God bestowed on the posterity of Adam. Qur'ān 18:50 repeats the Iblis incident that is also found in Qur'ān 7:11–18, 15:26–43, 17:61–65, and 38:67–88. Lastly God warns the children of Adam that they should not worship Iblis (Q36:60).

Account of the Adamic Narrative in the Bible

As was aforementioned, the Tawrāt (Pentateuch) is acknowledged in Islam as one of the Divine books and is also included in the Bible. Many similarities are found between the Adamic narrative of the Qur'ān and the Tawrāt. For ease of reference, biblical references will be used to discuss the contents of the Tawrāt.

In the Tawrāt, the Adamic narrative is recorded as a single narrative in Gen 1:26—3:34. The major texts of the Adamic narrative in the Qur'ān contain thirty-five elements as previously shown in Figure 3. Roughly seventeen story elements in Genesis overlap with the Qur'ānic account as shown in Figure 2.4.

Total Items of Adamic Narratives in the Qur'ān	Gen 1:26—3:34	Q 20:115–23	Q 7:11–25	Q 2:30–39
35 (100%)	17 (48.57%)	15 (42.86%)	19 (52.29%)	17 (48.57%)

Figure 2.4. Comparison of Adamic Narratives in the Qur'ān and the Bible

Since the three major texts of the Qurʾān are related but expand in detail from the previous text, and since the Tawrāt was written much earlier than the Qurʾān, it is not surprising that the Tawrāt contains elements that the later text does not repeat. The Adamic narrative in Genesis, therefore, has great number of story elements that are not recorded in the Qurʾān.[57]

The early Islamic commentators acknowledged the Adamic narratives of the Bible in their teachings. Brannon M. Wheeler, a well-known Islamic scholar, in his book *Prophets in the Qurʾān: An Introduction to the Qurʾān and Muslim Exegesis* (2002), collected evidences. He quotes the conversation between Ibn Abbas, a cousin of Muhammad, and Ibn Masud (d. 652), a companion of Muhammad, concerning the creation of a woman. "He (Adam) fell asleep once and when he woke up there was a woman sitting at his head whom God had created from his rib."[58] When Adam was asked why he named her Eve (*hawā*), he said, "because she was created from something living [*hayya*]."[59] These accountings are found in Genesis but are absent from the Qurʾān. Wheeler's collection of earlier commentators on the prophets in the Qurʾān includes additional examples. Ibn Ishaq says, "when Adam awoke from his sleep he saw her at his side and said, 'my flesh and my blood, and my spouse.'"[60] A similar accounting is found in Gen 2:23, "This is bone of my bones and flesh of my flesh."

The account narrated by Wahb b. Munabbih (d. 728/729) is also surprisingly similar to the biblical narrative.

> Iblis left the snake and picked the fruit. He took it to Eve saying how sweet it smelled, how good it tasted, how beautiful its color. Eve ate of the fruit and then repeated the same arguments to

---

57. Rule over all the creatures (1:26), God's own image (1:27), God blessed them (1:28–30), it was good on the sixth day (1:31), the completion of creation on the seventh day (2:1–3), the creation of the earth and of the garden (2:4–6, 8–14), God put the man in the garden of Eden to work it and take care of it (2:15), God's plan to create a helper (2:18), the creation of a woman (2:21–25), God's judgment on the serpent crawling on the belly and eating dust (3:14), enmity between the offspring of the serpent and of the woman (3:15), curse of woman in birth-giving pain and submission to man (3:16), curse of man in toils of labor (3:17–19), Adam naming of his wife, Eve (3:20), the making of garments of skin (3:21), banning from the tree of life (3:22), and the banishment of Adam and Eve from the garden of Eden (3:23–24).

58. Wheeler, *Prophets in the Qurʾān*, 19.

59. Wheeler, *Prophets in the Qurʾān*, 19.

60. Wheeler, *Prophets in the Qurʾān*, 19.

Adam, who also ate it. ... God cursed the earth from which Adam was created, changing fruits to thorns. Because Eve enticed Adam, pregnancy would be difficult and dangerous. Because the snake allowed Iblis to enter it, its feet were retracted into its belly and it was to eat from the earth, and be the enemy of the descendants of Adam. Wherever the snake encounters these descendants, it will hold onto their heel. Wherever they encounter the snake, they will crush its head.[61]

While these story elements were only found in the Bible and not in the Qur'ān, yet they were accepted as fact by the early Muslim believers. This supports the fact for a holistic view of the Adamic narrative, the Genesis accounting of the Adamic narrative needs to be considered as the backdrop from which all the following story elements in the Qur'ān can be pegged onto. In other words, it is reasonable to say that the Qur'ānic accounting of the Adamic narratives were meant to be built on the foundation of the biblical narrative so that new details can be given without repeating the old.

Prophecy of the First Prophet Adam

Thus far, the findings from the Qur'ān and the Bible have shown great similarities. The criteria for prophethood were similar as were the many story elements of the Adamic narrative. In this section, evidences for the prophethood of Adam will be extracted from the Qur'ān as well as the Bible to verify whether Adam can indeed be considered as a prophet.

Evidence for Adam's Prophethood in the Qur'ān

The first requirement for a prophet was the election of a prophet by God. Adam fully satisfies this requirement because he was the very first of the human kind. The fact that God had planned to create humankind (Q2:30), personally shaped Adam from clay and created him (Q7:11, 12), and taught him the names of his creation (Q2:31), all point to the fact that Adam was indeed chosen by God.

The second condition for a prophet is that they must be given a message, either verbally or in a written form, which is ordained by God. Several verses of the Adamic narrative record that Adam received the

---

61. Wheeler, *Prophets in the Qur'ān*, 24, 29.

"guidance" (Q2:38; 20:122, 123) and "words of inspiration" (Q2:37) from God. Before the fall, there was no need for the divine guidance for humanity. However, disobedience of Adam and his wife required "the beginning of the cycle of revelation."[62] In Qur'ān 2:38, God gives them a message saying, "Get ye down all from here; and if, as is sure, there comes to you *guidance* from Me, whosoever follows My guidance, on them shall be no fear, nor shall they grieve" (my emphasis).

The last requirement for prophethood is that that the prophet must be sent to the people to proclaim and convey the message. Since Adam, however, was the first man on the earth, he was sent to all humankind.[63] If they observe the guidance of God, their lives on earth will be protected from fear, grief, and sufferings of this world. Therefore, we can deduce that the guidance of God was given to humanity through Adam. Based on the conclusion from the study of the Qur'ān and of Islamic scholars, Adam meets all the conditions to be considered as a prophet of God.

Evidence for Adam's Prophethood in the Bible

Adam in the Bible is also not labeled as a prophet in any verse. The first test of prophethood is the calling from God. The explicit calling of God is not found in the Genesis narrative. However, unlike all other creation, which came into being through God's words, Adam was custom made and breathed upon to take on the image of likeness of God (Gen 1:26; 2:7). The fact that he was set apart and unique from the rest of the creation, attests to the fact that God chose him. Further, because Adam is the first of his kind, his creation can be equated as God appointment of Adam as the father of humanity.

Another indication of God's preferential treatment of Adam can be found in how two different words for "put" was used. The Genesis account records that God *placed* him in the garden of Eden with his purpose. The New International Version translated two different Hebrew words *yasem* (2:8, root *sym*) and *yanihehū*[64] (2:15, root *nūakh*) into the

62. Lumbard, *Prophets and Messengers of God*, 109.

63. The Qur'ān refers humankind as "the children of Adam" (*bani Adam*). Among the Adamic texts, Qur'ān 7:26–58 is solely dedicated for the children of Adam. This term also used in Qur'ān 7:172 and 36:60. *Bani Adam*, in fact, "signifies humanity as a whole." Sherif, *A Guide to the Contents of the Qur'ān*, 72.

64. The verb "to put" (root. *nūakh*) in this verse simply means "to settle down, to place, to deposit, and to leave behind." Köhler and Baumgartner, *Hebrew and Aramaic Lexicon*, 2:679–80.

same English verb, "to put." In Gen 2:15, "God took the man and *put* him into the garden of Eden to cultivate it and keep it." This verse explains God purpose for placing Adam in the garden of Eden[65] was to work in it.

The same verb "to put" (in Hebrew *yasem*) in verse 8, however, is not associated with any physical labor. The root form of Hebrew verb *sym* carries richer meanings of "to put, to install, to erect, to confirm, and to ordain."[66] Bruce K. Waltke explains that Adam was created and placed in the garden for a close fellowship with God.[67] This unique position of Adam's intimacy with God legitimizes his prophetic calling.

Another condition for prophethood in the Tawrāt was that the prophet needed to be sent to the people to relay the message God gave. Since Adam was the first man on earth, everyone alive until the Great Flood was his progeny. The fact that the story of creation and the fall was transmitted to be included in the Tawrāt attests to the fact that Adam did relay God's words. Adam's unique status without a people group does not disqualify him from becoming a prophet. According to the genealogy of Adam, he lived 930 years until Lamech, the father of Noah, became fifty-two years old (Gen 5:1–32). If we count all the people who lived with Adam, we may have multitude of Adam's contemporaries. Adam was responsibility for his progeny.

The third condition of Adam's prophethood is his message. In the Bible, God spoke to Adam, the head of humanity (Gen 1:28–30; 2:16–17; 3:8–19).[68] Genesis is not explicit about the message that Adam received from God. However, theologically, Adam is regarded as the messenger of God's redemptive plan. Willem A. VanGemeren extracts seven elements

---

65. A well-known commentator of Genesis adds that the garden of Eden is a "symbolic place where God dwells." Wenham, *Genesis 1–15*, 61. Wenham further explains that the garden of Eden can be rendered as "an archetypal sanctuary, prefiguring the later tabernacle and temples." Wenham, *Genesis 1–15*, 61.

66. Köhler and Baumgartner, *Hebrew and Aramaic Lexicon of the Old Testament*, 3:1321–26.

67. Waltke, *Genesis: A Commentary*, 86.

68. God's word in these verses contains blessings and dietary instructions (1:28–30), warning against the eating from the tree of the knowledge of good and evil (2:16–17), and dialogues after the fall (3:8–19). The last dialogue in Gen 3:8–19 is the last conversation Adam had with God and contain the curse of the serpent (3:14–15), the punishment of the woman (3:16) and Adam (3:17–19). The curse of the land (3:17b–18) is embedded in Adam's punishment. In this discourse, Adam is accused as the breaker of the divine commandment (3:17).

of *pre-Abrahamic* covenants[69] from the "early stage of the redemptive history," and points out that the redemptive message that Adam received after the fall was "the hope in the seed" recorded in Gen 3:15.[70] This future hope that the enemy that brought the fall of humanity will be defeated through the offspring of a woman was actually not spoken to Adam but was declared in a form of a curse for the serpent. The revelations of punishment and curses were witnessed by all of them.

The prophetic message recorded in the Bible bears the quality of foretelling what will happen in the future and thereby giving hope to the humankind. In Genesis, although not conveyed through words, God showed his grace through action by making garments of skin for Adam and his wife (Gen 3:21). While this action does not convey complete forgiveness, it is an act that conveys God's love and grace. Thus, Adam would have taught his offspring of how the disobedience had wrought suffering and how God had covered their nakedness and given them hope for future victory.

Conclusion and Suggestions

The investigation on the Adamic narratives in the Qur'ān and in the Bible provides valid evidences for the prophethood of Adam. While Adam satisfies all the criteria for prophethood, both in the Qur'ān and in the Bible, the message they receive and declare is quite different from each other.[71]

---

69. Key redemptive elements in the early stages of the history of redemption are of cosmic significance: (1) God's blessing on the family, (2) *the hope in "the seed" (Gen 3:15)*, (3) the hope in God's provision of rest and comfort (5:29), (4) God's blessing on the fallen creation (9:1), (5) the regularity of nature (8:22), (6) the hope in God's presence (9:27), and (7) God's special relationship with men of integrity (Enoch and Noah). VanGemeren, *Interpreting the Prophetic Word*, 86.

70. A German scholar, Ernst W. Hengstenberg, labeled this verse as "protoevangelium"(proto-gospel) in which the Messianic hope first rendered. Hengstenberg, *Christology of the Old Testament*, 13.

71. The difference exists because the consequence for disobedience to God is different. In the Qur'an, the outcome for disobeying God was falling in sin (Q7:19; 2:35) and being driven out of the garden and becoming miserable (Q20:117) which would cause them to be hungry, unsheltered, thirty, and suffer from heat (Q20:118, 119). In Genesis, however, the consequence for disobeying God and eating the tree of the knowledge of good and evil was a certain death (Gen 2:16). God does not warn Adam that if he disobeys, he will be evicted from the Garden or that he would suffer. The fact that the curses which were declared after the fall of Adam in Genesis are already mentioned before the fall of Adam in the Qur'ān is an added indication that the recorder of the Qur'ān had foreknowledge of the Adamic narrative in Genesis.

Since the penalty for disobedience is described differently, the subsequent message given to the prophet Adam for the humankind is also different. In the Qur'ān, the message Adam receives is geared toward avoiding the consequences of disobedience for it says, "but if, as is sure, there comes to you guidance from Me, whosoever follows My guidance, *will not lose his way, nor fall into misery*" (Q20:123b). In Genesis, however, the message is embedded in the curse of the serpent and is geared toward countering Satan's scheme by future victory of the seed of the woman over the seed of the serpent (Gen 3:15).

The guidance given to Adam in the Qur'ān bears qualities of guiding or counseling the people so that the listeners can be averted from sinning and suffering. The Qur'ān records in Qur'ān 20:122 that "He (God) turned[72] to him, and gave him guidance." After Adam and his wife were expelled from the paradise, God required them to follow the guidance of God (Q20:122,123; 2:37, 38) so as to not to fall into misery. The concept of *guidance* (and words of inspiration) is significant to humanity because it was the instruction given to Adam and his wife when God expelled him to the earth, right after their disobedience. It was given to guide their earthly lives and to their descendants as well. In the Bible, the message given to Adam does not give instructions for living as does the Qur'ān. The biblical message also does not show ways to avoid misery or suffering in this world. Instead, it contains an element of a promise for complete victory over Satan.

An investigation of Adamic narratives on the Qur'ān provides significant "theological foundations"[73] for the interfaith dialogues to the biblical scholars as well as to the Islamic scholars. Further investigations need to be conducted on the differences in the message given to Adam, in the concept and consequences of sin, and in the nature of forgiveness that Adam received, and salvation. The twenty-four biblical characters that are considered as prophets in the Qur'ān need to be comparatively studied in order to distill the messages God gave to the people through the prophets.

---

72. What does "turned to him (Adam)" mean? According to a fourteenth-century Islamic commentator, al-Imam Ibn Kathir (1301–72), God "accepted their repentance because it was sincere, and He told them that the earth would be their realm." Kathir, *Stories of the Prophets*, 21.

73. Moucarry discussed about the problem of sin, and the meaning of salvation in Islam based on the Adamic narrative in the Qur'ān. Moucarry, *Prophet & the Messiah*, 95–112.

Appendix 1. *Qur'ān* 20:115-23[74]

20:115. We had already, beforehand, taken the covenant of **Adam,** but he forgot: and We found on his part no firm resolve.

20:116. When We said to the angels, "Prostrate yourselves to **Adam**" they prostrated themselves, but not Iblis: he refused.

20:117. Then We said: "O **Adam**! Verily this is an enemy to thee and thy wife: so let him not get you both out of the Garden, so that thou art landed in misery.

20:118. "There is therein (enough provision) for thee not to go hungry nor to go naked,"

20:119. "Nor to suffer from thirst nor from the sun's heat."

20:120. But Satan whispered evil to him: he said "O **Adam**! Shall I lead thee to Tree of Eternity and to a kingdom that never decays?"

20:121. In the result they both ate of the tree and so their nakedness appeared to them: they began to sew together, for their covering, leaves from the Garden: thus did **Adam** disobey His Lord, and allow himself to be seduced.

20:122. But his Lord chose him (for His Grace): He turned to him, and gave him guidance.

20:123. He said: "Get ye down both of you, all together from the Garden, with enmity one to another; but if, as is sure, there comes to you guidance from Me, whosoever follows My guidance, will not lose his way, nor fall into misery

---

74. Ali, *Holy Qur'ān*. All the Qur'ānic verses in this paper, unless it is indicated otherwise, are quoted from this version.

Appendix 2. *Qur'ān* 7:11–25 (Ali's Version)

7:11. It is We who created you and gave you shape; then We bade the angels bow down to **Adam,** and they bowed down; not so Iblis; he refused to be of those who bow down.

7:12. (God) said: "what prevented thee from bowing down when I commanded thee?" He said: "I am better than he: thou didst create me from fire and him from clay."

7:13. (God) said: "Get thee down from this: it is not for thee to be arrogant here: get out for thou art of the meanest (of creatures)."

7:14. He said: "give me respite till the day they are raised up."

7:15. (God) said: "be thou among those who have respite."

7:16. He said: "because Thou hast thrown me out of the way lo! I will lie in wait for them on Thy straight way.

7:17. "Then will I assault them from before them and behind them from their right and their left: nor wilt Thou find in most of them gratitude (for Thy mercies).

7:18. (God) said: "Get out from this disgraced and expelled. If any of them follow thee hell will I fill with you all.

7:19. O **Adam**! dwell thou and thy wife in the garden and enjoy (its good things) as ye wish: but approach not this tree or ye run into harm and transgression."

7:20. Then began Satan to whisper suggestions to them bringing openly before their minds all their shame that was hidden from them (before): he said "Your Lord only forbade you this tree lest ye should become angels or such beings as live forever."

7:21. And he swore to them both that he was their sincere adviser.

7:22. So by deceit he brought about their fall: when they tasted of the tree their shame became manifest to them and they began to sew together the leaves of the garden over their bodies. And their Lord called unto them: "Did I not forbid you that tree and tell you that Satan was an avowed enemy unto you?"

7:23. They said: "our Lord! We have wronged our own souls: if Thou forgive us not and bestow not upon us Thy Mercy we shall certainly be lost."

7:24. (God) said: "Get ye down with enmity between yourselves. On earth will be your dwelling-place and your means of livelihood for a time."

7:25. He said: "therein shall ye live and therein shall ye die; but from it shall ye be taken out (at last)."

Appendix 3. *Qur'ān* 2:30-39 (Ali's Version)

2:30. Behold thy Lord said to the angels: "I will create a vicegerent on earth." They said "Wilt thou place therein one who will make mischief therein and shed blood? Whilst we do celebrate Thy praises and glorify Thy holy (name)?" He said: "I know what ye know not."

2:31. And He taught **Adam** the nature of all things; then He placed them before the angels and said: "Tell Me the nature of these if ye are right."

2:32. They said: "Glory to Thee of knowledge we have none save that Thou hast taught us: in truth it is Thou who art perfect in knowledge and wisdom."

2:33. He said: "O **Adam**! tell them their natures." When he had told them God said: "Did I not tell you that I know the secrets of heaven and earth and I know what ye reveal and what ye conceal?"

2:34. And behold We said to the angels: "Bow down to **Adam**"; and they bowed down. Not so Iblis: he refused and was haughty: He was of those who reject Faith.

2:35. We said: "O **Adam**! dwell thou and thy wife in the Garden and eat of the bountiful things therein as (where and when) ye will but approach not this tree or ye run into harm and transgression."

2:36. Then did Satan make them slip from the (Garden) and get them out of the state (of felicity) in which they had been. We said: "Get ye down all (ye people) with enmity between yourselves. On earth will be your dwelling place and your means of livelihood for a time."

2:37. Then learnt **Adam** from his Lord words of inspiration and his Lord turned toward him; for He is Oft-Returning Most Merciful.

2:38. We said: "Get ye down all from here; and if, as is sure, there comes to you guidance from Me, whosoever follows My guidance, on them shall be no fear, nor shall they grieve."

2:39. "But those who reject Faith and belie Our Signs they shall be Companions of the Fire; they shall abide therein."

Bibliography

Al-A'zamī, Muhammad Mustafā. *The History of the Qur'ānic Text: From Revelation to Compilation*. Leicester, UK: UK Islamic Academy, 2003.

Al-Ashqar, 'Umar S. *The Messengers and the Messages: In the Light of the Qur'ān and Sunnah*. Translated by Nasiruddin Al-Khattab. Islamic Creed Series 4. 2nd ed. Islamic Creed Series. Raleigh, NC: International Islamic Publishing House, 2005.

cAli ibn Balaban al-Farsi. *Ihsan bi-tartib Sahih Ibn Hibban*. 10 vols. Beirut: Dar al-Fikr, 1996.

Al-Hilali, Muhammad Taqi-ud-Din, and Muhammad Muhsin Khan. *Interpretation of the Meanings of the Noble Qur'ān: In the English Language with Arabic Text*. Riyadh, Saudi Arabia: Maktaba Dar-Us-Salam, 1993.

Al-ʿĀtī, Hammūdah ʿAbd. *Islam in Focus*. 4th ed. Cairo, Egypt: Al-Falah Foundation, 2003.
Ali, Abdullah Yusuf. *The Holy Qurʾān: Text, Translation and Commentary*. Washington, DC: Khalil Al-Rawaf, 1946.
Arberry, Arthur John. *The Koran: Interpreted*. Oxford World's Classics. Oxford: Oxford University Press, 1964.
Asad, Muhammad. *The Message of the Qurʾān*. Gibraltar: Dar al-Andalus, 1984.
Bell, Richard, and William Montgomery Watt. *Bell's Introduction to the Qurʾān*. Edinburgh: Edinburgh University Press, 1970.
Bukhari, Sahih. "Hadith of Sahih Bukhari, Book 93: Judgements (Ahkaam)." https://sunnah.com/bukhari/93.
Esposito, John L., ed. *The Oxford Dictionary of Islam*. New York: Oxford University Press, 2003.
Glassé, Cyril. *The New Encyclopedia of Islam*. Rev. ed. Walnut Creek, CA: AltaMira, 2001.
Gottwald, Norman Karol. *A Light to the Nations: An Introduction to the Old Testament*. New York: Harper, 1959.
Haleem, Muhammad Abdel. *Understanding the Qurʾān: Themes and Style*. New York: Tauris, 2011.
Haque, Ziaul. *Prophets and Progress in Islam*. Kuala Lumpur, Malaysia: Utusan, 2008.
———. *Revelation and Revolution in Islam*. Ocala, FL: Atlantic, 1996.
Hengstenberg, Ernst Wilhelm. *Christology of the Old Testament and a Commentary on the Messianic Predictions*. Grand Rapids: Kregel, 1970.
Kassis, Hanna E. *A Concordance of the Qurʾān*. Berkeley, CA: University of California Press, 1983.
Kateregga, Badru D., and David W. Shenk. *A Muslim and a Christian in Dialogue*. Scottdale, PA: Herald, 1997.
Kathir, al-Imam Ibn. *Stories of the Prophets*. Edited by Aelfwine Acelas Mischler. Translated by Muhammad Mustafa Gemeʾah. Mansoura, Egypt: OM Al KORA, 1997.
Köhler, Ludwig, and Walter Baumgartner. *The Hebrew and Aramaic Lexicon of the Old Testament*. Vol. 2. Study ed. Leiden, Netherlands: Brill, 1995.
———. *The Hebrew and Aramaic Lexicon of the Old Testament*. Vol. 3. 4 vols. Study ed. Leiden, The Netherlands: Brill, 1996.
Lumbard, Joseph. "Prophets and Messengers of God." In *Voices of Islam*, edited by Vincent J. Cornell, 1:101–22. Voices of Tradition. Westport, CT: Praeger, 2007.
Mawdūdī, Sayyid Abul. *Towards Understanding the Qurʾān*. Translated by Zafar Ishaq Ansari. Vol. 5, *Sūrahs 17–20*. Leicester, UK: The Islamic Foundation, 1995.
Merrill, Eugene H. *Deuteronomy*. The New American Commentary. Nashville, TN: Broadman & Holman, 1994.
Mir, Mustansir. "The Qurʾān, the Word of God." In *Voices of Islam*, edited by Vincent J. Cornell, 1:47–61. Voices of Tradition. Westport, CT: Praeger, 2007.
Moucarry, Chawkat Georges. *The Prophet & the Messiah: An Arab Christian's Perspective on Islam & Christianity*. Downers Grove, IL: InterVarsity, 2002.
Nickel, Gordon D. *Narratives of Tampering in the Earliest Commentaries on the Qurʾān*. Leiden, Netherlands: Brill, 2011.
Nickel, Gordon, and Andrew Rippin. "The Qurʾān." In *The Islamic World*, edited by Andrew Rippin, 145–56. London: Routledge, 2008.

O'Shaughnessy, Thomas J. *Creation and the Teaching of the Qurʾān*. Rome: Biblical Institute, 1985.
Reeves, John C. *Bible and Qurʾān: Essays in Scriptural Intertextuality*. Leiden, Netherlands: Brill, 2004.
Rippin, Andrew. *Muslims: Their Religious Beliefs and Practices*. New York: Routledge, 2005.
Saeed, Abdullah. "The Charge of Distortion of Jewish and Christian Scriptures." *Muslim World* 92.3–4 (2002) 419–36.
Shenk, David W. *Journeys of the Muslim Nation and the Christian Church: Exploring the Mission of Two Communities*. Scottdale, PA: Herald, 2003.
Sherif, Faruq. *A Guide to the Contents of the Qurʾān*. Berkshire, UK: Garnet & Ithaca, 1995.
Steenbrink, Karel A. *Adam Redivivus: Muslim Elaborations of the Adam Saga with Special Reference to the Indonesian Literary Traditions*. Zoetermeer, Netherlands: Meinema-Zoetermeer, 1998.
Tottoli, Roberto. *Biblical Prophets in the Qurʾān and Muslim Literature*. New York: Routledge, 2002.
Ur-Rahim, Muhammad Ata, and Ahmad Thomson. *Jesus: Prophet of Islam*. Rev. ed. Elmhurst, NY: Tahrike Tarcile Qurʾān, 1977.
VanGemeren, Willem A. *Interpreting the Prophetic Word: An Introduction to the Prophetic Literature of the Old Testament*. Grand Rapids: Zondervan, 1990.
Waardenburg, Jacques. *Muslims and Others: Relations in Context*. Berlin: Gruyter, 2003.
Wallace, Howard N. "Adam (Person)." In *Encyclopedia of the Bible and Its Reception*, edited by Hans-Josef Klauck, 300. Berlin: Gruyter, 2009.
Waltke, Bruce K. *Genesis: A Commentary*. Grand Rapids: Zondervan, 2001.
Wenham, Gordon J. *Genesis 1–15*. Waco, TX: Word, 1987.
Wheeler, Brannon. "Adam." In *The Qurʾān: An Encyclopedia*, edited by Oliver Leaman, 11–12. New York: Routledge, 2006.
———. "Arab Prophets of the Qurʾān and Bible." *Journal of Qurʾānic Studies* 8.2 (2006) 24–57.
———. *Prophets in the Qurʾān: An Introduction to the Qurʾān and Muslim Exegesis*. Annotated edition. London: Continuum, 2002.
Wood, Leon James. *The Prophets of Israel*. Grand Rapids: Baker, 1979.
Young, Edward J. *My Servants, the Prophets*. Grand Rapids: Eerdmans, 1952.

3

Prophet Nuh

The Proclaimer of Islamic Holism

Sam Kim

NOAH ("NUH") IS A representative figure in Islamic, Jewish, and Christian religious traditions.¹ In both Jewish and Christian faiths, Noah is one of the crucial patriarchs—an outstanding example of righteousness.² In Islamic tradition, Nuh narrative has many implicit meanings for Muslims in finding Allah within the holistic view. Allah sent Nuh as the first messenger (Awwal-irrasūl) to preach and warn the people of his day to worship Allah alone.³ I argue that the Nuh narrative resonates fundamental Islamic faith in the singularity of Allah and shows Nuh as a prototype for

---

1. In this paper, I differentiate Noah as a biblical character and Nuh as an Islamic figure in the Qur'ān. Nuh, however, is the same name used in the Arabic Bible and the Qur'ān. All quoted qur'ānic ayaat (verses) are from Yusuf Ali English translation and the Bible from NIV in English and Ketab il-haya in Arabic.

2. In Judaism, Noah's story is for Israel. Noah represents humanity in Islamic, Jewish, and Christian religious traditions. "We recall that the sages at hand find in the stories of creation and Noah reason to celebrate Israel's life and hope for Israel's salvation." Katsh, *Judaism in Islam*, 69.

3. Thirty men, one woman, and two archangels in the Bible appear in the Qur'ān, and six surahs have the names of biblical figures among them. Only Noah, Ishmael, Moses, Lot, and Jesus are called as messengers and prophets in the Qur'ān. Tottoli, *Biblical Prophets in the Qur'ān*, 72.

of the prophet Muhammad. To demonstrate this, I will research specific implicit meanings of the Nuh narrative and compare major differences between the Noah in the Bible and Nuh narratives in the Qurʾān.

I. Noah and Nuh Narratives

1. The Noah Narrative in the Bible

Noah's story can be broken down into three parts between Gen 6–9; before the flood, the flood, and after the flood. In the Bible, the Noah story is not a just punishment story of God's anger toward the sin of humanity, but a reverse creation narrative and new covenant between God and human beings. In Christianity, Noah is one of the patriarchs, not a prophet.

When God created creatures and human beings, he saw them as good (Gen 1:31, "God saw all that he had made, and it was good"). However, when God looked at human beings' wickedness, he was grieved (or "sad" in Arabic translation) in the times of Noah and decided to destroy everything he created.

> The Lord saw how great the wickedness of the human race had become on the earth, and that every inclination of the thoughts of the human heart was only evil all the time. The Lord regretted that he had made human beings on the earth, and his heart was deeply troubled. (Gen 6:5–6)

Noah, however, found favor in the sight of the Lord (Gen 6:8). Allah commanded Noah to build an ark (Gen 6:13–21). After Noah built the ark, he and his family embarked on the ark along with two of every kind of living animals (Gen 7:6–10). As God warned, there was a big flood for forty days and nights. Almost a year later, the ground was dried, God commanded Noah to get out of the ark, and he gave him authority over animals.

> Then God said to Noah, "Come out of the ark, you and your wife and your sons and their wives. Bring out every kind of living creature that is with you—the birds, the animals, and all the creatures that move along the ground—so they can multiply on the earth and be fruitful and increase in number on it." (Gen 8:16–17)

Noah made a burnt offering to God. God made the covenant in which he stated he will never again destroy all life "by the waters of flood" and he gave the rainbow as the sign of the covenant (Gen 8:21; 9:8–17). God also blessed Noah and his sons saying "Be fruitful and increase in number and fill the earth" (Gen 9:1).

In other passages of the Bible, Noah's story is related to the day of Judgment.[4] In Matthew and Luke, Jesus referenced Noah's flood story as an example of God's judgement. In 2 Pet 2:5, Noah was called a preacher of righteousness, and his faith and obedience were recognized by God in 1 Pet 3:20 and Heb 11:7 as well. In general, Noah and the ark are considered types or metaphors of the final judgement and the redemptional work of God. God invited Noah and his family into the ark to save them, and in the New Testament God invites his people into the faith of Jesus Christ to save.

2. The Nuh Narrative in the Qur'ān

The Nuh narrative is spread over the Qur'ān. In particular, as a symbol of punishment of Allah, Nuh is mentioned along with Hud, Salih, and Shu'aub—each one of them was also sent to people in their times (Q7:65, 73, 85). In the Qur'ān (like the Bible), Nuh was a son of Lamech, son of Methuselah, son of Enoch, son of Mahalalel, son of Kenan, son of Enosh, son of Seth, but Nuh's mother was Qaynush coming from Cain's descendants, according to ibn Abbas.[5] Tabari's describes that Nuh lived in the time of Bewarashb.[6] His ministerial area was considered to be Mesopotamia.[7] According to Abū Isḥāq, from the period of Adam, Allah had commanded "the children of Seth not to intermarry with the children of Cain."[8] However, in the course of time, two hundred sons of Seth disobeyed this command of Allah and married Cain's descendants. As a result, their intermarriage corrupted the earth, and people started to worship idols such as Wadd, Suwa, Yaghuth, Ya'uq, and Nasr (Q71:20–23).[9]

---

4. Cf. Isa 54:9; Ezek 14:14, 20.
5. Al-Thaʻlabī, *'Arāʼis al-majālis*, 92.
6. Al-Tabari, *History of al-Tabari*, 348.
7. Muhammad, *One God, One Creed*, 2.
8. Al-Thaʻlabī, *'Arāʼis al-majālis*, 92–93.
9. Gatje, *Qur'ān and Its Exegesis*, 143. In the days of tribesmen (*qaum*) of Noah, the tribe of "Kalb accepted Wadd, [the tribe of] Hamdan accepted Suwa', [the tribe of] Madhhij accepted Yaghuth, [the tribe of] Murad accepted Ya'qu, and [the tribe of] Himyar accepted Nasr. Thus, an Arab maybe named 'Abd Wadd [the servant of Wadd] or 'Abd Yaghuth [the servant of Yaghuth]." Al-Thaʻlabī, *'Arāʼis al-majālis*, 92–93.

Allah, therefore, sent Nuh when he was 480 years old to warn and convict the unjust and rebellious people by night and by day for 120 years (Q71:5; 53:52).[10] He asked people to worship Allah alone and warned that if they refused, there would be punishment from Allah. Most people, however, refused to take Nuh's warnings, and rather mocked and threatened, saying "you are . . . to be stoned or banished from the community" by people (Q 26:116; 54:9).[11] In fact, Allah foretold Nuh that none of the people would believe Nuh's warnings so that Nuh would not grieve for them (Q11:36–38; 9:41). The Qur'ān does not describe Allah's emotion of grief unlike the Bible. For Muslims, Allah is Omniscient and Omnipotent. It is not possible that Allah is regretted what he did.

After preaching over the years, Nuh prayed and requested that Allah give them whatever punishment they deserved. To answer Noah's request, Allah told Nuh that there would be an imminent flood and commanded to build the ark. Allah also sent the angel Gabriel to teach Nuh how to build it.[12] Nuh, therefore, planted teak trees and later used the lumber from these trees to build the ark. The size of the ark was "three hundred yards long, fifty yards wide and towered up to a height of thirty yards. There were three rooms inside . . . Noah took the body of Adam with him and laid it crosswise between the men and the women" in the ark.[13]

According to the commands of Allah, Nuh boarded the ark at the age of 600 years with family, his closest companions who followed Allah's

10. Al-Tabari, *History of al-Tabari*, 348.

11. Cf. "The term rujum in the Qur'ān is semantically connected to the term rajim—traditional understand thereof as 'deserving to be stoned,' but also banished or outcast. Marjum—which appears in the course of the unbeliever's threatening to stone him, but if this term is related to rajim they might rather be threatening him with banishment." Reynolds, *Qur'ān and Its Biblical Subtext*, 64. In the Bible, statements of people's insulting respond to Noah's warnings were little, but in the Qur'ān, it was detailed. It is because the Qur'ān followed and took Jewish Midrash versions of Noah stories. In Midrash descriptions, more active actions of Noah's warnings and hostile responses of people are founded. For instance, Tanchuma (one of midrash) states that "they mocked and laughed at him in their words," and Genesis Rabbah (the collection of rabbinic interpretation of the book of Genesis) examples that "people asked Noah why he was so busy with planting cedars and then later cutting them down. 'Because the Master of the Universe told me that he is bringing a flood to the world' was his reply." Peoples' response, however, was against Noah, and they ridiculed him. Lodahl, *Claiming Abraham*, 118.

12. Al-Tha'labī, *'Arā'is al-majālis*, 94.

13. Gatje, *Qur'ān and Its Exegesis*, 102–3. There are various opinions on the size of the ark. For example, "according to al-Hasan the Ark was a thousand two hundred yards long and six hundred yards wide long."

commands,[14] and two of each living creature.[15] However, the unbelievers and one of Nuh's son were drowned (Q11:42–43).[16] Nuh's children were Shem, Ham, Japheth, and Canaan or Yām, and "they all had the same mother."[17] After six month, all people and animals got off the ark following the commands of Allah at mountain Judi (Q11:44). After building the ark, Nuh lived 350 years more.[18] For 950 years, Nuh was faithful to Allah (Q29:14–15).

II. The Meaning of Nuh's Narrative for Muslims

1. The Manifestation of Allah's attributes

The Nuh narrative seeks to reveal Allah's justice and mercy through the messenger and the message. *'Adl* ("justice," العدل) means the system of laws that judges or punishes people.[19] In the Qur'ān, justice is described as an absolute basis of Allah's act. Justice is also key in the responsibilities of Muslims, as Allah commands, and includes broad "social and economic justice."[20] Ultimately, Allah sends messengers for the sole purpose of warning people of His justice.

> We sent aforetime our messengers with Clear Signs and sent down with them the Book and the Balance (of Right and Wrong), that men may stand forth in justice; and We sent down Iron, in which is (material for) mighty war, as well as many benefits for mankind, that Allah may test who it is that will help, Unseen,

---

14. According to Muqatil, there were over seventy people in the ark. Al-Tha'labī, *'Arā'is al-majālis*, 98.

15. Al-Tabari, *History of al-Tabari*, 348.

16. There are some arguments about this son. Some Islamic scholars such as Ali and al-Hasan asserts that this son was not Nuh's son, but his wife's. Gatje, *Qur'ān and Its Exegesis*, 104. Nuh's wife is mentioned as unfaithful betrayers against their husbands by rejecting their doctrine. Allah sets forth, for an example to the Unbelievers, the wife of Noah and the wife of Lut: they were (respectively) under two of our righteous servants, but they were false to their (husbands), and they profited nothing before Allah on their account, but were told: "Enter ye the Fire along with (others) that enter!" (Q66:10).

17. Gatje, *Qur'ān and Its Exegesis*, 368.

18. Al-Tabari, *History of al-Tabari*, 348.

19. See "Justice."

20. Aminu-Kano and FitzGibbon, *Islamic Development*, 15.

Him and His messengers: For Allah is Full of Strength, Exalted in Might (and able to enforce His Will). (Q57:25)

Nuh's narrative as purported by the Qur'ān is a typical example of Allah's punishment and a manifestation of his justice. Whenever the day of Judgment is mentioned in the Qur'ān, the statement that Allah sent his prophet Nuh along with Hud, Salih, and Shuaib is mentioned.[21] Therefore, Nuh's ark is a symbol of Allah's justice to judge the wickedness of human beings.

However, on the other hand, Muslims understand Allah's justice is another expression of his mercy. In Islam, "justice and awareness of human frailty are involved in the exercise of divine mercy. Because of mercy, persons who turn to God in sincere repentance and who then journey on the Straight Path will be forgiven by the gracious Master."[22] Nuh's ark represents Allah's compassion and mercy towards human beings. Nuh's ark was open to anybody who obeyed the guidance of Prophet Nuh from Allah. It goes beyond the tribal or clan limits. Allah's attributes of compassion and mercy allow his prophets and messengers to work on the earth and guide and help the needy.[23]

2. Islamic Holism—Tawhid and Ummah

Allah's commands through Nuh were not just moral codes. Nuh's religion is based on divine unity (Q71:3), so that Nuh invited people into this oneness of Allah. Submission to Allah through entering the ark, which reflects a belonging to Ummah to obey the prophet's warning, is the only path to save people's lives. Allah wanted to create a new human being community—Ummah. Noah's ark is to preserve the Tawhid faith and Ummah in which people have believed in the oneness of Allah

1) Holism in Islam

In Islam, we can find the biggest act of conformity through all beliefs, rituals, and practices. The religion of Islam is "one in which all life realms are

---

21. For examples, Q7:65, 73, 85 and so on.
22. Wagner, *Opening the Qur'ān*, 353.
23. Raser, "Compassion," 158.

consolidated into a harmonious whole."[24] This holism, therefore, is resonated in the universe, all religious rituals and structures, Muslims' practices such as daily confession of faith (Shahadha), the invocation of Allah (Biismilahiwarahman), Five pillars, Sharia and so on. Within this frame, Allah is described in Tawhid (monotheism, unity, or oneness) beliefs. This holistic understanding is reflected in Ummah towards human beings.

2) Tawhid

Muslim's understanding of the concept of wholeness is represented well in the concept of Tawhid towards Allah and Ummah towards human beings. Tawhid refers to the state of unity, oneness and uniqueness of Allah. The first statement of Muslim's daily faith confession (Shahadha) is that there is no other god, but Allah. This Tawhid unifies all creation under Allah's oneness.[25] Therefore, this Islamic holistic view of the oneness of Allah penetrates the existence of all humanity and the universe.

> Unity in Islam defines humankind's vertical relationship with God, an individual's relationship with himself or herself, human-to-human relationships and humanity's relationship with other creations.[26]

The Nuh narrative enhances the concept of Tawhid and declares that Nuh is "the proclaimer of the One—Only God and Straight Path (Q54:17–22)."[27]

3) Ummah

Ummah is the brotherly community which shares the same religious belief. In Q49:10, it declares that Muslim believers are "but a single brotherhood." In Q3:110 of the Mohsin Khan translation, it states that Ummah is a confession of monotheism and the prophethood of Muhammad.

> You [true believers in Islamic Monotheism, and real followers of Prophet Muhammad SAW and his Sunnah (legal ways, etc.)] are the best of peoples ever raised up for mankind; you enjoin Al-Ma'ruf [i.e. Islamic Monotheism and all that Islam has ordained]

---

24. Odessy, "Islamic Holistic Philosophy," 7.
25. Aminu-Kano and FitzGibbon, *Islamic Development*, 3.
26. Salek, *Faith Inspiration in a Secular World*, 353.
27. Wagner, *Opening the Qur'ān*, 3.

and forbid Al-Munkar [polytheism, disbelief and all that Islam has forbidden], and you believe in Allah. And had the people of the Scripture [Jews and Christians] believed, it would have been better for them; among them are some who have faith, but most of them are Al-Fasiqun [disobedient to Allah—and rebellious against Allah's Command].

Ummah goes beyond a bloodline. As it can be seen, the story of Nuh's drowned son (Q11:42–46) explicates how Ummah is bonded into faith in Allah. This is a unique story which cannot be found in Christian or Jewish traditions. Although he was a son of Nuh, Allah said to Nuh that his son was not his family because he did not believe in Allah and Nuh's warnings.

> And Noah called upon his Lord and said: "O my Lord! surely my son is of my family! and Thy promise is true and Thou art the Justest of Judges!" He said: "O Noah! he is not of thy family: for his conduct is unrighteous. So ask not of Me that of which thou hast no knowledge! I give thee counsel lest thou act like the ignorant!" (Q11:45–46)

The narrative of the drowned son highlights that "the bond of faith is greater than that of blood and that an intercession on behalf of unbeliever family member is of no value."[28] Wagner Walter also strongly argues that "the Ummah is constituted not by ethnicity or social rank but by the unity of believers confessing-worshiping-serving the one God."[29]

Furthermore, the meaning of entering the ark includes keeping the Divine law, Sharia, and is accomplishment of Tawhid confession as well.[30] Ibn al-'Arabi and his followers tried to use a "parallel exegesis," and in Nuh the exegesis argue "where the sea is related to matter and the saving ship to divine law, this approach of using parallels sees actual events and lawful decisions as symbols for the spiritual world."[31] In Islam Allah's revelation is "more about law than theology" and sharia is considered

---

28. Tottoli, *Biblical Prophets in the Qur'ān*, 22–23.

29. Wagner, *Opening the Qur'ān*, 353.

30. Another interpretation of the ark is for the ark of the covenant (Q2:248; 20:39). tabuut. Reynolds, *Qur'an and Its Biblical Subtext*, 100.

31. Gatje, *Qur'ān and Its Exegesis*, 40–41. "They maintain the character of reality of the external meaning; yet at the same time they see 'allusions' in this, which are important to understand. Since the external meaning is generally treated exhaustively in the traditional exegesis, not much of an effort is made towards an interpretation in this direction." In uncovering the inner meaning, a distinction is made between actual allegorical interpretation (ta'wil) and the 'uncovering of parallels'(tatbiq)."

Allah's "blueprint helping people to find the "straight path" that will lead to life in this world and the next."[32] Sharia is the Divine law which reflects Allah's attributes in implement of the law in every area of Muslims' life and to bind them as one brotherhood.

3. Prototype of the Prophet Muhammad

The conformity of Muhammad as the last prophet and messenger of Allah is crucial fundamental of Islamic doctrines.[33] The role of messenger is "the representative of God [Allah] among his people, with the responsibility and authority."[34] Nuh's situations and messages have mirrored Muhammad's contexts. Abū Isḥāq states that "in the Muslim typology of prophecy, Noah [Nuh] represents perhaps the ideal prototype of all prophets and foreshadows the early career of the Prophet Muhammad—until the success of the latter in spreading his message clearly averts such punishment from his people."[35]

1) The One message

Allah establishes the same religion and give the same message to all prophets. In Q4:163, Allah gave one message to Muhammad, which was precisely the same message given to Noah and other messengers.

> We have sent thee inspiration, as We sent it to Noah and the Messengers after him: we sent inspiration to Abraham, Isma'il, Isaac, Jacob and the Tribes, to Jesus, Job, Jonah, Aaron, and Solomon, and to David We gave the Psalms. (Q4:163)
>
> The same religion has He established for you as that which He enjoined on Noah—the which We have sent by inspiration to thee—and that which We enjoined on Abraham, Moses, and Jesus: Namely, that ye should remain steadfast in religion, and

---

32. Aminu-Kano and FitzGibbon, *Islamic Development*, 17.

33. "Of utmost importance is the fact that almost all of those verses in which Muhammad is referred to as nabī occur in the final period of the revelation, that is, in the Medinan verses. Muhammad is therefore identified as prophet predominantly in the last part of his mission and rather than at in the earlier Meccan period." Tottoli, *Biblical prophets in the Qur'ān*, 73.

34. Tottoli, *Biblical Prophets in the Qur'ān*, 73.

35. Al-Thaʻlabī, *ʻArāʼis al-majālis*, 71.

make no divisions therein: to those who worship other things than Allah, hard is the [way] to which thou callest them. Allah chooses to Himself those whom He pleases, and guides to Himself those who turn [to Him]. (Q42:13)

Nuh's message toward people which was essentially "worship Allah alone" was the same which Muhammad told the polytheist in Mecca (Q11:25–26). Allah commanded Muhammad to recite the Nuh story towards the Meccan people and encouraged Muhammad to go through the same difficult situations of Noah (Q10:71). As Noah and his companions had to enter the ark by the invitation of Allah, Muhammad and his companions made Hijra by the will of Allah. The drowned son's story reminds us of peoples in Muhammad's own experience from Mecca to Medina. As aforementioned, the people who got on the ark was the first Ummah which was community with one monotheistic religion.[36] Muhammad can use these illustrations for encouraging those companies who were worried about their relatives left behind in their migration to Medina.

> With this new twist in Noah's story, the Qur'ān underscores the idea that Islam creates a new kind of social arrangement, a polis or social identity that is not dependent upon blood kinship but rather upon submission to Allah's will. Indeed, that spirit of submission is embodied in the next slice of the Qur'ān's narrative.[37]

2) Persecutions

The Qur'ānic verses about persecutions in the Nuh narratives are regarded as the same contexts of Muhammad in Mecca. He was accused as a liar, sorcerer, or being possessed (Q51:52; 52:49; 68:2; 69:41; 81:22–25).[38] The message to Qurayshi leaders which Muhammad declared was the same as that proclaimed by Noah, and people's mocking to Muhammad was the same as well. For instance, in Q23:24 the people of Noah criticized Nuh that he wanted to establish his personal superiority, so that Allah should have sent them an angel to warn them, but not a human. In Q11:31, Noah himself affirms that he did not say "I am an angel" before God, but God sent him to warn his oppressors. This word was repeated when

---

36. Gatje, *Qur'ān and Its Exegesis*, 93.
37. Lodhal, *Claiming Abraham*, 121.
38. El-Badawi, *Qur'ān and the Aramaic Gospel*, 86.

God ordered Muhammad to declare his message. He told the Meccan people that he did not say he was an angel in Q6:50.[39] Nuh was the most suffering servant of Allah. Aḥmad ibn Muḥammad al-Thaʿlabī states that "none of the other Messengers did as much in their mission as he did, for he preached to his people day and night and no prophet suffered from his nation the blows, insults and types of injury and roughness that he received."[40] Muhammad also went through severe persecutions from the people in his day.

3) Intercession of Nuh and Muhammad

Nuh is not only the prototype of Muhammad, but he has the same spiritual status as Muhammad. In the Nuh narrative, Nuh cried out to Allah before the flood.

> [In the days of old], Noah cried to Us, and We are the best to hear prayer. And We delivered him and his people from the Great Calamity, And made his progeny to endure [on this earth]; And We left [this blessing] for him among generations to come in later times: "Peace and salutation to Noah among the nations! (Q37:75–79)

Muhammad is known as an intercessor for Muslims on the final judgement day.

> And pray in the small watches of the morning: [it would be] an additional prayer [or spiritual profit] for thee: soon will thy Lord raise thee to a Station of Praise and Glory! (Q17:79)

According to the account of Abu Hurayra, Muhammad also elevated Nuh as an intercessor for Muslims. When his companions asked about Nuh, Muhammad repeated a story in the times of Nuh where people asked Nuh to be an intercessor for themselves. "You are the first of the messengers sent to earth and God named you 'grateful servant', please intercede on our behalf with your Lord, don't you see what trouble we are in?"[41]

---

39. El-Badawi, *Qurʾān and the Aramaic Gospel*, 52.

40. Al-Thaʿlabī, *ʿArāʾis al-majālis*, 103.

41. Tottoli, *Biblical Prophets in the Qurʾān*, 116, re-quotation of Sahih Muslim I. 184–85 NO194.

IV. Comparison of the Noah and Nuh Narratives

1. The Titles

In the Bible, as one of the patriarchs, Noah is not identified as a prophet. Noah, however, is the first person called a righteous man. In Gen 6:9–11 and 7:5, Noah was a righteous man, blameless in his generation, and had walked with God. He has, also, an honorific title, "a herald of righteousness." In the Aramaic Gospel Tradition, the world for "righteous one" (*slihe*) became "the standard word for apostle in Syriac."[42]

> If he did not spare the ancient world when he brought the flood on its ungodly people, but protected Noah, a preacher of righteousness, and seven others. (2 Pet 2:5)[43]

Noah's faith is recognized by God and even his faith was able to condemn the world. By the grace and favor of God, he became heir of the righteousness. Not by his work, but by faith in God and grace of God, he and his family were saved.

> By faith Noah, when warned about things not yet seen, in holy fear built an ark to save his family. By his faith he condemned the world and became heir of the righteousness that is in keeping with faith. (Heb 11:7)

The Noah story reflects God's righteousness through his redemptional work through Noah's belief in God. In that sense, we can go further to see the typology of Jesus and his work. Many biblical exegesis scholars describe the ark as Jesus and his redemptional work.[44] Jesus is the shelter for the people of God. Noah's ark is not planned or designed from his own ideas, but God. After the flood, Noah was drunken and showed that he had weakness to need a savior.

Nuh in the Qur'ān is called a grateful servant (slavery) of Allah (الله عبد عظيم) and is identified as one of the prophets and messenger's lines. Nuh was faithful to the commands and the guidance of Allah. As in the Aramaic Gospel Tradition, the righteousness is also used for Allah's messengers and prophets.[45] This character is to prove their prophethood in

---

42. El-Badawi, *Qur'ān and the Aramaic Gospel*, 87.

43. لَمْ يَعْفُ اللهُ عَنِ الْعَالَمِ الْقَدِيْمِ، لَكِنَّهُ أَنْقَذَ نُوحَ الَّذِي كَانَ يَعِظُ مَنَادِياً بِحَيَاةِ الْبِرِّ، وَأَنْقَذَ سَبْعَةً آخَرِيْنَ مَعَهُ، عِنْدَمَا أَرْسَلَ الطُّوفَانَ عَلَى عَالَمِ الْأَشْرَارِ

44. Michaels, *Oxford Bible Interpreter*, 265–72.

45. El-Badawi, *Qur'ān and the Aramaic Gospel Traditions*, 87.

the Qur'ān. In the Qur'ān, Allah punished man's wicked generations in other prophets' times since Nuh. There was no special description such as is stated in Scripture when it says, "the times of the people of Noah were unique for their evil and rebellion."[46] Nuh carried out his commission from Allah as just a prophet and messenger among many.

> How many generations have We destroyed after Noah? and enough is thy Lord to note and see the sins of His servants. (Q17:17)

According to Ibn 'Abbas, between Adam and Noah, the people followed a single religion.[47] However, people's wickedness caused the anger of Allah, and Allah sent Nuh to them. Nuh was not only a prophet, but also a great exemplar for all Muslims in his righteous acts to obey Allah's commands (Q37:75–82) in his day.[48] Allah takes care of and responds to human merit. "The merit of Nuh consists in his admonishing his age, in obedience to God's message."[49]

2. The Purpose of the Flood Punishment

First Corinthians 10:11 says that the Old Testament shows many examples to warn or foretells for the believers. In 1 Pet 3:20–21, God waited patiently for people to repent from their wickedness while Noah was building the ark. The flood of Noah's time is used as "*antitupon*," in Greek origin a type, typology, or sign, as a type of baptism.[50] As Noah's family was saved in the ark from the flood, human beings are saved by the resurrection of Jesus Christ. In the Bible, God created a new Adam and generation through the flood. As one of the types and shadows of Jesus in the Old Testament, Noah's story has reflected the redemptional work of Jesus. Noah worshiped God and offered burnt offerings. He was called an heir of righteousness, because he found favor in God and faith in God. His drunkenness also showed that he was merely a human being who need Jesus.

In Islamic accounts, there is no specific statements after the flood incidents about Nuh story. The Nuh narratives aim to show the ideal

---

46. Lodhal, *Claiming Abraham*, 114.
47. Gatje, *Qur'ān and Its Exegesis*, 94–95.
48. Wagner, *Opening the Qur'ān*, 305.
49. Neusner, *Christian Faith and the Bible*, 85.
50. *Oxford Bible Interpreter*, 264–65.

Islamic community and the importance of belief in the oneness of God. In parallel exegesis of Ibn al-'Arabi and his followers, "where the sea is related to matter and the saving ship to divine law" in the Nuh narratives.[51] Only Ummah which is with Tawhid and divine law can be the only community survived from the final judgement.

IV. Conclusion

Noah in the Bible and Nuh in the Qur'ān is the pivotal figure in both traditions. After the Creation, God set the covenant and blessed him as he blessed Adam in Christianity. Noah's narrative symbolizes Jesus' redemptional life and ministries. We, therefore, can find a sign (typology) of Jesus' cross and resurrection and his redemptional work.

Nuh is considered the first messenger and leader of the first Ummah in Islam. The Nuh narrative has resonated in Islamic holism as forms of Tawhid and Ummah. Furthermore, Nuh within the line of prophet and messenger is a prototype of Muhammad and at the same time an excellent exemplar for all Muslims in his submission to Allah's commands and guidance.

Appendix 1. Important Qur'ānic Ayaat (verses)

Warning:

7:59–64 We sent Noah to his people. He said: "O my people! worship Allah! ye have no other god but Him. I fear for you the punishment of a dreadful day!"

Rejection:

14:9 Has not the story reached you (O people!), of those who (went) before you?—of the people of Noah, and 'Ad, and Thamud?—And of those who (came) after them? None knows them but Allah. To them came messengers with Clear (Signs); but they put their hands up to

---

51. "They maintain the character of reality of the external meaning; yet at the same time they see 'allusions' in this, which are important to understand. Since the external meaning is generally treated exhaustively in the traditional exegesis, not much of an effort is made towards an interpretation in this direction. In uncovering the inner meaning, a distinction is made between actual allegorical interpretation (ta'wil) and the 'uncovering of parallels' (tatbiq)." Gatje, *Qur'ān and Its Exegesis*, 40–41.

their mouths, and said: "We do deny (the mission) on which ye have been sent, and we are really in suspicious (disquieting) doubt as to that to which ye invite us."

17:17 How many generations have We destroyed after Noah? And enough is thy Lord to note and see the sins of His servants.

Allah Sent Noah

11:25 We sent Noah to his people (with a mission): "I have come to you with a Clear Warning:

26 "That ye serve none but Allah: verily I do fear for you the Penalty of a Grievous Day."

27 But the Chiefs of the Unbelievers among his people said: "We see (in) thee nothing but a man like ourselves: nor do we see that any follow thee but the meanest among us in judgment immature: nor do we see in you (all) any merit above us: in fact we think ye are liars!"

28 He said: "O my people! see ye if (it be that) I have a Clear Sign from my Lord and that He hath sent Mercy unto me from His own Presence but that the Mercy hath been obscured from your sight? Shall we compel you to accept it when ye are averse to it?

29 "And O my People! I ask you for no wealth in return: my reward is from none but Allah: but I will not drive away (in contempt) those who believe: for verily they are to meet their Lord and ye I see are the ignorant ones!

30 "And O my People! who would help me against Allah if I drove them away? Will ye not then take heed?

31 "I tell you not that with me are the Treasures of Allah nor do I know what is hidden nor claim I to be an angel. Nor yet do I say of those whom your eyes do despise that Allah will not grant them (all) that is good: Allah knoweth best what is in their souls: I should if I did indeed be a wrongdoer."

32 They said: "O Noah! thou hast disputed with us and (much) hast thou prolonged the dispute with us: now bring upon us what thou threatenest us with if thou speakest the truth!"

33 He said: "Truly Allah will bring it on you if He wills and then ye will not be able to frustrate it!

34 "Of no profit will be my counsel to you much as I desire to give you (good) counsel if it be that Allah willeth to leave you astray: He is your Lord! and to Him will ye return!"

35 Or do they say "He has forged it?" Say: "If I had forged it on me were my sin! And I am free of the sins of which ye are guilty!"

Allah Commanded Nuh to Build and Ark

36 It was revealed to Noah: "None of thy people will believe except those who have believed already! So grieve no longer over their (evil) deeds.

37 "But construct an Ark under Our eyes and Our inspiration and address Me no (further) on behalf of those who are in sin: for they are about to be overwhelmed (in the Flood)."

38 Forthwith he starts constructing the Ark: every time that the Chiefs of his People passed by him they threw ridicule on him. They threw ridicule on him. He said: "If ye ridicule us now we (in our turn) can look down on you with ridicule likewise!

39 "But soon will ye know who it is on whom will descend a Penalty that will cover them with shame will be unloosed a Penalty lasting."

Allah Commanded Nuh to Embark and Gather on Board the Believers and a Pair from Every Species

40 At length behold! there came Our Command and the fountains of the earth gushed forth! We said: "Embark therein of each kind two male and female and your family except those against whom the Word has already gone forth and the Believers." But only a few believed with him.

41 So he said: "Embark ye on the Ark in the name of Allah whether it move or be at rest! For my Lord is be sure Oft-Forgiving Most Merciful!"

Dialogue between Nuh, His Son, and Allah

42 So the Ark floated with them on the waves (towering) like mountains and Noah called out to his son who had separated himself (from the rest): "O my son! embark with us and be not with the Unbelievers!"

43 The son replied: "I will be take myself to some mountain: it will save me from the water." Noah said: "This day nothing can save from the Command of Allah any but those on whom He hath mercy!" and the waves came between them and the son was among those overwhelmed in the Flood.

44 When the word went forth: "O earth! swallow up thy water and O sky! withhold (thy rain)!" and the water abated and the matter was ended. The Ark rested on Mount Judi and the word went forth: "Away with those who do wrong!"

45 And Noah called upon his Lord and said: "O my Lord! surely my son is of my family! and Thy promise is true and Thou art the Justest of Judges!"

46 He said: "O Noah! he is not of thy family: for his conduct is unrighteous. So ask not of Me that of which thou hast no knowledge! I give thee counsel lest thou act like the ignorant!"

47 Noah said: "O my Lord! I do seek refuge with Thee lest I ask Thee for that of which I have no knowledge. And unless Thou forgive me and have Mercy on me I should indeed be lost!"

48 The word came: "O Noah! come down (from the Ark) with Peace from Us and Blessings on thee and on some of the Peoples (who will spring) from those with thee: but (there will be other) Peoples to whom We shall grant their pleasures (for a time) but in the end will a grievous Penalty reach them from Us."

Appendix 2 Differences between Noah and the Nuh Narratives

	Noah	Nuh
Covenant	Noahide covenant with rainbow sigh in Gen 9:20-25	Q33:7 And when we made a covenant with the prophets with thee, and with Noah, and Abraham, and Moses, and Jesus, the son of Mary; a solemn covenant we made with them.
Weakness of Noah	Being drunkenness of Noah and curse on Ham	No mention

	Noah	Nuh
Decreation	Gen 7:11–16 "The fountains of the great deep burst forth"—an act of divine decreation[52]	Q11:40–41 There is the mention of waters gushing forth from the earth and not simply rainfall; there is also the mention of two animals of every kind
Number of animals	"Two of every kind," of every living thing, of all flesh" in Gen 6:19, and "seven pairs of all clean animals and seven pairs of the birds of the air also" in Gen 7:2–3	Q11:40 "Two of every kind" animals on the board
Disembarkment	Genesis 8 Process of Disembarkment— Raven, Dove . . .	Q11:44/46 Earth swallowed waters and Heaven holed the rain. So the ark settled on al-Judi. No mention of a dove.

Bibliography

Al-Tabari, Abu Ja'far Muhammad b. Jarir. *The History of al-Tabari: General Introduction and from the Creation to the Flood*. Translated by Franz Resenthal. Albany, NY: State University of New York Press, 1989.

Al-Tha'labī, Aḥmad ibn Muḥammad. *'Arā'is al-majālis fī qiṣaṣ al-anbiyā': Lives of the Prophets*. Translated by William M Brinne. Leiden, Netherlands: Brill, 2002.

Aminu-Kano, Muhtari., and Atallah FitzGibbon. "Islamic Development." https://www.islamic-relief.org/.

El-Badawi, Emran Iqbal. *The Qur'ān and the Aramaic Gospel Traditions*. New York: Routledge, 2014.

Gatje, Helmut. *The Qur'ān and Its Exegesis: Selected Texts with Classical and Modern Muslim Interpretations*. Translated and edited by Alford T. Welch. Oakland, CA: University of California Press, 1976.

"Justice." https://dictionary.cambridge.org/dictionary/english-arabic/justice.

Katsh, Abraham I. *Judaism in Islam: Biblical and Talmudic Backgrounds of the Koran and Its Commentaries*. New York: New York University Press, 1954.

---

52. Lodhal, *Claiming Abraham: Reading the Bible and the Qur'ān Side by Side*, 114.

Lodahl, Michael. *Claiming Abraham: Reading the Bible and the Qur'ān Side by Side.* Grand Rapids, MI: Brazos, 2010.

Muhammad, T. *One God, One Creed: A Brief Analysis of the Undercurrents of Indian Thought.* Calicut, India: Islamic Publishing House, 1980.

Neusner, Jacob. *Christian Faith and the Bible of Judaism: The Judaic Encounter with Scripture.* Grand Rapids, MI: Eerdmans, 1987.

Odessy, Dina El. "Islamic Holistic Philosophy." Presentation at One World: Logical and Ethical Implications of Holism Conference, University of Essex, September 8. 2017.

The Oxford Bible Interpreter: 1 Peter and 2 Peter. Seoul, Korea: Disciples' Publishing House, 2006.

"The Prophet Nuh (as)—Second of the Great Ones." https://web.archive.org/web/20210414023724/http://circlegroup.org/the-prophet-nuh-as-second-of-the-great-ones/.

Raser, Harold E. "Compassion: Being the Hands and Feet of God." In *Missio Dei: A Wesleyan Understanding.* edited by Keith Schwanz and Joseph Coleson, 158–67. Kansas, MO: Beacon Hill, 2011.

Reynolds, Gabriel Said. *The Qur'ān and Its Biblical Subtext.* New York: Routledge, 2010.

Salek, Lucy V. "Faith Inspiration in a Secular World: An Islamic Perspective on Humanitarian Principles." *International Review of The Red Cross* 97.897/898 (2016) 345–70.

Tottoli, Roberto. *Biblical Prophets in the Qur'ān and Muslim Literature.* Translated by Michael Robertson. Surrey, UK: Curzon, 2002.

Wagner, Walter H. *Opening the Qur'ān: Introducing Islam's Holy Book.* Notre Dame, IN: University Notre Dame Press, 2008.

4

Textual and Contextual Reading of Biblical Abraham and the Qur'ānic 'Ibrāhīm

Il Joo Kong

I. Introduction

IN 2015, MUSLIM SCHOLARS reported that the world has recently been going through security, political, and intellectual crises, which have resulted in wrong practices in the Islamic world such as takfīr, atheism, jihād, and so on. Muslim scholars and thinkers hope to correct some misconceptions that may lead to extremism. In February 2019, Pope Francis and Ahmad al-Tayyib signed a document titled *Human Fraternity for Peace and Living together*. And the higher committee for human fraternity announced to house a mosque, a church, and a synagogue for inter-religious dialogue and exchange in Abu Dhabi.

To prevent some Muslims from leaning toward extremism today, Islamic governments and religious circles have given new concepts to key religious terms. On the other hand, religious leaders have said that the common ancestor of Judaism, Christianity, and Islam was Abraham. In this paper, we aim to investigate the similarities and differences between 'Ibrāhīm of the Qur'ān and Abraham of the Bible.

We prefer to read the Arabic Qur'ān to figure out the meaning of the Qur'ān, rather than an English translation of the Qur'ān. For example, literal translations of Arabic idioms and rhetorical questions often result in meaningless English. There are many mistranslations in it. One further cause for misinterpretation is the lack of awareness of the different meanings of a given word in different Qur'ānic contexts.

Context is crucial in interpreting the meaning of the Qur'ānic discourse. Traditionally, Arab Muslim exegetes divided interpretation of the Qur'ān into the two major types: Tafsīr bi- al-Ma'thūr (Interpretation of the Qur'ān by transmitted statements of Muḥammad, his Companions and their successors) and Tafsīr bi-al-Ra'y (Interpretation of the Qur'ān by personal opinion). According to the Sunni method of interpretation, tafsīr based on personal opinion (Tafsīr bi-al-Ra'y) completely supersedes tafsīr-based authentic narration (Tafsīr bi-al-Ma'thūr). Thus, the only acceptable tafsir for them is that which adheres to the following sequence: tafsīr of the Qur'ān by the Qur'ān, then by the Sunnah, then by the sayings of the Ṣaḥābah (Muslims who actually met Muḥammad) and Tābi'īn (Muslims who met Ṣaḥābah), then by the Arabic language, and finally by opinion, as long as it is based on the preceding four methods and does not contradict any of them.[1] They remained as such until modern times.

In our discussion, the term "context" is used to refer to two things: i) Parts of a statement that precede or follow a given word or phrase and influence its meaning, referred to in Arabic as *Siyāq* (context) or *Siyāq al-Naṣṣ* (textual context). ii) The context of the situation: the set of circumstances or facts that surround any statement in the Qur'ān.[2]

The textual context is based on the relationships of words in the structure of sentences to each other and the grammatical component in which the vocabulary is contained. The context of the situation is a set of specific characteristics of the social conditions within which the text is constituted.

The textual context is represented in the interpretation by transmission, and the context of situation is represented in the reason the Qur'ān verse came down ('asbāb al-nuzūl) and the sayings of the Companions who witnessed the situations and events. The methods of Qur'ānic interpretation among Sunni muslims prioritized the context of situation (i.e., sayings of the ṣaḥābah and Tābi'īn). This paper aims to compare the

---

1. Kong, *Qur'ānic Interpretation*, 122–24.
2. Haleem, "Role of Context," 47.

Qur'ānic 'Ibrāhīm with the Abraham of the Bible by examining the text itself as well as the context.

II. Textual Reading of 'Ibrāhīm in the Qur'ān and Abraham of the Bible

1. 'Ibrāhīm as a Ḥanīf

Some two hundred and forty-five verses in twenty-five sūras of the Qur'ān make reference to 'Ibrāhīm. The Qur'ān especially emphasizes his role as a precursor of Muḥammad and the establisher of the pilgrimage rites in Mecca. 'Ibrāhīm is also called "*ḥanīf*," usually translated as "upright" or "inclined to the true religion," in eight places (Q2:135; 3:67, 95; 4:125; 6:79, 161; 16:120, 123). The term appears elsewhere only twice, in both cases referring to Muḥammad (Q10:105; 30:30), and in the first of these he is called "*ḥanīf*" and not a polytheist, a phrase also several times applied to 'Ibrāhīm. It is to be assumed that Muḥammad's connection to this respected figure served to enhance his religious authority.[3]

Some researchers think that the word *Ḥanīf* is a foreign word in Arabic and that it is derived from the Aramaic word meaning "hypocrite, atheist, pagan, or infidel," but this is out of context because these meanings are completely contradictory to the context of that sentence.[4] In fact, the etymology of the word *Ḥanīf* is very obscure, but after its use in the Qur'ān, it has taken on a new meaning. A. J. Droge defined this as a gentile, but "a gentile" doesn't make sense for the context.

Elsaid M. Badawi and Muḥammad Abdel Haleem defined *ḥanīf* as "inclined towards (Allah), inclined away (from false deities) and so considered upright."[5] The Muslim view of Islam as a religion of *ḥanīf* is closely tied to 'Ibrāhīm. Religion of *ḥanīf* means "not crooked or deviated (in behavior, ethics and religion), but straight."

Muslims today define Islam as the religion of *ḥanīf* because the Qur'ān represents 'Ibrāhīm as a *ḥanīf* Muslim. 'Ibrāhīm was one of several prophets Allah sent to invite people to worship him alone. For Muslims, *ḥanīf* and Muslim are practically synonyms.

---

3. McAuliffe, *Encyclopedia of the Qu'rān*, 1:5.
4. Gom'ah, *al-Mawsū'ah al-'Islāmīyyah al-'Ammah*, 577.
5. Badawi and Haleem, *Arabic–English Dictionary*, 239.

'Ibrāhīm was not a Jew, neither a Naṣrānī (A follower of 'Isā, Not Jesus Christ) but he was a Muslim professing the Oneness of Allah and a ḥanīf who inclined away from all other religions towards the upright one; and he was never of the polytheists (mushrikūn). (Q3:67)

Since 'Ibrāhīm was a *ḥanīf* in the pre-Islamic period, a Muslim views 'Ibrāhīm as someone living in obedience to Allah. *Ḥanīf* is also used to describe the ascetic monotheists of Mecca who refused idolatry and its practices.[6] Muḥammad Sayyid Tantawi said that a *ḥanīf* Muslim is someone who inclined to the true religion.

Muslims connect Muḥammad and 'Ibrāhīm as prophets to endorse the prophetic mission of Muḥammad. Just as Allah blessed 'Ibrāhīm and his descendants, may Allah bless Muḥammad and his descendants as well,[7] showing Islamic view of the similar nature of prophethood between 'Ibrāhīm and Muḥammad. We can say that the Qur'ān reconstructed the story of Abraham within the framework of an Islamic prophets. The stories of 'Ibrāhīm unique to the Qur'ān can be categorized two ways: stories of events and stories of religious perspectives.

2. 'Ibrāhīm as an 'Ummah

'Ibrāhīm became an 'ummah (Q16:120), a model imam for later prophets. 'Ummah in Modern Standard Arabic means "community," but 'Ummah in a dictionary of Qur'ān means a leader,[8] or Imam doing a good deed or a perfect example of excellence.[9] It is worth noting that the 'Ummah has a different meaning in both modern Arabic and Qur'ānic Arabic. Islamic encyclopedia[10] defined 'Ummah as it is a group of people, most of whom are of one origin and are united by inherited traits, interests, and common aspirations, or by a same religion, place, or time. It was said that the nation ('Ummah) of Muḥammad is the one who was sent to him who believed in him or disbelieved, while the nation ('Ummah) of Islam is all Muslims.

---

6. Badawi and Haleem, *Arabic–English Dictionary*, 239.
7. Tantawi, *Al-Qur'ān al-Karīm*, 523.
8. Kassab, *Translation of the Meanings*, 463.
9. *Al-Montakhab*, 580.
10. Bearman et al., *Encyclopaedia of Islam*, 10:212.

Hasan al-Bash said that 'Ibrāhīm became the father and ancestor of the tribes which spread throughout Iraq, Palestine, and Ḥijāz. He asserted that 'Ibrāhīm became the ancestor of the Israelites. Furthermore, he became the ancestor of 'Ismāʻīl's descendants as well as the Midianite peoples. 'Ibrāhīm became the first leader of the *Tawḥīd* (monotheism) creed, to which his descendants adhered. And he became the founder of *Ḥanīf* Muslims. According to Islamic encyclopedia,[11] *Tawḥīd* is the knowledge of Allah in the Lordship and the recognition of unity, which is the essence of Islam, rather the essence of all the heavenly religions, and it is the call of the messengers and prophets from Adam to Muḥammad.

The reason 'Ibrāhīm is important to Muslims is that, first, he is *ḥanīf*, second, he is a Muslim, and third, he spread the doctrine of *Tawḥīd*. That is why Arab Muslims today have stressed that Islam is a *ḥanīf* religion, and they emphasize that Islam is a religion of *Tawḥīd*.

3. The Difference between the Qur'ānic 'Ibrāhīm and the Biblical Abraham

In both the Bible and the Qur'ān, Abraham/'Ibrāhīm departed his hometown and moved to another place and gave birth to two sons at an old age. God/Allah commanded him through a vision to offer his son as a sacrifice. In both texts, Abraham/'Ibrāhīm obeys God/Allah. Some of the accounts on 'Ibrāhīm in the Qur'ān are shared with the Torah and Mishnah, while other accounts are unique to the Qur'ān.

The most oft-repeated Abrahamic narrative in the Qur'ān, the story of his smashing the pagan idols (Q6:74–84; 19:41–50; 21:51–73; 26:69–86; 29:16–27; 37:83–98; 43:26–27; 60:4), has no biblical parallel, but is well-known in Jewish exegetical literature.[12]

(1) Difference in Lineage

'Ibrāhīm was born near Damascus. 'Azar was his uncle, not his father.[13] This genealogy of 'Ibrāhīm in the Islamic text differs from that in the Bible. Genesis 11:26 states, "Nahor was the father of Terah and Terah became the father of Abraham, Nahor and Haran."

11. Bearman et al., *Encyclopaedia of Islam*, 10:432.
12. McAuliffe, *Encyclopedia of the Qu'rān*, 1:6.
13. Al-ʻAqqad, *'Ibrāhīm Abu al-'Anbiya*, 83.

What interests Christians is Abraham's sacrifice of Isaac in Genesis 22:2, where God commands Abraham: "Take your son, your only son, Isaac, whom you love, and go to the region of Moriah. Sacrifice him there as a burnt offering on one of the mountains I will tell you about."

There is a controversy over which son 'Ibrāhīm sacrificed; some Muslim commentators say 'Isḥāq, while others say 'Ismā'īl. The Qur'ān only states: "Oh my son [*yābunayya*]" (Q37:102). Some Muslim commentators claim that 'Ismā'īl was the only son of 'Ibrāhīm before 'Isḥāq's birth, to argue that it was 'Ismā'īl, not 'Isḥāq, who 'Ibrāhīm attempted to offer in obedient sacrifice.[14]

In Gen 22:2 God commanded Abraham, "Take your son, your only son Isaac whom you love," but the Qur'ān only says a son was offered without providing his name. That is why some commentators after the time of Muḥammad argue that the son was 'Ismā'īl, and others argued for 'Isḥāq. The Qur'ān highlights 'Ibrāhīm and 'Ismā'īl, but not 'Isḥāq, the second-born son. "Praise be to Allah who has given me despite my old age 'Ismā'īl and 'isḥāq. Lo! my Lord is indeed the Hearer of supplication" (Q14:39). This Qur'ānic verse seems to highlight 'Ismā'īl over 'Isḥāq.

Muslims make a connection between Arabs and 'Ismā'īl bn 'Ibrāhīm as recorded in Genesis. They argue that the 'Isrā'īliyyāt sources did not include the beliefs of the pre-Islamic Arabs. In the Qur'ānic interpretation, the 'Isrā'īliyyāt is a legend and story drawn from many Jewish sources and a small number from Naṣārā's sources. The 'Isrā'īliyyāt that entered the commentaries of the Qur'ān are many and varied, as the Qur'ān talks about the Children of Israel a lot. Dr. Amal Muḥammad Abd al-Rahman, in her book entitled, "*al-'Isrā'īliyyāt fī tafsīr al-Tabarī*" made recommendations to start correcting the books of Qur'ānic commentaries and similar stories of the prophets to correct the concepts that settled in Muslims' minds. She also recommended that there be an introduction to each of these revised commentaries which warn against the danger of the 'Isrā'īliyyāt and emphasized the need to pay careful attention when using the commentaries, as they contain content that offends Islam and distorts its image.[15]

Early Muslim interpretations of the Qur'ān received help from converts from Judaism and Christianity because the Qur'ān was difficult to interpret as there were parts that were omitted or abridged. With this in

---

14. Al-'Aqqad, *'Ibrāhīm Abu al-'Anbiya*, 85.
15. Al-Raḥmān Rabī', *Al-'isrā'iliyyāt fī Tafsīr Al-ṭabarī*, 382–83.

mind, it would not be possible to correctly interpret the original meaning of the Qur'ān if present-day Muslims will only limit themselves to the 'Isrā'īliyyāt that does not go against Islamic theology and Islamic law.

Arabs considered themselves to be Nabat Ibn 'Ismā'īl.[16] However, 1 Chr 1:29 records that Nabayut was son of Ishmael. Some scholars believe the Nabat to be the ancestors from whom the nabateans, the builders of Petra in Jordan, traced their 'Ibrāhīmic ancestry. But Arab Christians do not know where the Nabateans lived. It is certain that they were Arab peoples who spoke Aramaic.

The Qur'ānic narrative continues when Allah chooses 'Ismā'īl as a prophet.[17] Baby 'Ismā'īl brings forth water from the Zamzam well. Hājar suffered from thirst, baby 'Ismā'īl touched the Zamzam rock, water gushed out. Hājar went back and forth seven times between al-Ṣafā and al-Marwah. Hajar's walk back and forth seven times became an important ritual for the pilgrimage to Mecca, including drinking water from the Zamzam well. More importantly, Muslims call the Ka'bah of Mecca "the house of Allah" and "*al-Bayt al-Ḥarām*."

When 'Ibrāhīm came back from Hebron, Allah tested 'Ibrāhīm by commanding him to sacrifice his son, and 'Ibrāhīm obeyed. Seeing his obedience, Allah redeemed 'Ismā'īl with a ram. When the two came back to the wadi, Allah ordered 'Ibrāhīm to lay the foundation for the Ka'bah. Upon completing it, 'Ibrāhīm and 'Ismā'īl invoke Allah to accept it. After that, 'Ibrāhīm returned to Hebron and the news from Allah that his wife Sarah was pregnant with a son. Sarah gave birth to a son, 'Isḥāq.

The Qur'ānic insertion of the story of 'Ismā'īl building the Ka'bah for Muslims brought about the idea that 'Ismā'īl, not 'Isḥāq, was the son offered in sacrifice. In fact, the name of the son to be sacrificed is not given in the Qur'ān. Qur'ān 2:127 says that 'Ibrāhīm and 'Ismā'īl established the foundations of the House (i.e., the Ka'bah). These two chapters of the Qur'ān establish a uniquely Islamic narrative: the owner of the Ka'bah was Allah, and the builders were 'Ibrāhīm and 'Ismā'īl. These stories in the Qur'ān find no parallel in either the Bible or later Jewish traditions.

---

16. Al-'Aqqad, *'Ibrāhīm Abu al-'Anbiya*, 81.
17. Al-Bash, *'Ibrāhīm*, 10.

(2) A Geographic Difference

'Ibrāhīm's prophetic mission inspired people in Iraq, Persia, the *Bilād al-Shām* (*Syria, Lebanon, Northern Jordan and Palestine*), Egypt as well as the Ḥijāz to follow the new straight path. Ḥijāz is a geographical region that comprises most of the western part of modern-day Saudi Arabia and is centered on the two Muslim cities—Mecca (also Makka; Makkah) and Madina (Medina; al-Madīnah).

One element of today's Muslim faith that is directly associated with 'Ibrāhīm is the pilgrimage to Mecca. In the Qur'ānic narrative, 'Ibrāhīm went to Mecca and set up the al-Bayt (*Kaʿbah*; Q2:125), and this is different from the biblical account. This story, of course, ties to Hajar and 'Ismāʿīl. 'Ibrāhīm was too old to have children, and he traveled to Egypt without a son. In Egypt, he invited the Egyptians to the Creed of Tawḥīd. The Egyptians accepted his creed and gave him a royal lady named Hājar as a gift. And with her, 'Ibrāhīm returned to Hebron. This woman gave birth to a son called 'Ismāʿīl. So Allah lifted Hājar above all people, to the highest position.[18] Allah sent Hājar and her son to a wadi near Kaʿbah, land unfit for agriculture. 'Ibrāhīm left Hājar and her son there and returned to Hebron, and this is different from the biblical account.

The Bible narrates Abraham's trail with detailed names and specific locations. However, in the Qur'ān, the main events are not mentioned in chronological order of his travel. For example, the episode of Sarah and Abraham in Egypt is mentioned three times in the Bible, but is absent in the Qur'ān.

While the story of Abraham in Gen 11 to Gen 25 is narrated in chronological order, the story of 'Ibrāhīm is scattered in various verses from chapter 2 to chapter 87 in the Qur'ān. Furthermore, in the Qur'ān, the style of narrative is not historical but didactic. The Qur'ān generally omits specific names of places, and Becca is the only location mentioned in the Qur'ānic narrative of 'Ibrāhīm's story. Most Muslims interpret Becca to be Mecca, believing this is where 'Ibrāhīm settled his family for their prayer life. As mentioned above, the biblical Abraham and Qur'ānic 'Ibrāhīm show differences in lineage and geographic location.

---

18. Al-Bash, *'Ibrāhīm*, 10.

(3) A Covenant Difference

The Islamic encyclopedia[19] defines the *'Ahd* as "a will left before a person's death, or a promise to protect non-Muslims, or a contract between slaves. In Arabic Bible the term *'Ahd* was used as a covenant. In Arab countries, the Christian community and the Muslim community sometimes use the same vocabulary, although the same terms often have different theological meanings. Some terms are frequently used in the Qur'ān with different meanings for different contexts, a feature known in Arabic as *al-Wujūh wa-al-Naẓā'ir*. These were recognized from the early days of Qur'ānic interpretation. *'Ahd* is commonly translated as "promise" in Modern Standard Arabic, whereas in the Qur'ān it has other meanings based on its contexts, including *'Imāmah* (leading position), *mawāthīq* (contracts), *'Amr* (Commandment), *Ḥalf* (oath), *Tawḥīd* (unity).[20]

Mark Durie told us that there are instances of *'Ahd* and *'ahida* in the account of the establishment of the house by 'Ibrāhīm and his son 'Ismā'īl (Q2:124–25).[21] Allah makes a promise to make 'Ibrāhīm a leader over his people, and Allah obligates 'Ibrāhīm to purify his house. Mark Durie concluded that this story has no reflex in the Bible and in any case does not provide any evidence of the concept of covenant.[22]

In the Old Testament, God assured Abram of the ultimate fulfillment of His promises (Genesis 18:7, 18–21). " *On the same day the Lord made a covenant with Abram*" (Genesis 16: 18 a). God made a formal treaty (covenant) with Abram. In other words, this was a unilateral covenant. So its promises in Genesis are absolutely sure, meanwhile there is no evidence of the Abrahamic covenant in the Qur'ānic verses.

III. Abraham's Religions in the Interfaith Dialogue

The Qur'ān says that there are two factions in *'ahl al-Kitāb*, i.e., Jews and Naṣārā[23] who have the book (Scripture). There are those who reject the

19. Bearman et al., *Encyclopaedia of Islam*, 10:1019.
20. Al-Damaghani, "Abd Allah Al-Husein bn Muḥammad," 2:78–79.
21. Durie, *Qur'ān and Its Biblical Reflexes*, 208.
22. Durie, *Qur'ān and Its Biblical Reflexes*, 208.
23. The prevailing scholarly opinion is that the Arabic term *al-Naṣārā* is derived from the name of Jesus' hometown of Nazareth in Galilee and that it literally means "Nazarenes," alternately "Nazoreans," that is to say, "people from Nazareth." McAuliffe, *Encyclopaedia of the Qur'ān*, 1:310. *al-Naṣārā* in the Qur'ānic Dictionary (*Mu'jam*

new Daʿwah (Q5:68) and those who say that they have "a common word" based on 'Ibrāhīm (Q3:64). Allah asked Muḥammad to engage the *'Ahl al-kitāb* (the people of the book).

> "Say, "Oh people of the book! Listen to a proposal that is equally fair (kalimah sawā') to us and to you: that we shall worship nobody save Allah; that we shall not attribute to Him any partner; that we shall not take one another as deities besides Allah." (Q3:64)

The Muslims' interpretation of the term "common word" is not the same as common Christian leaders would assume to understand it. And the interpretation of "common word" in the Qur'ān has been reinterpreted. An Islamic interpretation does not extend the meaning to be that we love God and our neighbors, as Muslim and Christian leaders concluded at the Yale Common Word Conference in 2008. The meaning of the "common word" in Q3:64 is to be understood in its context, which means to worship Allah and to reject of any form of *shirk* (polytheism).

In the eighth and ninth centuries, religious dialogues and arguments continued between Muslims and Christians. Social relations improved but doctrinal disputes increased. John of Damascus (d. 749) said that Islam does not belong to the 'Ibrāhīmic legacy.[24] Also in the eighth and ninth centuries, Muslims, especially those who were educated, encountered Christian polemical writings against Islam. Among educated Muslims arose a conflict over topics such as faith and fatalism. There was also a period of Christian apology during the periods of Abu Qurrah (d. 820) in early Abbasid time, and in the books of the ninth century there was a debate between Caliph al-Mahdī and the Christian Patriarch.

In the year 781, during the reign of al-Mahdī, the third of the Abbassid Caliphs in Bagdad, a two-day debate took place between the Patriarch of the Eastern Syrian Church and the Caliph himself. In this debate the theme of the 'Ibrāhīmic religion became a central topic. Muslims asked the Christians to recognize Muḥammad as a prophet. During the time of the Qur'ān and the companions of Muḥammad, Muslims attempted to gather the people of the three religions under the banner of the 'Ibrāhīm religion. The main argument centered on the prophethood of Muḥammad. Muslims at that time saw Muḥammad as the bearer of 'Ibrāhīmic heritage.

'Alfāẓ al-Qur'ān al-Karīm) was followers of al-Masīḥ: *Mu'jam 'Alfāẓ al-Qur'ān al-Karīm*, Part 2, 1104.

24. Al-Sayyid, "al-Diyanat al-'Ibrāhīmiyyah," 67.

Refutation by Christians and by Muslims continued. There was a refutation against Christianity by al-Jahiz (d. 868) as well as al-Kindi (d. 873), al-Qasim Ibn 'Ibrāhīm, Ali Ibn Rabban al-Tabarī (d. 870) and Abu 'isā al-Warraq. The critique against Christianity in the Qur'ān was sharper. Most obvious is that the al-Mu'tazilah commenced this polemics.

Christian thinkers had been using the logic of Aristotle. After them, al-Mu'tazilah employed logic for refutation. There were four topics in Muslim polemics: the nature of al- Masīḥ, the Person (*'uqnūm*) of God, the Bible (esp. the gospel) and Christian religious life and priesthood. Muslims insisted that these four areas of doctrine deviated from Islamic *waḥdaniyyah* (Oneness of Allah). Mutual refutation continued for 800 years. Christians, especially religious people and businessmen, were persecuted in all four periods.[25]

More educated Muslims saw that the West encouraged Christian evangelism (*tabshīr*) during the colonial era. Muslims in eastern Arabia (*al-Mashriq*) were defensive because Western Christians and Catholic missionaries were actively engaged in apologetics. In other words, during the Middle Ages, the dominant Muslims led to the proof that Islam was right, but in the colonial era, some Western disputants led the controversy with evidence that Christianity was right (al-Sayyid 2018, 73).[26]

In the nineteenth and early twentieth centuries, the influence of the Crusades increased the encounter between Christians and Muslims. There were two major debates: one in 1854, the debate between Karl Gottlieb Pfander (1803–65) and Rahmat Allah (1818–91) in Lahor.[27] However, Muslims gaining familiarity with Western culture initiated a new debate from 1850 to 1950 in defense of Islam. Religious debate went together with the fight against colonialism.

In the early twentieth century and beyond, Christians participated in the debate. At the end of the nineteenth century new participants outside of Protestant and Catholic circles entered the discussion. Anthropologists, sociologists, philosophers, and liberal theologians began writing articles about world religions.

As their view of religion changed, the view on Judaism changed and then Catholics and some Christians began to change their view of Islam. Among them, Catholic theologians and Orientalists who lived with

---

25. Al-Sayyid, "al-Diyanat al-'Ibrāhīmiyyah," 72.
26. Al-Sayyid, "al-Diyanat al-'Ibrāhīmiyyah," 73.
27. Azumah and Sanneh, *African Christian and Islam*, 230.

Muslims for a long time became acquainted with the legacy of Islamic religion and began to change the traditional view of Islam. Some Christians identified Islam as an independent religion, but that like Judaism, it must be in the family of Abraham.

In the early 1950s, requests for dialogue with Muslims began between Protestants, Catholics, and Orientalists. Some Christians who participated in this dialogue had an open mind about common faith and political motives. The Second Vatican Council (1962–1965) recognized Judaism and Islam as faiths included in the spiritual and genetic heritage of the family of Abraham.[28] This led the Catholic church and some Protestant institutions to dialogue with Islamic religious organizations. On the way to unity in the religious dialogue with Muslims, a Catholic theologian Hans Küng promoted the view that there will be no peace in the world without peace between the churches.[29]

In September 2006 Pope Benedict XVI caused a furor in the Islamic world when he made a speech at a German university. In a lecture titled "Faith, Reason and the University." Benedict quoted, without endorsing, the words of a Byzantine emperor who declared that Islam's prophet had brought into the world "things only evil and inhuman, such as his command to spread by the sword the faith he preached."[30]

A week later, on September 20, 2006, in his general address in St. Peter's Square, the Pope made it clear that he does not agree with the statement he quoted from the fourteenth-century Christian ruler. Pope Benedict stated:

> In no way did I wish to make my own the words of the medieval emperor. I wished to explain that not religion and violence, but religion and reason, go together. I hope that my profound respect for world religions and for Muslims, who worship the one God and with whom we promote peace, liberty, social justice, and moral values for the benefit of all humanity, is clear.[31]

More than sixty years after the Second Vatican Council, in February 2019 in Abu Dhabi, Pope Francis and Ahmad al-Tayyib (the Egyptian Grand Imam of al-Azhar) signed a document titled *Human Fraternity*

---

28. Al-Sayyid, "al-Diyanat al-'Ibrāhīmiyyah," 75.
29. Al-Sayyid, "al-Diyanat al-'Ibrāhīmiyyah," 76.
30. Fisher, "Vatican Says Pope Benedict Regrets," para. 9.
31. Kasimow and Drake, "Pope Benedict XVI, Islam, and Interreligious Dialogue," para. 3.

for Peace and Living Together. This document begins with the following statements. "Faith leads a believer to see the other brother or sister to be supported and loved. Through faith in God, who has created the universe, creatures and all human beings (equal on account of his mercy), believers are called to express this human fraternity by safeguarding creation and the whole universe and supporting persons, especially the poorest and those most in need."[32] The document assumes a unity of faith between the Catholic church and Islam.

Over the past decade or so, the term "Religions of Abraham" has been used in academic and ecumenical circles to refer to Judaism, Christianity, and Islam. The term has become widespread among those who wish to promote peaceful interaction between those of the three religions.

IV. Abraham in the New Testament

How is Abraham in the Old Testament understood in the New Testament? The interplay of dialogue between one text used in a different context was termed as an "intertextuality." This is also used to study the reuse of passages of the Old Testament in the context of the New Testament. In other words, intertextuality is to consider how the dialogue between the original meaning (the Old Testament context), Jewish understanding, and the new meaning (the New Testament context) has developed.[33] Osborne confirmed that the New Testament writers were cognizant of the Old Testament context and applied it in the light of the Christ event.[34]

The Gospel of Matthew begins with the genealogy of Jesus Christ, the son of David, and the son of Abraham. The first page of the New Testament shows the relationship between the New Testament and the Old Testament, and the Gospel of Matthew associates Jesus with David as the Jewish Messiah.

Among Paul's epistles, in Romans, Abraham is described as a model of faith, and believers are said to be children of the promise. Paul identifies the children of Abraham as children of the promise. In Galatians, Christ is the singular offspring of Abraham and all who believe in him become children of Abraham. However, in Romans, those who have faith

---

32. "Document on Human Fraternity," para. 1.
33. Osborne, *Hermeneutical Spiral*, 331.
34. Osborne, *Hermeneutical Spiral*, 332.

like Abraham become his children. In the Gospel of John, Abraham is used in polemics between Johannine Christians and their opponents.

Moreover, the Gospel of John makes a distinction between the descendants of Abraham (John 8:33) and the children of Abraham (John 8:39). The former refers to genetic lineage and the latter refers to spiritual descent.

In Hebrews, Christ and Abraham meet indirectly, insofar as Christ in the person of Melchizedek encounters Abraham, but according to the logic of the typology, Christ appears before the Levitical priesthood.[35] The book of James introduces Abraham as a man of faith.

The New Testament always makes faith the channel through which we receive salvation. But, of course, faith must have the right object to be effective, and the object of saving faith is Jesus Christ. "And if you are Christ's, then you are Abraham's seed, and heirs according to the promise" (Galatians 3:29).

Christ is the seed of Abraham (Gal 3:16), and the one who believes in Christ is the seed of Abraham (Gal 3:29). Abraham is the one who inherits the inheritance. To be a descendant of Abraham is to belong to Christ.

Bradley R. Trick defines two categories: "sons of Abraham" and "children of Promise." He contends that "sons of Abraham" in 3:7 designates the Jews, i.e., those physical descendants of Abraham who also share his faith. In contrast, "children of promise" in Gal 4:28 designates the gentiles who have through faith received the Abrahamic blessing, i.e., the Spirit of sonship that makes them children of God.[36]

While descendants of Abraham share his faith, the object of saving faith is Jesus Christ. Therefore, to determine whether a person is a descendant of Abraham, you must ask whether he is adopted through a son of God (Jesus Christ) and received the Holy Spirit.

V. Conclusion

Some consider the 'Ibrāhīm of the Qur'ān and the Abraham of the Bible to be the same and call Judaism, Christianity, and Islam the religions of Abraham. However, there is a difference in the method of interpretation of each scripture, and even within the same religion, differences in

---

35. Bakhos, *Family of Abraham*, 73.
36. Trick, "Sons, Seed, and Children of Promise," iv–v.

the interpretation can be observed both between the various traditions within Islam, and between different periods in history.

Furthermore, some terms in the Qur'ān have been reshaped to serve the Qur'ān's distinctive theological agenda. There are numerous concepts of the Qur'ān which illustrate this feature, including *ḥanīf*. Many Muslims today emphasize that Islam is the religion of *ḥanīf*. Muḥammad's religious roots are traced to the *ḥanīfiyyah* tradition with its pronounced identification with the figure of 'Ibrāhīm.

Section II examined the textual comparison between the Qur'ānic 'Ibrāhīm and the biblical Abraham. The Jewish Abraham founds an elect nation; the Christian Abraham founds a salvific faith for other nations; the Muslim 'Ibrāhīm offers a model of anti-idolatrous obedience for all nations. The Qur'ān adjusted the stories of the Bible in order to emphasize their unique religious values. In doing so, their adherents define themselves as entities distinct and separate from one another. Each text has different and exclusive theological implications.

Section III noted the rhetoric of twentieth-century ecumenical advocacy of religious tolerance and understanding. During the engagement of Christians and Muslims since the seventh century, many have tried to maintain dialogue by emphasizing the common ancestry of faith in Abraham. Over the past decade or so, the term "Religion of Abraham" has been used in academic and ecumenical circles to refer to Judaism, Christianity, and Islam. The term has become widespread among those who wish to promote peaceful interaction between those of the three religions.

Section IV examined how this thesis demonstrates that the faith of the Qur'ān is not a saving faith according to the New Testament. Jesus Christ is understood as the fulfillment of the covenantal promise, the seed of Abraham through whom all nations will be blessed. The passage in Gal 4:29–30 states that the full typology of the free children of promise ultimately finds fulfillment only in the union of Jewish Christians (i.e., the children of the free woman) and gentile Christians (i.e., the children of promise) in Christ. While descendants of Abraham share his faith in God, the object and medium of saving faith is Jesus Christ.

When we compare Abraham in the Bible with 'Ibrāhīm in the Qur'ān, there are notable differences in their narratives as well as theological discourse found in the Qur'ān which is unique to it. And we conclude that Abraham in the Bible was repurposed by the Qur'ān, rather than inherited from the Bible.

Bibliography

'Abd Al-Raḥmān Rabīʿ, 'āmāl Muḥammad. *Al-'Isrā'iliyyāt fī Tafsīr Al-ṭabarī*. Cairo: Supreme Council for Islamic Affairs, 2015.
Al-ʿAqqad, Abbas Mahmud. *'Ibrāhīm Abu al-'Anbiya*. Cairo: Dar Nahdah Misr, 2014.
Al-Bash, Hasan. *'Ibrāhīm*. Cairo: Dar al-Qutaybah, 2009.
Al-Damaghani, ʿAbd Allah Al-Husein bn Muḥmmad. *Al-Wujūh wa-l-Naẓā'ir*. Vol. 2. Cairo: Wizarah al-'Awqaf, 2012.
Al-Montakhab. Cairo: Supreme Council for Islamic Affairs, 2017.
Al-Montakhab (in English). Cairo: Ministry of al-'Awqāf, 2017.
Al-Sayyid, Radwan. "al-Diyanat al-'Ibrāhīmiyyah min al-'Ikhtilaf ila al-'I'tilāf." *At-Tafāhum* 61 (2018) 63–78.
Azumah, John, and Lamin Sanneh. *The African Christian and Islam*. Carlisle: Langham, 2013.
Badawi, Elsaid M., and Muḥammad Abdel Haleem. *Arabic–English Dictionary of Qurʾānic Usage*. Leiden: Brill, 2008.
Bakhos, Carol. *The Family of Abraham: Jewish, Christian, and Muslim Interpretation*. New Haven: Harvard University Press, 2014.
Bearman, P. J., et al. *The Encyclopaedia of Islam*. Vol. 10, T–U. Leiden: Brill, 2015.
"Document on Human Fraternity for World Peace and Living Together: Full Text." *Vatican News*, February 4, 2019. https://www.vaticannews.va/en/pope/news/2019-02/pope-francis-uae-declaration-with-al-azhar-grand-imam.html.
Droge, A. J. *The Qurʾān—A New Annotated Translation*. Sheffield: Equinox, 2013.
Durie, Mark. *The Qurʾān and Its Biblical Reflexes*. Lanham: Lexington, 2018.
El-Awa, Salwa M. S. *Textual Relations in the Qurʾān, Relevance, Coherence and Structure*. London: Routledge, 2006.
Elias, Amira. "The Comparative Textual Study of the 'Abraham Story' in the Bible and the Qurʾān." Master's thesis, Concordia University, 2000.
Fisher, Ian. "Vatican Says Pope Benedict Regrets Offending Muslims." *The New York Times*, September 17, 2006. https://www.nytimes.com/2006/09/17/world/europe/17pope.html#:~:text=ROME%2C%20Sept.,the%20sensibility%20of%20Muslim%20believers.%E2%80%9D.
Friedrich, Gerhard, et al., eds. *Theological Dictionary of the New Testament*. 10 vols. Grand Rapids: Eerdmans, 1995.
Gleave, Robert. *Islam and Literalism: Literal Meaning and Interpretation in Islamic Legal Theory*. Edinburgh: Edinburgh University Press, 2012.
Gomʿah, Muḥammad Mukhtar. *al-Mawsūʿah al-'Islāmīyyah al-'Ammah*. Cairo: Wizārah al-'Awqāf, 2015.
Haleem, M. A. S Abdel. "The Role of Context in Interpreting and Translating the Qurʾān." *Journal of Qurʾānic Studies* 20.1 (2018) 47–66.
Kasimow, Harold, and George Drake. "Pope Benedict XVI, Islam, and Interreligious Dialogue." https://www.grinnell.edu/news/pope-benedict-xvi-islam-and-interreligious-dialogue#:~:text=In%20meeting%20with%20a%20Muslim,reduced%20to%20an%20optional%20extra.
Kassab, Rashid Said. *Translation of the Meanings of the Glorious Qurʾān*. Amman: Maṭābiʿ al-ʿīmān, 1994.
Kong, Il Joo. *Abrahamic Religions (in Korean)*. Seoul, Korea: Salim, 2019.

———. "Does "ẓāhir" in the Qur'ān Refer to Literal Meaning?" *Journal of Arab and Islamic World Studies* 6 (2019) 53–103.
———. *Qur'ānic Interpretation, Origin, Development and Modern Trends.* Seoul: CLC, 2021.
———. "A Semantic Study of the Arabic Language and Translation of the Meaning of the Qur'ān." *Journal of Mediterranean Area Studies* 23.2 (2021) 1–41.
Lippman, Thomas. *Understanding Islam.* New York: Meridian, 1995.
Lowin, Shari L. "The Making of a Forefather: Abraham in Islamic and Jewish Exegetical Narratives." PhD diss., The University of Chicago, 2002.
McAuliffe, Jane Dammen, ed. *Encyclopaedia of the Qur'ān.* Vol. 1, A–D. Leiden: Brill, 2001.
Mirza, Younus Y. "Ibn Kathir *(D.774/1373)*: His Intellectual Circle, Major Works and Qur'ānic Exegesis." PhD diss., Georgetown University Press, 2012.
Mu'jam 'Alfāẓ al-Qur'ān al-Karīm. Part 1. Cairo: Majma' al-Lughah al-'Arabiyyah, 1989.
Mu'jam 'Alfāẓ al-Qur'ān al-Karīm. Part 2. Cairo: Majma' al-Lughah al-'Arabiyyah, 1990.
Munayyi', Abd al-Halim Mahmud. *Abu al-'Anbiya' 'Ibrāhīm.* Cairo: Matba'ah al-Madani, 2004.
Osborne, Grant R. *The Hermeneutical Spiral: A Comprehensive Introduction to Biblical Interpretation.* Downers Grove, IL: IVP Academic, 2006.
Rabī', 'āmāl Muḥammad 'Abd al-Raḥmān. *Al-'isrā'īliyyāt fī Tafsīr al-Ṭabarī.* Cairo: Lajnah 'iḥyā' al-Turāth al-'islāmī, 2015.
Swanson, Mark N. *Folly to the Hunafa'*. Pontificium Institutum Studiorum, 1995.
Tabari, Abu Ja'far. *Jāmi' al-Bayān 'an- Taw'īl 'āy al-Qur'ān.* Cairo: Dar ibn Hazm, 1954.
Tantawi, Muḥammad Sayyid. *Al-Qur'ān al-Karīm wa at-Tafsīr al-Muyassar.* Matabi' Zamzam, 2012.
Trick, Bradley R. "Sons, Seed, and Children of Promise in Galatians: Discerning the Coherence in Paul's Model of Abrahamic Descent." PhD diss., Duke University Press, 2010.
'Umar, 'Ahmad Mukhtār. *Mu'jam al-Lughah al 'Arabiyyah al-Mu'āsirah.* Part 1. 'ālam alkutub, 2008.

5

The Joseph Narrative in the Bible and Qur'ān

Peter G. Riddell

The Qur'ān is the first and most important source for those who wish to understand Islam, both for Muslims and non-Muslims alike.[1]

Introduction: Principles of Narrative

The Yusuf narrative, which occupies the entire twelfth chapter of the Qur'ān, is the longest and most detailed prophetic narrative in Islam's sacred text. Similarly, the Joseph narrative, which runs from chapters 37 to 52 in the book of Genesis, is one of the most extensive narratives in the Bible. At face value, there are striking similarities between the Yusuf and Joseph accounts. Indeed, in the early twenty-first century with so much attention given to interreligious bridge-building, there is pressure to acknowledge the similarities and downplay the differences between the sacred texts of Islam and Christianity. However, we must avoid assumptions

---

1. Abu-Zayd, "Others in the Qur'ān," 281.

in that regard, but rather subject both the narratives to scrutiny at various levels in order to determine whether they are more similar to or different from each other in key ways.

We need to clarify terminology at the outset, particularly concerning the use of the term "narrative." Are the Qur'ānic and biblical narratives in fact the same kind of literary text? Addressing that question will help us determine whether the Yusuf and Joseph accounts really have the same kind of function. Robert E. Longacre of the Summer Institute of Linguistics developed a useful theory of the internal structure of biblical narrative discourse. He argued that biblical narrative typically consisted of the following elements:[2]

- Aperture: a formulaic beginning to the narrative
- Stage: an early identification of a paradox or problem
- Episodes: segments in the narrative. These episodes could be differentiated by various means: formulaic, temporal, locational markers; other syntactic features; shifts in genre, content, or characters; when in conversation, sub-genre shifts as the patterns of dialogue change; e.g., question, rejection, commendation
- Peak (discussed below)
- Closure: the wrap-up of the discourse
- Finis: a formulaic ending to the narrative

In later research, Longacre refined this structure around elements which he termed Stage, Inciting Incident, Mounting Tension, Climax, Denouement, Closure.[3] Longacre's important research into the literary structure of the Bible was key in the emergence of the theory of discourse Peak:

> If we grant that any discourse is going somewhere, it follows that it does not simply start and stop but that it may have some sort of culminative expression between.[4]

Ralph Terry, building on Longacre's research, defines Peak as "a zone of grammatical or stylistic turbulence within a discourse that corresponds to its climax and/or denouement." He further argues that all

2. Longacre and Levinsohn, *Field Analysis of Discourse*, 104–5.
3. Longacre, *Top-Down, Template-Driven*, 140–41.
4. Longacre, *Grammar of Discourse*, 20.

languages indicate that "standard grammatical rules and stylistic conventions... change around those parts of a text which show the most conceptual tension."[5]

Most research into Peak has focused on the study of narrative discourses, where it is normal to find a Peak towards which the narrative advances and from which there is rapid descent. Peak can be seen as the point of the story, when a question is answered that was previously posed, or a paradox is resolved that was previously presented. In terms of its relation to other elements in Longacre's structure of narrative, Peak resolves thematic questions that were raised when the Stage is set.

It is therefore important to identify the Peak of a narrative text, which represents the culmination of the text. If readers identify a false Peak they may well miss the point of the entire text. Equally if authors are unclear in presenting the Peak, the audience may well fail to perceive it and the narrative will seem anti-climactic, leaving the audience with a sense of "so what?" Some books of the Bible may have a single Peak, while others may have a series of Peaks. Where there are multiple Peaks, the book may contain a number of unrelated themes (found in separate Stages), with each independently resolved by its Peak, or the Peaks may represent a gradual advance on the main Peak.

In considering the similarities and differences between Qur'ān and Bible in our chosen narrative, it will be important to determine whether these principles, that have been developed from the study of the biblical text, also apply in the case of the Qur'ān. Longacre argues that there are various ways for authors to signal the narrative Peak:[6]

1. Concentration of Participants: Longacre says "One hallmark of peak... is the crowded stage."

2. Rhetorical Underlining is another device. Longacre explains that "The narrator does not want you to miss the important point of the story so he employs extra words at that point [of Peak]." This can be seen in the use of rhetorical questions in Job 38–41. Other devices can include parallelism, paraphrase, and tautologies.

3. Heightened Vividness. Here Longacre points to a shift in the nominal-verbal balance, or a change of tense, person, grammar, form, or locus.

---

5. Terry, *Discourse Analysis of First Corinthians*, 9.
6. Longacre, *Grammar of Discourse*, 39–43.

4. Change of pace may also signal a forthcoming Peak, with a shift to short, fragmentary, crisp sentences which emphasise the change of pace, or the opposite may occur.

Finally, Longacre also suggests "some stories may have a *didactic* (or *thematic*) peak, as well as an action peak. . . . A didactic peak is a special elaboration of some episode which precedes or follows the action peak. Essentially action ceases at a didactic peak and participant(s) speak out in a monologue/dialogue which develops the theme of the story."[7]

The Materials from Bible and Qur'ān

Turning our attention to the characters in focus, Joseph in the Bible and Yusuf in the Qur'ān, the former only makes brief appearances apart from the main discussion extending from Gen 37:2 to 50:26. Apart from that lengthy section, which will form the main focus of our study, there is a brief mention of Joseph's birth at Gen 30:24–25, plus later New Testament back-references the story of Joseph in Acts 7:9–18 (a brief summary of the Joseph narrative) and Heb 11:21–22 (a brief reference to the deaths of Jacob and Joseph).

Similarly, the Yusuf narrative is focused on a single chapter of the Qur'ān 12:1–111. This chapter is late Meccan according to the Nöldeke chronology, which is consistent with Durie's study of the "eschatological transition."[8] The only other passing references to Yusuf are Q6:84, also late Meccan, where he is simply listed among a group of biblical prophets, and Q40:34, similarly late Meccan, which refers to how Yusuf encountered doubt in spite of the signs that he brought to the community of believers. The biblical narrative is rich in detail. The main events are summarized in the following Table 5.1.

---

7. Longacre, *Grammar of Discourse*, 37–38.

8. Though interestingly al-Zanjani places it earlier in the Meccan period. Cf. Riddell, "Reading the Qur'ān Chronologically," 304; Nöldeke et al., *History of the Qur'ān*, 124; Durie, *Qur'ān and Its Biblical Reflexes*, 93.

Bible Event	Genesis
Joseph is Jacob's favored son; receives coat; has dream	37:2–11
Sold into slavery by brothers	37:12–36
Imprisoned because of Potiphar's wife's ruse	39
Interprets royal officials' dreams	40
Interprets Pharaoh's dreams	41:1–36
Appointed as 2IC to Pharoah	41:37–57
Has two sons, Manasseh and Ephraim	41:50–52
Famine drives brothers to Egypt; Joseph tests brothers	42
Second journey to Egypt with Benjamin	43
The silver Cambridge University Press ruse	44
Joseph reveals himself; brothers return to Jacob with the good news	45
Jacob goes to Egypt, meets Joseph; the family settles there	46:1—47:12
Joseph and the famine	47:13–31
Jacob blesses Manasseh and Ephraim	48
Jacob blesses all his sons; dies	49
Joseph mourns his father; reassures his brothers; dies in Egypt	50

Table 5.1. Biblical Events of Joseph Narrative

The Qur'ānic Account: An Episodic Analysis

For the Qur'ānic account of the Yusuf story, we will subject Sura 12 to an analysis of episodes according to Longacre's framework. The Qur'ānic account extracts the Yusuf story from the broader context of the Jacob story, so central to the biblical account. Episode 1, vv. 1–7, serve in this role. The characters are introduced, and arguably the main character, Allah, is introduced early, with his sovereign purposes being stated succinctly at vs. 6: "This is about how your Lord will choose you, teach you to interpret dreams, and perfect His blessing on you and the House of Jacob, just as He perfected it earlier on your forefathers Abraham and Isaac: your Lord is all knowing and wise."

Episode 2 runs from vv. 8–18. Yusuf's brothers hatch their plot and carry it out. There is rapid progress in the story, with comparatively little interest in the narrative detail (unlike the biblical account). Allah frequently appears to reassure Joseph in his dark moments of the eventual outcome (v. 15). These pervasive appearances of the divine authority have the effect of preventing development of the dramatic tension that is normal for narrative in general and biblical narrative in particular.

In Episode 3 (vv. 19–20), Yusuf is saved and sold into slavery. There is initially hope and then deception when the travellers who extricate him from the well turn him to monetary gain. Again the principal actor, never far from the action, comments: "God was well aware of what they did." Episode 4 runs from vv. 21–29. We are reminded that Allah is in control: "In this way We settled Joseph in that land and later taught him how to interpret dreams: God always prevails in His purpose, though most people do not realize it." Yusuf is tempted by the wife of his owner but again, the principal actor steps in; Allah is present to guide Yusuf away from natural lusts: "he would have succumbed to her if he had not seen evidence of his Lord—We did this in order to keep evil and indecency away from him, for he was truly one of Our chosen servants."

In Episode 5 (vv. 30–35) we encounter the ruse of his owner's wife in getting the women in the city to fall for Yusuf's beauty. To avoid further temptations, Yusuf asks Allah to place him in prison. Allah obliges, though Yusuf's innocence is never really in doubt in the story. Episode 6 (vv. 36–42) focuses on the dreams of Yusuf's fellow prisoners and his interpretation of these dreams. In fact, Yusuf spends more time preaching than interpreting the dreams, drawing on a rhetorical question at verse 39 as a pedagogical device. In the final verse of this episode we see the intervention of Satan (making the servant forget Joseph) to temporarily derail the inexorable march of the divinely predestined story. Episode 7, which is brief and only occupies vv. 43–45, presents Pharaoh's dreams, setting up the story for significant forward movement. Episode

8, similarly small (vv. 46–49), changes the location to the prison, where Yusuf interprets Pharaoh's dreams.

Episode 9 (vv. 50–57) begins with a repair insert, resolving the earlier false accusation against Yusuf by the owner's wife. Then Yusuf is brought before Pharaoh and rewarded by being appointed to a senior administrative position. There is a paradox in this episode concerning Allah's guidance. On the one hand we encounter the statement "God does not guide the mischief of the treacherous" (v. 52), but at the same time readers are reminded of the divine hand in phrases such as "man's very soul incites him to evil unless my Lord shows mercy" (v. 53) and "We grant Our mercy to whoever We will and do not fail to reward those who do good" (v. 56). In Episode 10 (vv. 58–62) Yusuf's brothers come before Yusuf, who devises a trick in planting their goods back in their saddle bags. This episode lacks the force of the biblical account because it is so short on narrative detail. We encounter a change of locale to Canaan (unnamed) in episode 11 (vv. 63–67) where the brothers come before their father (unnamed), who pronounces a firm statement stressing the authority of Allah: "God is the best guardian and the Most Merciful of the merciful."

In Episode 12 (vv. 68–82), Yusuf's brothers return before Yusuf with their youngest brother. There is a carry-over statement from Episode 10 that their father knew the outcome anyway; he had the hidden knowledge of events which prophets had. Yusuf reveals himself to (the unnamed) Benjamin but not to the other brothers. There is the trick of planting the drinking cup at which Benjamin is detained. The other brothers attempt unsuccessfully to persuade Joseph to release Benjamin. Some confusion surrounds vv. 82–83 where the transition and change of locale is not clear. In Episode 13 (vv. 83–87) we encounter the agony of the unnamed Jacob, yet he seems to know of Joseph's survival: "I have knowledge from God that you do not have. My sons, go and seek news of Joseph and his brother."

Episode 14 (vv. 88–93) involves another change of locale when the brothers return before Yusuf in Egypt. He reveals himself, doing so very quickly and without buildup in the immediately surrounding verses. Episode 15 (vv. 94–98) focuses on another rapid transition to Canaan, where Jacob (both unnamed) is apprised of developments. But he knew all along: "Did I not tell you that I have knowledge from God that you do not have?" The penultimate Episode 16 (vv. 99–101) involves the descent of the whole family to Egypt. Vv. 100–101 include a strong statement of God's purpose and that Allah "is most subtle in achieving what He will." The original dream of Yusuf is explained. All the characters are assembled together.

The final episode 17 (vv. 102–11) serves as closure and wrap-up. Muhammad reappears as the addressee. Allah explains the purpose of story and warns disbelievers of forthcoming punishment, explaining to readers that prophets (such as Yusuf) indicate the path to be followed. The various episodes of the Qur'ānic account can be assembled in comparative form with the biblical account in the following Table 5.2:

Genesis	Qur'ān 12
37:2–11: Joseph is Jacob's favored son; receives coat; has dream	Ep1: vv. 1–7: characters introduced; dream
37:12–36: Sold into slavery by brothers	Ep2: vv. 8–18: the plot hatched, carried out, reported Ep3: vv. 19–20: slavery
39: Imprisoned because of Potiphar's wife's ruse	Ep4: vv. 21–29: temptation by wife of his owner Ep5: vv. 30–35: Wife's ruse; Joseph chooses prison
40: Interprets royal officials' dreams	Ep6: vv. 36–42: Dreams of fellow prisoners; Joseph's interpretation; Joseph preaches; Satan intervenes
41:1–36: Interprets Pharaoh's dreams	Ep7: vv. 43–45: Pharaoh's dreams Ep8: vv. 46–49 Change of locale to prison; Joseph interprets Pharaoh's dreams
41:37–57: Appointed as 2IC to Pharoah	Ep9: vv. 50–57: Joseph brought before Pharaoh; appointed to senior admin position
41:50–52: Has two sons, Manasseh and Ephraim	n/a

42: Famine drives brothers to Egypt; Joseph tests brothers	Ep10: vv. 58–62: Joseph's brothers come before Joseph (first trip to Egypt); Joseph's trick
43: Second journey to Egypt with Benjamin	Ep11: vv. 63–67: Change of locale to Canaan (unnamed)
	Ep12: vv. 68–82: Brothers return before Joseph (second trip to Egypt);
44: The silver Cambridge University Press ruse	the drinking Cambridge University Press ruse;
45: Joseph reveals himself; brothers return to Jacob with the good news	brothers return to Jacob with the bad news
	Ep13: vv. 83–87: The agony of Jacob
	Ep14: vv. 88–93: Brothers return before Joseph (third trip to Egypt); Joseph reveals himself
	Ep15: vv. 94–98: Rapid transition to Canaan; Jacob apprised of developments
46:1—47:12: Jacob goes to Egypt, meets Joseph; the family settles there	Ep16: vv. 99–101: Redescent to Egypt; Joseph's prayer
	Ep17 vv. 102–11: Close and wrap-up; Muhammad reappears on stage as addressee; Allah explains purpose of story. Warns disbelievers of forthcoming punishment. God explains to readers that prophets (such as Joseph) show the path to be followed
47:13–31: Joseph and the famine	
48: Jacob blesses Manasseh and Ephraim	
49: Jacob blesses all his sons; dies	
50: Joseph mourns his father; reassures his brothers; dies in Egypt	

Table 5.2. Comparison of Joseph Narratives

Is There a Peak?

As we saw at the outset of this paper, in narrative scripture, Peak represents a significant moment of disclosure, understanding, and resolution after a careful build-up of suspense and uncertainty. In consideration of this, a strong case could be made for a Peak in the Genesis account of Joseph to be found at Gen 45:3:

וַיֹּאמֶר יוֹסֵף אֶל-אֶחָיו אֲנִי יוֹסֵף.

At this point in Egypt, most of the key characters have been gathered together. Joseph reveals his identity to his brothers after the lengthy suspense created by the series of events that followed his brothers' plot in the early part of the narrative. The sense of shock the brothers experience is clear in the verse: "Joseph said to his brothers, 'I am Joseph! Is my father still living?' But his brothers were not able to answer him, because they were terrified at his presence."

In the case of the Qur'ānic account of the Yusuf story, however, the problem with identifying Peak relates to the genre. Commentary by Allah is frequently inserted into the story line, pointing out to readers the significance of event X or statement Y. The following selection of verses is far from comprehensive but sufficient to illustrate the point:

- [6]This is about how your Lord will choose you, teach you to interpret dreams, and perfect His blessing on you and the House of Jacob, just as He perfected it earlier on your forefathers Abraham and Isaac: your Lord is all knowing and wise.'
- [7]There are lessons in the story of Joseph and his brothers for all who seek them.
- [15]We inspired him, saying, "You will tell them of all this [at a time] when they do not realize [who you are]!"
- [19]God was well aware of what they did
- [21]God always prevails in His purpose, though most people do not realize it. [22]When he reached maturity, We gave him judgement and knowledge: this is how We reward those who do good.
- [24]... he would have succumbed to her if he had not seen evidence of his Lord—We did this in order to keep evil and indecency away from him, for he was truly one of Our chosen servants.

- ³⁴and his Lord answered his prayer and protected him from their treachery—He is the All Hearing, the All Knowing.
- Intervention of the great adversary: ⁴²Joseph said to the one he knew would be saved, "Mention me to your master," but Satan made him forget to do this.
- ⁵⁶In this way We settled Joseph in that land to live wherever he wished: We grant Our mercy to whoever We will and do not fail to reward those who do good. ⁵⁷ The reward of the Hereafter is best for those who believe and are mindful of God.
- ⁷⁶In this way We devised a plan for Joseph—if God had not willed it so, he could not have detained his brother as a penalty under the king's law—We raise the rank of whoever We will. Above everyone who has knowledge there is the One who is all knowing.
- Joseph's concluding prayer: ¹⁰¹"My Lord! You have given me authority; You have taught me something about the interpretation of dreams; Creator of the heavens and the earth, You are my protector in this world and in the Hereafter. Let me die in true devotion to You. Join me with the righteous."
- ¹¹¹There is a lesson in the stories of such people for those who understand. This revelation is no fabrication: it is a confirmation of the truth of what was sent before it; an explanation of everything; a guide and a blessing for those who believe.

While Muslims view the Qur'ānic text as being Allah's word, communicated through Muhammad, a non-Muslim view of the above verses which stress the sovereignty of Allah might be to see these verses as interruptions by a storyteller, ensuring his audience/s get the point of the story. But whatever the explanation, it is the case that the uncertainty on the part of the reader, so important in biblical narratives, does not occur to the same degree in the Qur'ān because of the pervasive presence of and commentary by the narrator, Allah. Hence a clear Peak, resolving this uncertainty, is more difficult to identify than would be the case if Allah were less visible in the story.

Episode 14, the counterpart to biblical Peak when Yusuf reveals himself, could not be considered Peak in the Qur'ānic account, because though it explains the significance of the story, it is merely repeating what has been said on a number of occasions previously in the chapter. An argument could be made for a narrative Peak to occur in Episode 16, verse 100: "This," said Joseph to his father, "is the meaning of my old vision." At this point the meaning of original dream is resolved, thus resolving the problem presented in the stage. But it is a Peak lacking the kind of impact that normally results from a build-up of suspense among readers. A didactic Peak could be proposed for verse 110, when Allah's lesson is encapsulated overtly and clearly for the audience at the end of the story: "When the messengers lost all hope and realized that they had been dismissed as liars, Our help came to them: We saved whoever We pleased, but Our punishment will not be turned away from guilty people."

Variations in Detail between Biblical and Qur'ānic Accounts

From a distance, the reader is struck by the similarities between the two narrative accounts of the biblical Joseph and Qur'ānic Yusuf. Favored by his father, he falls victim to a plot hatched by his jealous brothers. Their plot results in him being in servitude in Egypt, and then prison. His ability to interpret dreams earns the favor of the Pharoah, who appoints him to a high position in the kingdom of Egypt. His brothers descend to Egypt from famine-stricken Canaan, seeking relief for themselves and their aged father, who remains in Canaan. Through a sequence of events involving some trickery on the part of Joseph, and Joseph revealing his identity, he succeeds in having his brothers bring his father to Egypt where the family is reunited.

However, if a reader looks beyond the macro-elements to consider a more detailed analysis of the two narrative accounts, differences in detail emerge at frequent points of the stories. As Noegel and Wheeler observe, "The basic outline of the Joseph story in the Bible and Qur'ān agree, though the details differ and the focus of interpretation by Jews and Muslims tends to diverge."[9] The following discussion offers a selection rather than a comprehensive listing of those differences in detail. In terms of context, the biblical account reports that just prior to Joseph's dream and his brothers implementing their plot, he was seventeen years of age (Gen 37:2). However, the Qur'ānic exegetical literature offers an alternative account. Al-Suyuti (d. 1505) reports that "Hasan al-Basri says

---

9. Noegel and Wheeler, *A to Z of Prophets*, 175.

that Joseph was thrown into the pit when he was twelve years old."[10] This kind of difference in detail permeates the biblical and Qur'ānic accounts.

With regard to Josephs' dream, both Bible and Qur'ān agree that eleven stars, the sun and the moon bowed down before Joseph. However, in the Bible account in Gen 37, Joseph tells both Jacob and his brothers about his dream, whereas in the Qur'ān Joseph only tells Jacob, who warns him not to tell his brothers. In the biblical account, Jacob sends Joseph off to join his brothers who are already with the flocks. However, in the Qur'ān the brothers persuade Jacob, against his will, to allow Joseph to accompany them with the flocks. The Bible relates that the plot is hatched after Joseph has come to join his brothers, whereas in the Qur'ān the plot is hatched before the brothers persuade Jacob to release Joseph to their care. Reuben is identified by name as the cautious brother in the biblical account, whereas none of the brothers is named in the Qur'ān.

In the Bible Joseph's brothers sell him to passing merchants, whereas in the Qur'ān the brothers have already left the scene. Joseph is found by passers-by in the well and is sold to a merchant. In Gen 39, details are given about the interaction between Joseph and Potiphar's wife. Potiphar is deceived by his wife into thinking that Joseph is guilty. However, in Q12:21–35, Joseph is vindicated before the (unnamed) Potiphar but with continuing temptation Joseph suggests himself that he be imprisoned. The Qur'ān mentions that Joseph himself was tempted by lust, whereas there is no reference to this in the biblical account. Moreover, in Q12:30 the Qur'ān relates that women in the city discussed the seduction of Joseph, but this account does not appear in the Genesis account.

Genesis 40 relates the account of the cupbearer and baker in prison, providing considerable narrative detail, demonstrating Joseph's wisdom and gifts. However, Q12:36–42 includes a reduced version of the same account, devoting most attention to expounding theological truths. The narrative is relegated to this exposition, with Joseph seen as devout rather than specially gifted. Note that in both accounts Joseph is forgotten by the cupbearer, but the Qur'ān specifies that this occurs under Satan's influence.

Genesis 41 is concerned with Pharaoh's dreams. Joseph is rehabilitated and placed in a position of authority in a purely narrative account. Q12:43–57 contains the core of this story, but with extra elements. The cupbearer goes to prison where Joseph interprets Pharoah's dream for him, whereas in the biblical account, Joseph is brought to Pharoah's

---

10. Wheeler, *Prophets in the Qur'ān*, 127.

court to interpret the dream. Q12:50–52 is inserted to resolve the earlier account of the slandering of Joseph by the women, which caused his imprisonment. Q12:56–57 includes a direct didactic exposition by God, spelling out in clear terms the theological lessons to be drawn.

In Gen 42 Joseph's brothers visit Egypt. The Qur'ānic account of this visit (Q12:58–67) makes no mention of leaving one of the brothers (Simeon in the Bible) as hostage. Other differences can be noticed: the Qur'ānic account refers to loading camels (v. 65) rather than the Genesis reference to donkeys (v. 26). Furthermore, in this part of the respective narratives, Jacob appears more trusting of God in the Qur'ān (v. 64) than in the Bible (vv. 36–38). Genesis 44 recounts how Joseph's steward searches in the brothers' bags for the missing drinking cup, whereas the parallel account in Q12:76 has Joseph himself searching in the bags. In a key point in both accounts, Joseph reveals his identity. However, in Gen 45 Joseph reveals himself to all the brothers at the same time, whereas in Q12:69 Joseph had revealed himself to Benjamin secretly before the others to reassure him about the ruse that was being played on the other brothers.

Staying in Gen 45, when the brothers return to Egypt after the second visit to Jacob with Benjamin withheld, Joseph has already revealed himself to them all so Jacob is joyful. However, in the Qur'ānic account there is confusion in the story at vv. 82–83, with the result that Joseph has not yet revealed himself so Jacob is in agony, thinking Benjamin is lost.

Purposes of the Two Accounts

The Biblical Account

First, let us consider certain features of the Joseph account in Genesis that distinguish it from other narrative accounts in the Bible. Gerhard von Rad makes the following observation:

> It differs from the earlier patriarchal stories that spoke more about God. Where in this story do we ever read a statement like "God appeared" "God spoke," "God gave heed"? etc. In comparison with all these stories, the Joseph story is distinguished by a revolutionary worldliness, a worldliness that unfolds the entire realm of human life, with all its height and depths, realistically and without miracle.[11]

---

11. Moberly, *Theology of the Book of Genesis*, 227.

In somewhat similar vein, Walter Brueggemann commented:

> The purposes of God are not wrought here by abrupt action or by intrusions, but by the ways of the world which seem to be natural and continuous. There is no appeal for faith or response, for the main point is that the ways of God are at work, regardless of human attitudes or actions.[12]

So within the biblical account there is an absence of theophanies compared with previous accounts of other patriarchs in Genesis. Joseph's life and its faithfulness serves as a model of righteousness for readers, without God being inserted directly into the narrative to emphasise the point. Furthermore, it is argued that Joseph sits within a stream of prophetic experience leading to Christ. James Hamilton compared the persecution Joseph suffered at the hands of his brothers with the stories of Cain and Abel, Ishmael and Isaac, and Esau and Jacob, observing that it

> could have been understood as *prospective* in that they generated the expectation that future individuals in the line of promise, who experienced God's favor and kindness, would be expected to experience similar treatment.[13]

Hamilton continues:

> There is historical correspondence between the way wicked opponents have treated the righteous prophets, and the pattern undergoes a heightening or escalation of significance when the Messiah himself experiences the fullest expression of this pattern of events and is crucified. The pattern is typologically fulfilled in Jesus.[14]

By this account, Joseph is essentially positioned to function as a saviour in Egypt to all the community, not just his own people, in the face of famine, similar to the later core function of Jesus Christ himself.

---

12. Brueggemann, *Genesis*, 289.
13. Hamilton, "Was Joseph a Type," 53.
14. Hamilton, "Was Joseph a Type," 53.

The Qur'ānic Account

Goldman reminds us that the Yusuf account is the 'Qur'ān's longest sustained narrative' particularly about an individual person's life.[15] Some also argue that it is the best story of all the prophetic stories, a claim inspired by Q12:3: "We tell you [Prophet] the best of stories in revealing this Qur'ān to you." For example, the famous Jalalayn commentary explains this verse in terms of the following: "We will relate to you the best of narratives in what We have revealed, in Our revealing, to you this Qur'ān . . ."[16] The modern scholar Mahmood Shakir Saeed agreed, offering two specific reasons for its special status: "The story of Joseph, peace be upon him, represents the peak of all the Qur'ānic stories with regard to its topical unity and its artistic appeal, and also with regard to the lessons of faith which the story contains."[17] However, some other commentators suggest that the story is rather a more general statement on the nature of Qur'ānic narratives.[18]

On this debate it is worth turning to the *Stories of the Prophets* (*Qisas al-anbiya' [QA]*), a narrative genre through which the story of Yusuf has been widely disseminated across the Islamic world. The QA typically takes narratives which occur in the Qur'ān and embellishes them with additional details from diverse sources in order to maximise their appeal to audiences. There have been several iconic collections of the QA throughout Islamic history, as well as a plethora of popular versions produced for mass consumption. The famous collection by the eleventh century scholar Muhammad ibn Abd Allah al-Kisa'i does not address the reason why the Yusuf account is described as "the best of narratives."[19] The collection by the fourteenth century theologian Ibn Kathir (d. 1373) quotes Q12:3 but does not consider the meaning of "best of narratives."[20] However the version of the QA by the Turkish author Nasir al-Din b. Burhan al-Din Rabghuzi (d. 1310) goes to some lengths to provide

---

15. Goldman, "Joseph," 55.
16. Al-Mahalli and Al-Suyuti, *Tafsir al-Jalalayn*, 241.
17. Saeed, *Model for a Muslim Youth*, 5.
18. Goldman, "Joseph," 55.
19. Al-Kisa'i, *Tales of the Prophets*.
20. Ibn Kathir, *Stories of the Prophets*. This work represents a compilation of information on lives of the prophets extracted from Ibn Kathir's famous *Al-bidaya wa'l-hidaya* (*The Beginning and the End*).

different scholarly explanations why the Yusuf story is described as the best of narratives, listing the following reasons offered in the literature:[21]

1. "Of all the stories in the Qur'ān the richest in entertaining episodes and most plentiful in instructive points is the Story of Joseph."

2. "This story lasted forty years from beginning to end; eighty years according to others."

3. "The Story of Joseph has come down right to its conclusion in one chapter of the Qur'ān."

4. "The other stories took place between strangers. But the Story of Joseph happened between parents and their children."

5. "There are three aspects to this story: maintaining obedience to the Lord in good and bad times, acting decently toward people at large, and being generous in times of affluence as well as in times of scarcity."

6. "Joseph treated his brothers well while enduring their cruelty."

7. "This story begins with a dream, there is a dream in the middle, and it ends with a dream."

8. "This story comes to an end with love."

9. Muhammad said, "if someone wishes to be delivered from... [various] sorts of calamity [ungratefulness, theft, poverty, sorrow, hypocrisy, anger, unbelief/polytheism, sorcery], he must recite the chapter entitled Joseph, because the Story of Joseph contains all calamities together."

Though these various perspectives point to some level of debate among Muslims, it is clear that there is widespread agreement on the crucial importance of Sura Yusuf in the life of Muslim communities down the centuries. Within the Qur'ānic account, the theme of Yusuf as one of Allah's signs is paramount: "Joseph came to you before with clear signs, but you never ceased to doubt the message he brought to you" (Q 40:34). It would be helpful to pursue this theme via another literary genre: that of *Friday sermons*. The theme of Yusuf as one of Allah's signs is emphasized in a sermon that was issued to all mosques in Singapore in 2017 by the Singapore Council of Islamic Scholars, as follows:

---

21. Rabghuzii, *Stories of the Prophets*, 137–38.

> When we discuss about sabr [patience], we cannot deny the importance of studying the lives of the Prophets ... for they ... faced all sorts of tests from Allah s.w.t. Among them, Prophet Yusuf a.s.... In fact, the Qur'ān affirms his patience as a sign and an example for those who wish to emulate.[22]

The twin themes of being tested and the importance of patience are underscored throughout this sermon:

> The story of Prophet Yusuf a.s. teaches us the true meaning of being tested, and also of patience (sabr).... Prophet Yusuf a.s. were [sic] tested with such major challenges, yet, he continued to be firm in his faith, resilient, and faced the tests with patience and in firm belief that Allah s.w.t. knows best.[23]

The centrality of testing is an important device to remind the reader of the role of the divine narrator, whose overriding sovereignty is being emphasised throughout the story. Human participants are support actors, important to fill the stage but destined to follow the divine script. The Singapore sermon draws on the Hadith to reiterate that authority lies with Allah:

> At times, a person is tested even though he is the most beloved servant of Allah s.w.t. There are those who are tested because these challenges are *kaffarah* or an expiation of their past sins. Let us look at a hadith of our beloved Prophet Muhammad s.a.w. that was recorded by Imam Bukhari: ... "No fatigue, nor disease, nor sorrow, nor sadness, nor hurt, nor distress befalls a Muslim, even if it were the prick he receives from a thorn, but that Allah expiates some of his sins for that."[24]

In line with these ideas, University of Melbourne scholar Abdullah Saeed comments:

> The primary purpose of these narratives does not seem to be simply to tell a story, but rather to relate the struggles of the Prophet Muhammad to those of earlier prophets. When Muhammed was having difficulties in his mission, these stories

---

22. Singapura, "Lessons from the Story," 2.
23. Singapura, "Lessons from the Story," 3.
24. The Hadith reference is taken from *Sahih Bukhari* Book 75, Hadith 2 (5641, 5642).

would remind him that earlier prophets had to face similar challenges.[25]

Here we find an echo of Mark Durie's discussion of what he terms "Messenger Uniformitarianism," which he defines as follows:

> Allah's procedure with messengers has always been the same in the past, so the Messenger's current experiences only repeat those of earlier messengers, including some which might seem frustrating or difficult. The intended application of this teaching is that because messengers have experienced these difficulties in the past and persevered, present difficulties are no reason for the believers to fall away, nor for the Messenger to lose heart.[26]

Saeed elaborates:

> According to the Qur'ān, all of them taught the same basic message of belief in the One God, Creator and Sustainer of the universe, and that human beings should recognize God's Oneness and lead an ethical and moral life.[27]

Roberto Tottoli similarly sees a trajectory in function from Yusuf to Muhammad in writing:

> [Yusuf] is to be considered a figure who was similar to Muhammad who was also constrained to escape to Medina, but by the end of his life came to know triumph and, like Joseph, was generous with his brothers, the Meccans, who had rejected and despised him.[28]

Brannon Wheeler seems to dispute this angle on the Yusuf narrative in the Qur'ān. He writes:

> the story of Joseph does not easily conform to the story of other prophets in the Qur'ān. Joseph is not sent as a prophet to a particular people, nor does he claim a particular message. His story does not appear to relate directly to events occurring in the life of the prophet Muhammad.[29]

---

25. Saeed, *Qur'ān*, 67.
26. Durie, *Qur'ān and Its Biblical Reflexes*, 136.
27. Saeed, *Qur'ān*, 66–67.
28. Tottoli, *Biblical Prophets in the Qur'ān*, 31.
29. Wheeler, *Prophets in the Qur'ān*, 175.

However, this is missing the point that is shared in the statements by Durie and Saeed. What is at issue in prophetic stories in the Qur'ān is not a resemblance between specific events that affect the lives of the various prophets, but rather the role of the actors in the story and the function of the narrative in pointing the way ahead for its readers. Aisha Stacey puts it well in saying:

> The essence of the story of Joseph is patience in the face of adversity and sorrow. Joseph faced every trial with patience and complete trust in God. His father Jacob bore his grief and misery with patience and submission. All the chapters of Qur'ān [sic] were revealed at particular times, in response to particular situations . . . the road may be long and difficult but the ultimate victory belongs to those with God consciousness and patience. The story of Joseph is a lesson for us all. True patience, what the scholars of Islam call beautiful patience is a key to the gate of Paradise.[30]

The Qur'ānic story of Yusuf is relevant to Christians who are searching for the "salvation" theme in the Qur'ān. It demonstrates the role of prophets in guiding believers onto the straight path (cf. Q1:6). This sets believers up for a good outcome on the Day of Judgment.

Conclusion

Despite the obvious similarities between the biblical and Qur'ānic versions of the Joseph story, it is important to note the significant and various differences. First, some of the essential features of narrative, relating to reader suspense and uncertainty about the direction of the story, are clear in the Bible but absent from the Qur'ānic account. While both accounts may be the product of storytellers, the biblical storyteller knew how to hold his readers in suspense. In contrast the Qur'ānic storyteller was far less interested in such features of building and maintaining narrative suspense and far more committed to reminding his readers on a regular basis of the overall element of divine sovereignty and providence.

In the Bible, the function of Joseph is not to illustrate how God deliberately tests us but rather to demonstrate how a faithful life in the face of adversity bears fruit. In the Qur'ān, the Yusuf account indicates how each believer will be tested by Allah and if they endure with patience as

---

30. Stacey, "Story of Joseph," part 7, para. 12.

Yusuf did, they may find salvation on the last day. It is argued by some Muslim scholars that among all the prophetic stories in the Qur'ān, the Yusuf account is the best in achieving this goal.

While God is clearly sovereign in the biblical account, he is barely visible in the surface structure of the narrative, and the reader does not have God's overarching sovereignty broadcast loudly to him frequently during the story. By contrast, in the Qur'ānic account the reader is left in no doubt who is in charge; namely, Allah, who placed a series of obstacles in the way of his prophet, and will do the same for every believer, to test them out as a precursor for the Day of Judgement.

Bibliography

Abdel-Haleem, M. A. S. *The Qur'ān*. Oxford: Oxford University Press, 2004.

———. *Understanding the Qur'ān: Themes and Style*. London: Tauris, 2011.

Abu-Zayd, Nasr. "The 'Others in the Qur'ān: A Hermeneutical Approach." *Philosophy Social Criticism* 36 (2010) 281–94.

Al-Kisa'i, Muhammad ibn 'Abd Allah. *Tales of the Prophets (Qisas al-anbiya')*. Edited by Wheeler M. Thackston. Chicago: Great Books of the Islamic World, 1997.

Al-Mahalli, Jalal al-Din, and Jalal al-Din Al-Suyuti. *Tafsir al-Jalalayn*. Edited by Ghazi Bin Muhammad Bin Talal. Amman: Royal Aal al-Bayt Institute for Islamic Thought, 2007.

Bal, Mieke. *Narratology: Introduction to the Theory of Narrative*. Toronto: University of Toronto Press, 1999.

Brueggemann, Walter. *Genesis*. Atlanta: John Knox, 1982.

Durie, Mark. *The Qur'ān and Its Biblical Reflexes: Investigations into the Genesis of a Religion*. Lanham, MA: Lexington, 2018.

Goldman, S. "Joseph." In *Encyclopaedia of the Qur'ān: J–O*, by Jane D. McAuliffe, 3:55. Boston: Brill, 2003.

Hamilton, James M. "Was Joseph a Type of the Messiah? Tracing the Typological Identification between Joseph, David, and Jesus." *The Southern Baptist Journal of Theology* 12.4 (2008) 52–77.

Ibn Kathir, Ismail. *Stories of the Prophets*. Riyadh: Darussalam, 1999.

Longacre, Robert E. *The Grammar of Discourse*. New York: Springer US, 1996.

———. "A Top-Down, Template-Driven Narrative Analysis, Illustrated by Application to Mark's Gospel." In *Discourse Analysis and the New Testament*, edited by Stanley Porter and Jeffrey Reed, 140–68. Sheffield: Sheffield Academic, 1999.

Longacre, Robert E., and Steven Levinsohn. "Field Analysis of Discourse." In *Current Trends in Textlinguistics*, edited by Wolfgang Ulrich Dressler, 102–22. Berlin: de Gruyter, 1978.

Moberly, R. W. L. *The Theology of the Book of Genesis*. Cambridge: Cambridge University Press, 2009.

Noegel, Scott B., and Brannon M. Wheeler. *The A to Z of Prophets in Islam and Judaism*. Lanham, MD: Scarecrow, 2010.

Nöldeke, Theodor, et al. *The History of the Qur'ān*. Leiden, Natherlands: Brill, 2013.

Rabghuzii, Nosiruddin Burhonuddin. *Al-Rabghuzi. The Stories of the Prophets Qisas al-anbiya': an Eastern Turkish version.* Edited by H. E. Boeschoten and J. O'Kane. Leiden, Netherlands: Brill, 2015.

Rad, Gerhard von. *Genesis: A Commentary.* Edited by John Marks. Philadelphia: Westminister, 1961.

Riddell, Peter G. "Reading the Qur'ān Chronologically: An Aid to Discourse Coherence and Thematic Development." In *Islamic Studies Today: Essays in Honor of Andrew Rippin*, edited by M. Daneshgar and W. Saleh, 296–316. Leiden, Natherlands: Brill, 2016.

Roth, Elana. "The Story of Joseph." https://www.myjewishlearning.com/article/the-story-of-joseph/.

Saeed, Abdullah. *The Qur'ān: An Introduction.* London: Routledge, 2008.

Saeed, Mahmoud Shakir. *A Model for a Muslim Youth in the Story of Joseph (Yusuf).* Edited and translated by Khalid Ibraheem al-Dossary. World Assembly of Muslim Youth, 1998.

Singapura, Majlis Ugama Islam. "Lessons from the Story of Prophet Yusuf a.s." https://www.muis.gov.sg/-/media/Files/OOM/Khutbah/English/PDF/2017/E17Sep22-Lessons-from-the-Story-of-Prophet-Yusuf.pdf.

Stacey, Aisha. "The Story of Joseph." https://www.islamreligion.com/articles/1790/viewall/story-of-joseph/.

Terry, Ralph. *A Discourse Analysis of First Corinthians.* Publications in Linguistics 120. Arlington, TX: University of Texas at Arlington Press, 1995.

Tottoli, Roberto. *Biblical Prophets in the Qur'ān and Muslim Literature.* London: Routledge, 2002.

Wheeler, Brannon M. *Prophets in the Qur'ān: An Introduction to the Qur'ān and Muslim Exegesis.* London: Continuum, 2002.

6

Variant Versions of the Moses Story in the Qur'ān

Gordon D. Nickel

The stories of biblical characters in the Qur'ān have attracted a great deal of attention from academic scholars of Islam. One of the main reasons for interest in these stories has been to compare the Qur'ānic narratives with the corresponding accounts in the Bible. Analysis of the differences between the biblical and Qur'ānic narratives then turns toward such questions as how to characterize the relationship between the scriptures, and the possible provenance of non-biblical details in the Qur'ānic stories. From there the discussion may lead into vigorous and even polemical arguments over such questions as borrowing, dependence, influence and originality.[1] The relationship between the Bible and the Qur'ān has been the subject of some extensive and excellent studies during the past decade.[2]

Noticeably less scholarly attention has been devoted to the phenomenon of the repetition of stories of biblical characters within the Qur'ān

---

1. Waldman, "New Approaches," 47–64.
2. For example, Reynolds, *Qur'ān and Its Biblical Subtext* and *Qur'ān and the Bible*; Durie, *Qur'ān and Its Biblical Reflexes*. Amir-Moezzi and Dye, *Le Coran des historiens*.

itself, and to the questions surrounding the differences among the various versions. The story of Noah, for example, appears in seven variant versions, as does the story of Iblīs and Adam. The story of Lot appears in eight versions, and the messengers visit Abraham in five different suras. The versions of the same story in the Qurʾān display many differences in a wide range of types from apparently incidental to strikingly fundamental.

The subject of repetition as an observation of the literary character of the Qurʾān has seldom been the object of sustained academic research,[3] even though John Wansbrough wrote in 1977 that "variant traditions are present in such quantity as to deserve some attention in a description of the process"[4] by which a collection of units of what he calls "prophetical *logia*" became Muslim scripture. More recently Joseph Witztum repeated the appeal, arguing that "a systematic study of parallel passages in the Qurʾān is long overdue in order for us to answer basic questions concerning the formation of the Qurʾān."[5]

When noted by academic scholars in the past, Qurʾānic repetition sometimes appears as a theme in largely negative lists of first impressions of the literary nature of the book. In quite recent times, however, a number of prominent Western scholars of the Qurʾān have been characterizing repetition of formulae, verses, and whole narratives as indications of coherence and even carefully composed excellence in literary style. Some Muslim writers in turn have highlighted these scholarly hypotheses as support for Muslim truth claims for the Qurʾān as a literary miracle.

Of all the biblical characters in the Qurʾān, the figure of Mūsā—the Qurʾānic Moses—provides the largest number of versions of his story. There are also many distinct episodes in the Qurʾānic versions of his story that can be conveniently compared. After making some general observations about the Moses stories in the Qurʾān, this essay examines three sets of variant versions in more detail and analyzes similarities and differences for what they might tell us about the nature of the Qurʾān.

The question of multiple versions of stories of biblical characters in the Qurʾān, and the differences among them, bears more than purely

3. Nöldeke and Schwally suggested that repetition of the same material in the Qurʾān might offer clues to the relative chronology of Qurʾānic sūras, but they did not use this to determine their dating scheme. Nöldeke, *Geschichte des Qorans*, 1.63.

4. Wansbrough, *Quranic Studies*, 21.

5. Witztum, "Variant Traditions," 2. Witztum has highlighted—as well as perhaps stimulated—other recent studies, including Pohlmann, *Die Entstehung des Korans*, and Dye, "Le Coran et le Problème Synoptique," 234–61, cf. Dye, "Le Corpus Coranique," 806–22.

academic interest. In the history of Muslim polemic against the Bible, some of the most vigorous accusations have targeted differences of detail among the Gospel accounts. One scholar working in an intense Muslim environment found that for Muslims considering the Gospel accounts, "[p]arallel passages with variants and differences seem . . . incongruous in a book that is put forward as holy Scripture."[6] The scholar suggested that the conversation might become more sympathetic if Muslims could note and acknowledge variant versions of prophetic stories in the Qur'ān.

The Material on Moses in the Qur'ān

The material on Moses in the Qur'ān is substantial, varied, and interesting. His name appears some 136 times. Verses related to Moses number between 502 and 510 in a book of some 6236 verses. Some thirty-six of the Qur'ān's 114 suras mention Moses in fifty separate pericopes.[7] This is more material than about any other figure: more than twice as much as the material on Abraham, the next most mentioned figure; and more than five times the material on 'Īsā, the Qur'ānic Jesus.

Even more striking than this abundance of material is the special profile which the Qur'ān seems to give to Moses. In the canonical progression of the Qur'ān this is first signaled in the fourth Sura, where after a list of names of prophets which appear repeatedly, we read, "Allah spoke to Moses directly (*kallama taklīman*)" (Q4.164).[8] Further on, in a scene of divine revelation to Moses, Allah says, "Moses! I have chosen you over the people for my messages and for my word" (Q7.144). Later, the Qur'ānic voice declares about Moses, "We called him from the right side of the mountain, and we brought him near in conversation" (Q19.52). Similarly high statements are indicated in the description of versions of the "burning bush" episode below.

These are remarkable expressions in the total context of the Qur'ān. In fact, none of these expressions occurs in association with any other figure. Wansbrough concluded from these passages, "the scriptural material may be enlisted to support the particular position of Moses in the prophetical

---

6. Elder, "Parallel Passages," 255.

7. Clark, "Biblical and Early Islamic Moses," 28n32; Moubarac, "Moïse dans le Coran," 375.

8. Qur'ān translations are those of A. J. Droge from Nickel, *Quran with Christian Commentary*, except for the Qur'ānic "Allah" in place of Droge's "God."

hierarchy, but hardly that of Muhammad."[9] Wansbrough meant that though Muslims believe that the words of the Qur'ān were revealed to Muhammad, the name of Islam's messenger only appears four times in Muslim scripture. It is true that Muslim doctrine developed a claim for Muhammad's superiority over other prophets, but of this doctrine "there is no unequivocal trace" in the Qur'ān, according to Wansbrough.[10]

Characteristics of Narrative Repetition

Of the fifty or so pericopes which mention Moses, a number are more extensive. This may be seen in the chart of elements in the Qur'ānic variant versions, which plots a list of narrative elements familiar from the Hebrew Bible (below Table I, left side) against the Moses passages in the Qur'ān (across the top). The narratives with the greatest number of familiar elements are those in Suras 7, 20 and 28. Suras 2 and 26 also contain substantial narratives; and the narratives in Suras 10 and 27, though not as long, are also important passages. Scholars most frequently describe these various narratives with non-committal terms such as "accounts."[11] E. E. Elder called the various narratives "parallel passages."[12] Wansbrough described the repeating stories as "variant traditions,"[13] a term which reflects a dimension of analysis examined below. More recently, Andy Bannister has proposed that the seven versions of the Iblis and Adam story be described as oral "performance variants."[14]

The narrative elements which appear most often in the many variants in order of frequency are the scene with Moses in Pharaoh's court (element VIII), the deliverance of the children of Israel from the pursuing Pharaoh (XI), and Allah's sending of Moses to Pharaoh (VI).

The chart shows that the variant versions are significantly different from each other in the number of narrative elements they include and in the order in which they present the elements. Suras 28 and 20 recount a good number of familiar elements in a familiar order. The reason for

9. Wansbrough, *Quranic Studies*, 56.

10. Wansbrough, *Quranic Studies*, 55.

11. Clark, "Biblical and Early Islamic Moses," 30; Johns, "Moses in the Qur'ān," 125.

12. Elder, "Parallel Passages," 255.

13. Wansbrough, *Quranic Studies*, 20.

14. Bannister, *Oral-Formulaic Study*, 29.

the inversion of the familiar order at the top of the column for Sura 20 is that after Allah encounters Moses at the fire in the wilderness, Allah recounts to Moses events from his past in which Allah showed him favor. What this chart does not show is the differences in the presentation of individual elements.

Table I: Elements in the Quranic stories of Moses plotted against the main Moses passages in the Quran

NARRATIVE ELEMENTS	Sura 2.49-93	5.20-26	7.103-71	10.75-93	18.60-82	20.9-98	26.10-66	27.7-14	28.3-46	37.114-21	40.23-54	44.17-33	79.15-25
I. Baby Moses saved									1				
II. Moses kills a man									3				
III. Moses' sojourn in Midian									4				
IV. Moses sees a fire						1		1	5				1
V. God encounters Moses						2		2	6				2
VI. God sends Moses to Pharaoh			1	1		3, 8	1				1	1*	3
VII. Moses asks for help from Aaron						4	2		7				
VIII. Scene in Pharaoh's court			2	2		9	3	3	8		3	2*	
IX. God sends the plagues			3										
X. God tells Moses to lead Israel out of Egypt						10	4					3*	
XI. God delivers the children of Israel	1		4, 5	3		11	5		10	1	6	4*	
XII. God sends manna and quails	5		12			12							
XIII. Moses draws water from rock	7		11										
XIV. Moses goes away for 40 nights	2		6										
XV. Moses appoints 70 leaders			10										
XVI. God gives Moses the Tablets			8							2			
XVII. God gives Moses 'the book'	4, 10								11				
XVIII. Children of Israel worship a calf	3, 11		9			14							
XIX. Moses asks to see God			7										
XX. Moses commands to enter the land		1											
A. Allah says enter a township prostrate	6		13										
B. Allah raises a "mount" above the people	8, 12		15										
C. Children of Israel transgress the Sabbath	9		14										
D. Pharaoh believes before he dies				4									
E. Moses follows a strange ridding "servant"					1								
F. A Samaritan leads the people astray						13							
G. Pharaoh's wife asks that Moses be spared									2				
H. Pharaoh tells Haman to build a tower									9		5		
I. Haman and Qarun present with Pharaoh											2		
J. A "believer" defends Moses in court											4		

Numbers in each column indicate which narrative elements appear, and the order in which they appear. * - this version does not mention Moses

A number of narrative elements listed in the lower part of the table appear in the Qur'ānic versions but not in the Bible. Most of the episodes appear only once, but several repeat. To explain just two that repeat: Element A is about how Allah commands the children of Israel to enter an unidentified town, then specifies that they enter prostrate and pronounce the word *ḥiṭṭitun* as they enter. According to the Qur'ān, the evildoers among the people substitute another word for what Allah commanded them to say, so Allah punishes them (Q2.58, 59). As for Element B, Allah raises "the mount" above the children of Israel at the time he made a covenant with them, saying, "Hold fast what we have given you, and remember what is in it, so that you may guard (yourselves)" (Q2.63).

Three passages that have intrigued many Muslims as well as non-Muslim academic scholars are (F) an account of Israel's worship of the calf in which a Samaritan is culpable for leading the people astray (Q20.85–99); (J) an extensive defense of Moses from a "believer" in Pharaoh's court (Q40.28–45); and (E) a mysterious tale in which Moses follows a riddling "servant" and sees him do a series of surprising acts—incomprehensible right up to the end when the servant explains his actions to Moses' satisfaction (Q18.60–82). None of these episodes appears elsewhere in the Qur'ān, and indeed none resembles any other known source.

Comparison of Variant Versions of Three Episodes

From among the many interesting episodes in the Qur'ānic versions of the Moses story, this section examines three for their similarities and differences. The first episode, Moses at the burning bush, focuses the names that the deity gives for himself to Moses. The second example looks at an episode with a great number of details, the scene in the court of Pharaoh. Finally, the episode of the (golden) calf provides an opportunity to observe and consider both significant and fundamental differences.

1. *Names of the Deity at the Burning Bush*

The episode of God's encounter with Moses in the wilderness comes in three different narratives in the Qur'ān, in Suras 20, 27, and 28. In my description and discussion of these versions, "God" serves as a general term for the deity, because a central concern of the episode itself is how the deity names himself. Elder pointed out some of the differences among the three versions of the burning bush scene in one of the few scholarly articles on Qur'ānic repetition of stories and their differences.[15] Elder immediately spotted many differences of Arabic vocabulary and inclusion or omission of various narrative elements.[16] The following comparison focuses the names that the deity gives for himself in the three versions.

In the first canonical account of the episode,[17] Moses is attracted to a fire while traveling with his family in Midian. Moses tells his family to stay behind while he goes to investigate the fire. He adds that he hopes to bring a brand from the fire, and to find guidance there. When he arrives at the fire, a voice calls to him: "Moses! Surely I am your Lord [*rabb*], so take off your shoes. Surely you are in the holy *wādī* of *Ṭuwā*. I have chosen you, so listen to what is inspired. Truly I am *Allāh*—[there is] no god [*ilāha*] but me" (Q20.11–14).

The deity continues to speak to Moses, showing him two "signs" (*āyāt*): the staff which turns into a serpent, and the whitening of Moses' hand when he places it into his armpit. Then God commands Moses to go to Pharaoh. Moses asks God to give him Aaron for a helper, and God grants the request.

This version inserts into the middle of God's commands to go to Pharaoh (Q20.24, 43) a kind of flashback to Moses' childhood, his killing of a man, and his sojourn in Midian (Q20.37–41). In this speech, God says to Moses, "I cast love on you from me" (Q20.39) and "I have brought you up for myself" (Q20.41). This is the only appearance of this particular noun for love, *maḥabba*, in the Qur'ān. Once more God urges Moses and Aaron to set out and confront Pharaoh. When the two brothers express their fear about the mission, God encourages them with "Do not be afraid! Surely I am with both of you. I hear and I see" (Q20.46).

In this passage, therefore, the deity names himself to Moses as your (sing.) Lord (*rabb*) (20.12); and *Allāh*, adding "[there is] no god but me" (Q20.14).

---

15. Elder, "Parallel Passages," 254–59.
16. Elder, "Parallel Passages," 256–57.
17. Q20.10–48. Though Muslim scholars formulated schemes of dating the suras of the Qur'ān chronologically in a way which does not match their canonical sequence, most Muslims read, memorize and recite the Qur'ān in its canonical order. Commentaries also treat the material canonically, and thus initial interpretation of any theme is reflected in subsequent treatments of the same theme.

When Moses is called in Sura 27, a voice introduces a new name, "Lord of the worlds" (*rabb al-ʿālamīn*, 27.8). Here also the deity says he is *Allāh* (Q28.9, cf. 28.8), and he further describes himself as the mighty (*ʿazīz*) and wise (*ḥakīm*) (27.9), and as forgiving (*ghafūr*) and merciful (*raḥīm*) (Q27.11). God's speech here (vv. 9–12) is much shorter than in Sura 20, does not recount Moses' childhood, and does not lead into an extensive scene in the court of Pharaoh. This version seems to characterize the two signs to Moses as "among nine signs for Pharaoh and his people" (v. 12). Again God reassures Moses with "Do not fear," perhaps scolding his messenger by adding, "Surely in my presence the envoys do not fear" (v. 10).

In Sura 28, the encounter between God and Moses appears after an extensive narrative about Moses' childhood (Q28.7–14), his killing of a man (verses 15–21), and how he found a wife in Midian (vv. 22–28). The story of the divine encounter (vv. 39–35) specifies that Moses was called "from the right side of the *wādī*, in the blessed hollow, from the tree" (v. 30), but does not identify the *wādī* (valley) as *Ṭuwā*, as in 20.12 (the name appears once more in Q79.16). God names himself "*Allāh* Lord of the worlds" (v. 30), as in 27.8, but otherwise give no other name or description. The two signs to Moses are here called "proofs" (*burhānān*, v. 32). One other difference in this version is that in God's conversation with Moses—here also shorter than in Sura 20—Moses gives a particular reason for his fear that Pharaoh and his chiefs will kill him: because "I have killed one of them" (Q28.33).

2. Diversity of Details in Pharaoh's Court

The scene in the court of Pharaoh is the episode of Moses' story that appears both most frequently and most extensively in the Qurʾān. Many Qurʾānic portrayals of the scene actually provide more material on a theological exchange between Moses and Pharaoh than does the Exodus account. A. H. Johns suggests that "the qurʾānic description of Moses before Pharaoh is one of the most gripping scenes in the Qurʾān. The language is charged with a tremendous tension."[18]

---

18. Johns, "Let My People Go!," 144.

Prophets in the Qur'ān and the Bible

Table II: Details of the scene in Pharoah's court among 9 suras

DETAILS OF EPISODE	Sura 7.103f.	10.75f.	20.49f.	26.10f.	27.13f.	28.36f.	40.23f.	44.17f.	79.20f.
Moses introduces self	verse 104								
No mention of Moses								v. 17	
Aaron accompanies	111	v. 75	v. 47	v. 36					
Haman and Qarun in scene						v. 37	v. 24		
Pharoah questions Moses			49, 51	23					
Moses bears witness	105a		50, 52-5	24, 28					
Moses demands freedom	105b								
"An honorable messenger" demands								18-21	
Pharoah claims deity	106			29		38a			
Pharoah asks for sign			56	31					
Moses shows signs	107-8			32-33	v. 13	36a	23		20
Signs denied					14	36b	24		21
Pharoah asks Haman to make tower						38b			
A "believer" defends Moses							28-45		
Pharoah sends for magicians	109-12	79		36-38					
Magicians negotiate reward	113-14			41-42					
Magicians initiate "casting"	115-16		65-66						
Moses asks magicians to cast		80		43					
Moses speaks against magic		81-82							
God reassures Moses			68-69						
Moses casts and prevails	117-19			45					
Magicians believe in the Lord	120-21		70	47-48					
No one believes Moses		83							
Pharoah threatens magicians	123-24		71	49					
Magicians remain firm	125-26		72-73	50-51					

The scene in the Egyptian court is referred to in nine suras, and the greatest amount of detail is found in the versions in Suras 7, 20 and 26. Table II gives the details of the Qur'ānic versions down the left side and the Qur'ān passages across the top, to show which details appear in each passage. In this chart, verse numbers are given for each detail in the passage. The chart illustrates the actual proliferation of narrative detail in any one episode from among the Qur'ānic versions of the Moses story, as well as the striking range of difference in the content and sequence of detail between versions.

The wide range of variation seems to demand a way to categorize the kinds of differences from seemingly incidental or superficial, to significant, to fundamental. In Table II a number of fundamental differences are suggested in bold type. Chief of these is the detail in Sura 40 that a "believer" from the Pharaoh household dominates the scene for nineteen verses to preach to the Egyptians in Moses' defense (Q40.28–46). No such character appears in any of the other Moses versions.

Two other fundamental differences relate to the presence of Hāmān in Pharaoh's court. Suras 28 and 40 have Pharaoh asking Hāmān to make a tower so that Pharaoh might see Moses' god (*ilāha Mūsā*, Q28.38, 40.37). In Sura 40, however, Hāmān is joined by Qārūn (Q40.24, cf. 29.39), who elsewhere is a character in a different part of the Moses story that resembles Num 16 (Q28.76–82).

That the Qur'ān should present a brief version of the court scene in Sura 44.17–33 without mentioning the name of Moses (also very briefly in Q73.15–16) raises meaningful questions about both the provenance of—and the audience for—this recitation. Here the people of Pharaoh (verse 17) and the sons of Israel (v. 32) are specified, but the lead character in the scene is simply "an honorable messenger" (Q44.17; similarly Q73.15–16, "a messenger").

An interesting set of variants that may perhaps be described as significant without being fundamental are the names and descriptions of the deity in the scenes. When Moses first appears as messenger to Pharaoh in the canonical reading of the Qur'ān, he immediately announces, "Pharaoh! Surely I am a messenger from the Lord of the worlds" (Q7.104). Moses tells the court that he is also speaking for *their* Lord (*rabbikum*) (Q7.105). There is a contest of signs with the Egyptian wizards, which Allah inspires Moses to win. At their defeat, the wizards fall down prostrate and declare, "We believe in the Lord of the worlds, the Lord of Moses and Aaron" (Q7.121–22).

In Sura 20, when Moses and Aaron first appear in the Egyptian court, Pharaoh seems to have the first word. He asks them, "Who is your Lord, Moses?" (Q20.49). Moses answers, "Our Lord is the one who gave everything its creation, then guided" (Q20.50). After a second question from Pharaoh, Moses adds, "My Lord does not go astray, nor does he forget. Who made the earth as a cradle for you and put ways in it for you, and sent down water from the sky" (Q20.52–53). Here again the wizards are defeated by Moses in the contest of signs and cry out, "We believe in the Lord of Aaron and Moses." Pharaoh threatens the wizards with a painful punishment, but they stand firm and end up confessing to the ruler, "Surely we have believed in our Lord, so that he may forgive us our sins and the magic you forced us to [practice]. *Allāh* is better and more lasting" (Q20.73).

Further in Sura 26, Allah commands Moses and Aaron to announce to Pharaoh, "Surely we are the messenger (sing.) of the Lord of the worlds" (Q26.16). When the brothers appear before him, Pharaoh says that he recognizes Moses and knows of his earlier crime. He then queries, "What is the Lord of the worlds?" (Q26.23). Moses gives a threefold description in response to Pharaoh, while the ruler seems to interject objections to the courtiers: "The Lord of the heavens and the earth and whatever is between them" (Q26.24); "*Your* [pl.] Lord and the Lord of your fathers of old" (Q26.26); and "Lord of the East and the West and whatever is between them" (Q26.28). In this account, the wizards of Pharaoh once more declare their faith in "the Lord of the worlds, the Lord of Moses and Aaron" (Q26.47–48).

3. *Responsibility for the Calf*

References to the episode of the calf taken as a god come in Suras 2, 7, and 20. Sura 2 makes two brief mentions of the calf as part of a larger passage of polemic with the Sons of Israel (Q2.40–123). Sura 20 offers the longest treatment of the calf episode, again as part of a longer Moses passage (Q20.9–98). Once more there are many details that could be examined. This section traces in particular the assignment of responsibility and the language of wrongdoing.

The Qur'ān's first reference to the calf in the canonical progression seems to assume some knowledge of the details and place of the episode in the larger context of the Moses story (Q2.51–54, 92–93). Verse 51 declares "you took the calf" and "you were evildoers" (*ẓālimūn*). Allah pardons the Sons of Israel, but Moses says to them, "Surely you have done yourselves evil (*ẓalamtum anfusakum*) by taking the calf," and commands them to repent and kill one another (Q2.54). This command only appears in the Sura 2 version. Then Allah turns to the people in mercy (v. 54). Later in the same Moses passage and apparently still addressed to the Sons of Israel, the Qur'ān repeats "you took the calf" and "you were evildoers" (Q2.92). Here, however, there is no mention of mercy, but rather the Qur'ān comments, "they were made to drink the calf in their hearts because of their unbelief" (Q2.93). This punishment is only included in Sura 2. It is also worth noting that there is no mention here of Aaron or anyone else who might have led the people into idolatry.

The Sura 7 version of the calf episode starts out by telling that the people of Moses use their ornaments to make a calf, here described as a body with a mooing sound (Q7.148). By doing so the people become evildoers (*ẓālimūn*), then realize they have gone astray and ask the Lord for forgiveness (vv. 148–49). When Moses returns to his people from the mountain, he is angry and tells the people that they have done evil (*bi'sa*, v. 150), then seizes his brother. Aaron (see v. 142) seems to make the excuse that he was obliged to let the people make the calf and begs not to be included among the *ẓālimūn* (v. 150). Moses asks for forgiveness for himself and his brother, which seems to indicate Aaron's guilt (v. 151). But it is those who made the calf who have done evil deeds (*sayyāt*, v. 153); the anger of the Lord will reach them, and they will live with humiliation "in this present life" (v. 152).

Readers following the calf episode in the Qur'ān's canonical progression may be surprised by the differences in the extensive version at 20.83–98. First of all, in this version Allah informs Moses of an unspecified problem before Moses returns to his people. Second, Allah assigns blame before Moses has a chance to adjudicate the problem: "al-Sāmarī has led them astray" (v. 85). Moses arrives angry and questions his people about breaking their appointment with him (v. 86). The people say they did not want to break the appointment but say that the "burdens of the ornaments of the people" became so heavy that they "cast them" (v. 87). Here the mysterious "al-Sāmirī"—a character not mentioned or explained elsewhere in the Qur'ān—also casts and "brings forth" a calf (as in Sura 7 a "body" with a mooing sound). They then say, "This is your god (*ilāhukum*), and the god of Moses" (v. 88).

This version says that Aaron warned the people and asked them to obey him, but the people refuse (Q20.90–91). Moses questions Aaron, and Aaron explains that he was afraid of what Moses might say (vv. 92–94). Moses then confronts "al-Sāmarī" and receives from him a very enigmatic answer (v. 96). Finally, Moses banishes "al-Sāmarī" and forecasts his judgment. Moses says he will burn the "god" and "scatter it as dust in the sea" (v. 97).

The central role of "al-Sāmarī" in this version of the calf story must be considered a fundamental difference with the two other versions.[19] Along with that, variations in the assignment of responsibility for the idolatry in the three versions is a significant—if not fundamental—difference. In Sura 20 there is no prayer of forgiveness for Aaron, indicating his guilt. Instead, after Aaron gives his excuse, which in turn is different from his excuse in 7.150, Moses addresses al-Sāmarī. Even for al-Sāmarī there is no language of wrongdoing similar to that used in the other two versions for the Sons of Israel (Q2.54, 92; 7.148, 150, 153) and for Aaron (Q7.150–51). The Sura 20 version mentions leading astray (v. 85) and going astray (v. 92), but there is no language here of sin, repentance, and human need for forgiveness, or of forgiving or turning on the part of Allah.

Immediately following this version of the episode comes the self-referential claim that "we recount to you [sing.] some of the stories of what has already gone before" (Q20.99). And yet this telling or news (*anbāʾ*) of the calf episode departs wildly not only from the other two Qurʾānic versions, but also from the account in Exodus 32.

Traditional Muslim Discussions of Repetition

Muslims scholars recognized and acknowledged repetition in the Qurʾān from the earliest years of confessional discussion of its nature. For example, al-Rāmahurmuzī (d. 971) claimed the support of al-Ḥasan al-Baṣrī (d. 728) in writing that Allah had told stories in the Qurʾān of former times and that these are found repeated in different parts of the book.[20] The repetitions use different words and different word order but carry the same meaning, claimed al-Rāmahurmuzī, who openly acknowledged that "The different versions show omission (*hadhf*), ellipsis (*ilghāʾ*), addition (*ziyāda*) and condensation (*naqṣān*)."[21]

If the *Itqān fī ʿulūm al-qurʾān* of al-Suyūṭī (d. 1505) can be said to represent the accumulation of Muslim resources on the Qurʾānic sciences, Muslim thought on repetition of stories has been thoroughly confessional. The *Itqān*'s section on this theme (*takrīr al-quṣaṣ*) assumes

---

19. Witztum calls it the "[m]ost dramatic" difference. "Variant Traditions," 35; and Nicolai Sinai "conspicuous divergence." Sinai, "Two Types of Inner-Qurʾānic Interpretation," 278n59.

20. Speight, "Look at Variant Readings," 178.

21. Speight, "Look at Variant Readings," 178, from al-Rāmahurmuzī's *al-Muḥaddith al-fāṣil bayn al-rāwī wa al-wāʿī*.

above all other considerations that repetition was intended and executed by Allah.²² Al-Suyūṭī lists seven "benefits" of the repetition of stories that stem mainly from Muslim claims for the eloquence and inimitability of the Qurʾān. Al-Suyūṭī attributed these points to another early figure, Badr ibn Jamāʿa (d. 733), in the *al-Muqtinaṣ fī fawāʾid takrar al-qaṣaṣ*. Interestingly, al-Suyūṭī gives nearly the same amount of space to the question of why the story of Joseph only appears once.²³ One of the five reasons al-Suyūṭī lists is that the story contains the "flirtatious conduct" of women and their infatuation with an exceptionally beautiful human being, and therefore the story should not be repeated!²⁴

Muslim material on repetition of stories in the Qurʾān does not seem to have drawn much attention from academic scholars. In a recent article, however, Faraan Alamgir Sayed describes a traditional Muslim work written on repetition by al-Kirmānī (d. 1111), as well as the chapter on repetition in the *Burhān fī ʿulūm al-Qurʾān* of al-Zarkashī (d. 1392).²⁵ Al-Kirmānī's *al-Burhān fī tawjīh mutashābih al-Qurʾān* is given to repetition of verses, which al-Kirmānī explains as differing according to context.²⁶ In his *Burhān*, al-Zarkashī offers points similar to those in al-Suyūṭī's later *Itqān*, claiming beauty and power for the Qurʾān. For example, al-Zarkashī argued that if a story occurred only once in the recitations, skeptics could easily challenge the messenger to "bring another like this."²⁷ Another interesting argument in *al-Burhān*, evidently made prior to al-Zarkashī by Ibn Qutayba (d. 889), is that repetition of stories was essential so that the recitations could reach the various parts of the Arabian Peninsula.²⁸

---

22. Al-Suyūṭī, *al-Itqān fī ʿulūm al-qurʾān*, 2:189–92.
23. Al-Suyūṭī, *al-Itqān fī ʿulūm al-qurʾān*, 2:191–92.
24. Al-Suyūṭī, *al-Itqān fī ʿulūm al-qurʾān*, 2:191.
25. Sayed, "Repetition in Qurʾānic Qaṣaṣ," 53–75.
26. Sayed, "Repetition in Qurʾānic Qaṣaṣ," 57.
27. Sayed, "Repetition in Qurʾānic Qaṣaṣ," 57.
28. Sayed, "Repetition in Qurʾānic Qaṣaṣ," 57. Ibn Qutayba discussed repetition in his *Taʾwīl mushkil al-Qurʾān*. Sayed himself argues confessionally that the purpose of repetition in the Qurʾān's Moses stories is for literary and thematic reasons. *Repetition in Qurʾānic Qaṣaṣ*, 58–70. Joseph Witztum also cites the remark of al-Bāqillānī (d. 1013) in his *Iʿjāz al-Qurʾān*, that "repeating a story in different words which convey the same meaning is a difficult matter in which eloquence manifests itself and good style becomes evident." Witztum, "Variant Traditions," 2.

Modern Academic Writing on Variation

Western scholarly discussion of repetition in the Qur'ān has often depended on the acceptance of various Muslim versions of the Muhammad story (*sīra, maghāzī, ṭabaqāt, ta'rīkh*), at least in their main outlines, and the chronological arrangement of the suras that Muslims devised from the Muhammad story.[29] With this framework in mind, some Western scholars have then developed from the various versions of Qur'ānic stories a kind of psychological history of Muhammad's changing attitudes. There seems to be a sense of settled consensus in the 1953 statement of Richard Bell:

> In the telling of these stories Muhammad adapted them to what was occurring in his own mission ... the scheme is filled out by variable accounts of what was said by the messenger and by his opponents. ... We are justified therefore in taking these variable parts of the stories as reflecting what happened in his own experience.[30]

Many Western scholars have made the assumption that Muhammad chose to recite particular aspects of the Moses story according to his preaching needs at the time. For example, Bernard Heller asserted that in the Qur'ān, "Mūsā is considered as the precursor of, the model for, and the annunciator of Muḥammad."[31] For Heller this accounts for the frequency of the material on Moses and the particular features in Muhammad's recitation of the story on any specific occasion. Julian Obermann wrote that the differences in the diverse Moses narratives could be explained by the particular materials which Muhammad heard from the Jews at different parts of his career.[32]

Some recent strong and even insistent approaches to the Qur'ān are more careful about uncritical acceptance of the Muslim traditional narratives of Islamic origins but still retain the basic framework of the Muslim traditional story. Angelica Neuwirth explains the repetition of prophetic stories and the differences between them as reflecting a process whereby initial recitation, "communication," or "proclamation" of a story was followed by interaction between "the Prophet" and his audience about the

---

29. Laid out early in the western critical study of the Qur'ān by Nöldeke, *Geschichte des Qorâns*, 52–174.
30. Bell, *Introduction to the Qur'ān*, 127–28.
31. Heller, "Mūsā," 638.
32. Obermann, "Koran and Agada," 28.

story, including liturgical use of the story, resulting in later updates or rewrites of the story to fit into new social contexts. Neuwirth attempts to support this theory by appeal to the variant versions of a number of prophetic figures and episodes, none more so than the Qur'ānic Moses and especially the Moses episode versions that have been compared above. For example, in her article "Erzählen als kanonischer Prozeß" Neuwirth examines seven Moses passages according to her scheme of "Meccan" and "Medinan" periods and for each discusses the "life situation (*Sitz im Leben*) and progress in the canonical process."[33]

Joseph Witztum interacts with the "diachronic" views of Neuwirth, as well as those of Nicolai Sinai,[34] questions their dating of sūras, and suggests that clues to the relative dating of parallel accounts may be found at the level of philology.[35] He offers a very close study of the language of the calf story versions in Suras 7 and 20 described above,[36] and argues that priority of the two accounts may be established through a detail like the word "haste" (*'ajal*)—interestingly because he finds one of the two versions to be more similar to the Syriac translation of Exod 32:8 (cf. Syriac Deut 9:12, 16).[37]

Wansbrough chose to investigate the Qur'ān outside of the constraints of both Muslim tradition and chronology. Literary analysis of Muslim scripture "may properly disregard such criteria," Wansbrough explained in *Quranic Studies*. He found repetition to be a central characteristic of the text and suggested that what he termed "variant traditions" held clues for how the Qur'ān may have come together.[38] Muslim commentary on the Qur'ān explained, or "evaded," unmistakable repetition in the text by claiming a chronology of revelation. Wansbrough suggested rather that analysis of variant versions indicates "the existence of independent, possibly regional, traditions incorporated more or less intact into the canonical compilation, itself the product of expansion and strife

---

33. Neuwirth, "Erzählen als kanonischer Prozeß," 328–42.
34. From Sinai's *Fortschreibung und Auslegung* and "Qur'an as Process."
35. Witztum, "Variant Traditions," 10–12.
36. Witztum, "Variant Traditions," 28–43.
37. Witztum, "Variant Traditions," 41–43.
38. Wansbrough, *Quranic Studies*, 20–52.

within the Muslim community."[39] Then he compared three versions of the story of Shu'ayb to test his hypothesis.[40]

Wansbrough wrote that especially in the Qur'ān's stories about prophetic figures, "ellipses and repetition are such as to suggest not the carefully executed project of one or of many men, but rather the product of an organic development from originally independent traditions during a long period of transmission."[41] Interestingly, Wansbrough's theory runs opposite to the argument of al-Zarkashī: instead of attributing narrative repetition to diffusion of recitations to various regions of the Arabian Peninsula, Wansbrough pictured a gathering together of variant traditions from the different communities within which they originated.[42]

A recent article by Devin Stewart picks up on Wansbrough's hypothesis of variant traditions to argue for an alternate conclusion from the Qur'ānic evidence.[43] Stewart suggested, rather, that the versions of the Shu'ayb story serve as examples in suras "that adopt the form of a sermon."[44] The versions differ because the verbal/literary contexts in which they appear differ, asserts Stewart, arguing that the versions in Suras 7, 11, and 26 have been adapted to fit in with the pattern of the main parenetic intent in each sura.[45] Stewart includes a helpful and insightful analysis of methodology borrowed from biblical studies, highlighting the oral formulaic approach, oral performance theory, and redaction criticism.[46] Interestingly, Stewart recommends that scholars consider the editing of Qur'ānic suras in a manner similar to how New Testament scholars have examined the Gospel accounts, and he makes the striking suggestion that

---

39. Wansbrough, *Quranic Studies*, 21.

40. Wansbrough, *Quranic Studies*, 21–25.

41. Wansbrough, *Quranic Studies*, 47.

42. Wansbrough, *Quranic Studies*, 50.

43. Stewart, "Wansbrough," 17–51.

44. Stewart, "Wansbrough," 29.

45. Stewart, "Wansbrough," 34–40.

46. Stewart, "Wansbrough," 42–46. Related to the oral-formulaic approach, Stewart neglects to mention Bannister, *Oral-Formulaic Study*. Bannister examines the seven Qur'ānic versions of the Iblis and Adam story and proposes that the different versions be described as oral "performance variants" (29, 95, 259, 271–81). Since the publication of Stewart's article, see also Mark Durie's discussion of both philological and oral-formulaic approaches in *Qur'ān and Its Biblical Reflexes*, 218–23.

The presence of several similar versions of accounts in the synoptic Gospels . . . may be seen to exist in the Qur'ān, which has several versions of particular narratives, including many of the biblical narratives in the text. . . . [T]he ways in which the Qur'ān and the New Testament were produced may have been quite similar so that it is at least worthwhile comparing the corresponding historical processes of collection, compilation, redaction, and canonization.[47]

Variant Versions and Interfaith Conversation

Stewart's suggestion that repetition of narratives in the Qur'ān—and the differences among variant versions—be examined by methods similar to those used in the academic study of the New Testament leads this essay back to an active interfaith circumstance indicated in the introduction. Ever since the writings of Ibn Ḥazm (d. 1064), Muslim polemicists have attacked the integrity and reliability of the Gospel accounts on the basis of both their multiplicity and the differences among them.[48] The *Iẓhār al-ḥaqq* of Raḥmat Allāh Kayrānwī (1818–91) continues to circulate this attack widely throughout South Asia and many other parts of the world to this day.[49]

It seems that relatively few academic scholars have attempted to pick up on the similarities between repetition and difference among the Gospel accounts on the one hand, and the variant versions of prophetic stories in the Qur'ān on the other.[50] One scholar who could not ignore this theme while living in early twentieth-century Cairo, E. E. Elder, wondered whether Muslims would consider differences among the Gospel accounts less polemically if they were better informed about variance among Qur'ānic narratives. Elder suggested that Qur'ānic differences are "very much like many of those made so much of by Moslem critics of the Bible."[51]

---

47. Stewart, *Wansbrough*, 44.

48. Ibn Ḥazm, *al-Fiṣal fī l-milal*, 2:2–81, esp. 10–38. Monferrer Sala, "Kitāb al-fiṣal fī l-milal."

49. Kayrānwī, *Iẓhār al-ḥaqq*, 1:147–200. Nickel, *Gentle Answer*, 159–67.

50. Very recently, however, Guillaume Dye provides an example of how this might be done. "Le Coran et le Problème Synoptique," 235–40, 258–59.

51. Elder, "Parallel Passages," 359.

Witztum notes and also quotes from Elder's article, then writes that his own essay "steers away from theology."[52] One wonders, however, whether an academic decision to explain the Qur'ān apart from Islamic claims for its provenance and contents can ever not be theological in the minds of Muslims. Witztum and others write freely, for example, about multiple human composers for the various parts of the Qur'ān, a serious departure from Muslim faith in Allah revealing through Gabriel to Muhammad. They also seem to suggest that among their academic colleagues are some who skew the evidence on variant versions in the Qur'ān in favor of Islamic confessional views.[53] In such a climate, scholars need not hesitate to follow the literary evidence through into the living ways in which Christians and Muslims frequently converse.

Repetition is a major feature of the literary character of the Qur'ān. This feature has been demonstrated in this essay through the observation of the outlines of thirteen different Moses narratives in general, and through comparison of the variant versions of three Moses episodes in particular. The same could be done for variant versions of the Qur'ānic stories of Adam, Noah, Abraham, Lot, and other figures. The differences among the variant versions of prophetic episodes in the Qur'ān show a wide range of degrees of difference, from the apparently incidental or superficial to the strikingly fundamental. No system of categorizing these types of difference seems yet to be available in the secondary literature for the purpose of analysis. If so, this could be a useful avenue for scholarly initiative.

Once variance among accounts is acknowledged on both sides, however, an interesting discussion could proceed into the analysis and evaluation of differences. For example, if differences among Gospel accounts are judged to signify a lack of integrity and reliability, what is the implication for differences among the prophetic narratives of the Qur'ān? Alternately, if Muslims declare repetition and variation of Qur'ānic stories like the story of Moses to be signs of divine eloquence and inimitability, for what reason should the same be denied to variation among the Gospel accounts?

Such considerations seem to point past the literary form and structure of religious scriptures to the message between their covers. In this discussion of the contents of scriptures, Elder proposed that "The basis for rejecting the authority or authenticity of a book is not to be the

---

52. Witztum, "Variant Traditions," 3.

53. Witztum, "Variant Traditions," 12. See especially Dye, "Le Coran et le problème synoptique," 246–52.

finding of variant readings or differences in parallel passages. The truth of a book claiming to be a revelation rests not in its outward form, but in its intrinsic values and effect."[54] In other words, only by reading the scriptures themselves—including variant versions of the same stories—with an open heart and mind, can the reader gauge their qualifications for integrity and reliability.

Bibliography

Al-Suyūṭī, Jalāl al-Dīn ʿAbd al-Raḥmān ibn Abī Bakr. *al-Itqān fī ʿulūm al-qurʾān*. Riyad: Maktaba al-maʿārif, 1992.

Amir-Moezzi, Mohammad Ali, and Guillaume Dye. *Le Coran des historiens*. Paris: Les éditions du Cerf, 2019.

Bannister, Andrew G. *An Oral-Formulaic Study of the Qurʾān*. Lanham, MD: Lexington, 2014.

Bell, Richard. *Introduction to the Qurʾān*. Edinburgh: Edinburgh University Press, 1953.

Clark, Malcolm. "Biblical and Early Islamic Moses." In *A Biblical Itinerary in Search of Method, Form, and Content: Essays in Honor of George W. Coats*, edited by Eugene E. Carpenter, 20–38. Sheffield: Sheffield Academic, 1997.

Durie, Mark. *The Qurʾān and Its Biblical Reflexes: Investigations in the Genesis of a Religion*. Lanham, MD: Lexington, 2018.

Dye, Guillaume. "Le Coran et le Problème Synoptique: Quelques Remarques Préliminaires." In *Die Entstehung einer Weltreligion VI: Vom umayidischen Christentum zum abbadischen Islam*, edited by Marcus Groß and Robert M. Kerr, 234–61. Berlin: Hans Schiler & Tim Mücke, 2021.

———. "Le Corpus Coranique: Contexte et Composition." In *Le Coran des historiens*, edited by Mohammad Ali Amir-Moezzi and Guilaume Dye, 1:733–846. Paris: Éditions du Cerf, 2019.

Elder, E. E. "Parallel Passages in the Koran (The Story of Moses)." *The Muslim World* 15 (1925) 254–59.

Heller, Bernard. "Mūsā." In *The Encyclopaedia of Islam: New edition*, edited by C. E. Bosworth, 7:638–39. Leiden: Brill, 1993.

Ibn Ḥazm, Abū Muḥammad ʿAlī ibn Aḥmad ibn Saʿīd. *al-Fiṣal fī l-milal wa-l-ahwāʾ wa-l-niḥal*. 5 vols. in 2 vols. Cairo: Būlāq, 1899–1903.

Johns, A. H. "Let My People Go! Sayyid Quṭb and the vocation of Moses." *Islam and Christian Muslim Relations* 1.2 (1990) 143–70.

———. "Moses in the Qurʾān." In *Charles Strong Lectures, 1972–1984*, edited by Robert B. Crotty, 123–38. Leiden: Brill, 1987.

Kayrānwī, Raḥmat Allāh ibn Khalīl al-Raḥmān al-ʿUthmānī. *Iẓhār al-ḥaqq*. Beirut: al-Maktabat al-ʿIḍariyya, 1998.

Monferrer Sala, Juan Pedro. "Kitāb al-fiṣal fī l-milal wa-l-ahwāʾ wa-l-niḥal." In *Christian-Muslim Relations 600–1500*, edited by David Thomas, n.p. https://referenceworks.brillonline.com/browse/christian-muslim-relations-i.

54. Elder, "Parallel Passages," 359.

Moubarac, Youakim. "Moïse dans le Coran." In *Moïse: L'homme de l'alliance*, edited by H. Cazelles et al., 373–91. Paris: Desclée & Cie., 1955.
Neuwirth, Angelika. "Erzählen als kanonischer Prozeß: Die Mose-Erzählung im Wandel der koranischen Geschichte." In *Islamstudien ohne Ende. Festschrift für Werner Ende zu seinem 65. Geburtstag*, edited by Rainer Brunner et al., 323–44. Würzburg: Ergon Verlag, 2002.
Nickel, Gordon. *The Gentle Answer to the Muslim Accusation of Biblical Falsification*. Calgary: Bruton Gate, 2015.
———. *The Quran with Christian Commentary*. Grand Rapids: Zondervan Academic, 2020.
Nöldeke, Theodore. *Geschichte des Qorans*. Edited by Fredrich Schwally. Leipzig: T. Weicher, 1909.
———. *Geschichte des Qorâns*. Göttingen: Verlag der Dieterichschen Buchhandlung, 1860.
Obermann, Julian. "Koran and Agada: The Events at Mount Sinai." *American Journal of Semitic Languages and Literatures* 58 (1941) 23–48.
Pohlmann, Karl-Friedrich. *Die Entstehung des Korans: Neue Erkenntnisse aus Sicht der historisch-kritischen Bibelwissenschaft*. Darmstadt: Wissenschaftliche Buchgesellschaft, 2015.
Reynolds, Gabriel Said. *The Qurʾān and Its Biblical Subtext*. London: Routledge, 2010.
———. *The Qurʾān and the Text and Commentary*. New Haven, CT: Yale University Press, 2018.
Sayed, Faraan Alamgir. "Repetition in Qurʾānic *Qaṣaṣ*: With Reference to Thematic and Literary Coherence in the Story of Moses." *Journal of Islamic and Muslim Studies* 2 (2017) 53–75.
Sinai, Nicolai. *Fortscheibung und Auslegung: Studien zur frühen Koraninterpretation*. Wiesbaden: Otto Harrassowitz, 2009.
———. "The Qurʾān as Process." In *The Qurʾan in Context: Historical and Literary Investigations into the Qurʾānic Milieu*, edited by Angelika Neuwirth et al., 407–39. Leiden: Brill, 2010.
———. "Two Types of Inner-Qurʾānic Interpretation." In *Exegetical Crossroads: Understanding Scripture in Judaism, Christianity and Islam in the Pre-Modern Orient*, edited by Georges Tamer et al., 253–88. Berlin: De Gruyter, 2019.
Speight, R. Marston. "A Look at Variant Readings in the *ḥadīth*." *Der Islam* 77 (2000), 169–79.
Stewart, Devin J. "Wansbrough, Bultmann, and the Theory of Variant Traditions in the Qurʾān." In *Qurʾānic Studies Today*, edited by Angelika Neuwirth and Michael A. Sells, 17–51. London: Routledge, 2016.
Waldman, Marilyn R. "New Approaches to 'Biblical' Materials in the Qurʾān." In *Studies in Islamic and Judaic Traditions*, edited by William M. Brinner and Stephen D. Ricks, 47–64. Atlanta: Scholars, 1986.
Wansbrough, John. *Quranic Studies: Sources and Methods of Scriptural Interpretation*. Oxford: Oxford University Press, 1977.
Witztum, Joseph. "Variant Traditions, Relative Chronology, and the Study of Intra-Qurʾānic Parallels." In *Islamic Cultures, Islamic Contexts. Essays in Honor of Professor Patricia Crone*, edited by Behnam Sadeghi et al., 1–50. Leiden: Brill, 2015.

7

Dawud

Mark Durie

The Seven Oft-Repeated and Their Punishment Stories

OF THE NUMEROUS FIGURES referred to as *rasūl*, "messenger," or *nabī*, "prophet"[1] in the Qur'ān, the most prominent appear in stories of divine punishment.[2] Seven prophetic figures in particular are mentioned frequently in connection with such stories, where they are paired with the peoples to whom they were sent as "warners." These seven are Nuh and his people; Musa and the Egyptians; Lut and his people; Hud and the people of 'Ad; Salih and the people of Thamud; Shu'ayb and the people of Madyan; and Ibrahim and his people. Four of these seven are biblical figures. These are presumably the "seven oft-repeated" of Q15:87. A similar list in Q9:70 mentions five of these peoples, and "overthrown towns" (perhaps including "Lut's people" or Sodom and Gomorrah) to whom messengers were sent.

These punishment stories follow a standard outline in which Allah sends a messenger to a particular people (or town). The messenger calls

---

1. In the Qur'ān, "prophet" is a sub-category of "messenger." See Durie, *Qur'ān and Its Biblical Reflexes*, 132–33.

2. Tottoli, *Biblical Prophets in the Qur'ān*, 4–7.

the people to repent, but his warnings are not heeded. After rejecting the messenger, the people or town suffer violent punishment from Allah, delivered in a variety of ways—"whenever we have sent a prophet to a town, we have seized its people with violence and hardship" (Q7:94)—and the messenger is rescued.

Dawud—A Messenger Without a Punishment Story

In addition to messengers who figure in punishment stories, there are people identified by the Qur'ān as messengers or prophets, but no punishment stories is provided. In a mid-Medinan surah, which occurs later than the messenger stories, the Qur'ān states, "We have already told you the story of some messengers, but of some we have not" (Q4:164). One such figure is Dawud (David),[3] identified as a *nabī*, "prophet," three times, in Q4:163, Q6:89, and Q17:55. Altogether his name is mentioned sixteen times in nine passages, six of which are found in Meccan surahs. Most of these passages occur in what might be called litanies of past messengers, in which a series of messengers' names are invoked, either in a concentrated list, or in collections of messenger stories.

Surahs containing the five passages which mention Dawud appear in clusters, one of which is in the middle "Meccan" period of Nöldeke's classification.[4] There is also a later "Meccan" reference, and the remaining are early "Medinan."[5] The longest passage, Q38:17–30, is also the earliest in time. It includes a story of two people who were disputing about a ewe and appealed to Dawud for judgement. Subsequent references to Dawud are brief and allusive, no more than one or two verses each. The following figure depicts the distribution of the Dawud passages along a Qur'ānic timeline, in a chronological plot of surahs using a two-dimensional stylistic chronology.[6] The timeline stretches from the lower left (early Meccan)

---

3. The correct spelling of Dawud (also Da'ud) is a complex issue, due to variant spellings in the manuscripts. In the standard text the *rasm* spelling is d-alif-w-d, but see Puin, *Vowel Letters and Ortho-Epic Writing in the Qur'ān*, 158 for discussion of other early manuscript variants which have d-w-alif-d, as well as discussion by Horovitz, *Koranische Untersuchungen*, 109–11.

4. Nöldeke and Schwally, *Über den Ursprung des Qorans*, 117–43.

5. Meccan and Medinan are placed in quotes because of concerns about the validity of the conventional Qur'ān origin story: see Durie, *Qur'ān and Its Biblical Reflexes*, 11–20. Further references to the Meccan/Medinan contrast are to be read as if in quotes.

6. See Durie, *Qur'ān and Its Biblical Reflexes*, 77–83.

to the upper right (late Medinan). The gap in the middle reflects a hiatus between Meccan and Medinan surahs.

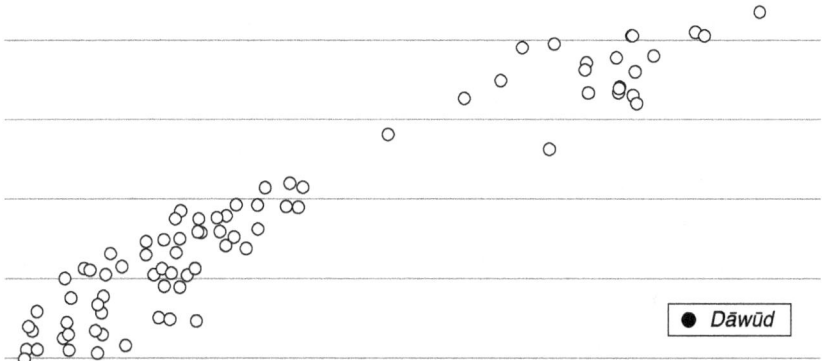

Figure 7.1. Surahs Which Mention Dawud

Since the Dawud passages involved are not long, I have reproduced them in full below in chronological order.[7] The English version here is based on Droge's translation, with some modifications:[8]

Middle Meccan

Q38:17–30

17 Bear with what they say, and remember Our servant Dawud, a man of strength. Surely he turned regularly [in repentance].

18 Surely We subjected the mountains [along] with him to glorify [Us] in the evening and at sunrise,

19 and the birds, gathered together, all regularly turning to Him [in praise].

20 We strengthened his kingdom, and gave him wisdom and a decisive word.

---

7. The chronological order followed is that of Durie, "A stylistic, non-biographical chronological ordering of the surahs of the Qurʾān." This chronology is based on stylistics.

8. The spellings of proper names have been Islamized, and there are a few other minor changes.

21 Has the story of the dispute come to you? When they climbed over the wall of the place of prayer,

22 when they entered upon Dawud, and he was terrified of them, but they said: "Do not fear! [We are] two disputants: one of us has acted oppressively toward the other. So judge between us in truth, and do not be unjust, and guide us to the right path."

23 Surely this is my brother. He has ninety-nine ewes, and I have [only] one ewe. He said "Give her into my charge," and he overcame me in the argument.

24 He said, "Certainly he has done you evil in asking for your ewe [in addition] to his ewes. Surely many [business] partners indeed act oppressively toward one another, except those who believe and do righteous deeds—but few they are." And Dawud guessed that We had tested him, so he asked his Lord for forgiveness, and fell down, bowing, and turned [in repentance].

25 So We forgave him. Surely he has intimacy indeed with Us and a good [place of] return.

26 Dawud! Surely We have made you a ruler [*khalifah*] on the earth, so judge among the people in truth, and do not follow [vain] desire, or it will lead you astray from the way of Allah. Surely those who go astray from the way of Allah—for them [there is] a harsh punishment, because they have forgotten the day of reckoning."

27 We did not create the sky and the earth, and whatever is between them, without purpose. That is the conjecture of those who disbelieve. So woe to those who disbelieve on account of the Fire!

28 Or shall We treat those who believe and do righteous deeds the same as the ones who foment corruption on the earth? Or shall We treat the ones who guard [themselves] the same as the depraved?

29 A blessed Book—We have sent it down to you, so that those with understanding may contemplate its verses [or signs] and take heed.

30 To Dawud We granted Sulayman—an excellent servant he was! Surely he turned regularly [in repentance].

27:15–16

15 Certainly We gave Dawud and Sulayman knowledge, and they said, "Praise [be] to Allah, who has favored us over many of His believing servants!"

16 Sulayman inherited [it] from Dawud, and said, "People! We have been taught the speech of birds, and we have been given [some] of everything. Surely this—it indeed is clear favor."

21:78–80

78 And Dawud and Sulayman—when they rendered judgment concerning the field, when the people's sheep had grazed in it—We were witnesses to their judgment.

79 We caused Sulayman to understand it, and to each We gave judgment and knowledge. [Along] with Dawud We subjected the mountains and the birds to glorify [Us]—We were the doers [of it].

80 We taught him the making of clothing[9] to protect you from your violence. Are you thankful?

17:55 Your Lord knows whatever is in the heavens and the earth. Certainly We have favored some of the prophets over others, and We gave Dawud [the] Psalms.

34:10–13

10 Certainly We gave Dawud favor from Us: "You mountains! Return [praises] with him, and you birds [too]! And we made iron malleable for him:

11 "Make full [coats of armor], and measure [well] in the sewing [of them]." And: "do righteousness, [for] surely I see what you do.

12 And to Sulayman [We subjected] the wind, its morning was a month's [journey], and its evening was a month's [journey], and We made a spring of molten brass to flow for him. And among the jinn, [there were] those who worked for him by the permission of his Lord. Whoever of them turns aside from our command—We shall make him taste the punishment of the Blaze.

13 They made for him whatever he pleased: places of prayer, and statues, and basins like cisterns, and fixed cooking pots. "House of Dawud! Work in thankfulness, [for] few of My servants are thankful!"

9. This "clothing" which protects from violence is most likely the chain mail of Q34:11.

Late Meccan

6:84–87

84 And We granted him Ishaq and Ya'qub—each one We guided, and Nuh We guided before [them]—and of his descendants [were] Dawud, and Sulayman, and Ayyub, and Yusuf, and Musa, and Harun—in this way We repay the doers of good . . .

87 . . . We chose them and guided them to a straight path.

Early Medinan

2:251 And they routed them by the permission of Allah, and Dawud killed Jalut, and Allah gave him the kingdom and the wisdom, and taught him about whatever He pleased. If Allah had not repelled some of the people by means of others, the earth would indeed have been corrupted. But Allah is full of favor to the worlds.

5:78 Those of the Sons of Israel who disbelieved were cursed by the tongue of Dawud and 'Isa, son of Maryam—that was because they disobeyed and were transgressing.

4:163 Surely we have inspired you as We inspired Noah and the prophets after him, and as We inspired Ibrahim, and Isma'il, and Ishaq, and Ya'qub, and the tribes, and 'Isa, and Ayyub and Yunus, and Harun, and Sulayman, and We gave Dawud the Psalms . . .

It is striking that Dawud is not associated in the Qur'ān with a punishment story and there is no report of him being sent to a specific people: we will discuss the question of Dawud's people further below. What Dawud is remembered for is being a wise king or *khalif* (Q38:20, 26),[10] as well as a warrior, a "man of strength" (Q38:17) who slew Jalut (Goliath; 2:251).[11] There is also the short story told about Dawud in Q38:21–24. This account of two disputants appears to be a reflex[12] of the parable told

---

10. The Shi'a came to consider Dawud as one in a line of caliphs, which included Adam, Harun and 'Ali: see Kister, "Legends in Tafsir and Hadith Literature," 96.

11. The strength of David is a theme of rabbinical literature: see Ta-Shma, "David: in the Aggadah," 452.

12. The word "reflex" is used to identify a correspondence which implies a connection, without specifying the nature of the connection.

by the Nathan the prophet (2 Sam 12:1–13) after David committed adultery with Bathsheba. There also appears to be some influence from Matt 18:12, since the "large number of sheep and cattle" of 2 Sam 12:2 have become ninety-nine ewes in the Qurʾān. The role of the prophet Nathan has been lost in the transmission.

This tale portrays Dawud as a model of piety,[13] who turned to Allah (Q38:17, 25) seeking forgiveness (Q38:24–25).[14] However, and notwithstanding the warning to Dawud in Q38:26 not to follow his own desires, the Qurʾān's account presents his plea for forgiveness in Q38:24 as a *non sequitur*, without the context of his adultery with Bathsheba. Indeed the biblical context of 2 Sam 11–12 has been rejected by Muslim scholars because it conflicts with the Qurʾānic doctrine of the moral infallibility (*ʿismah*)[15] of messengers as righteous, God-fearing, and rightly-guided (Q4:69; Q6:84, 87; Q21:26).

The closing application of this story, which is given in Q38:28, reminds hearers that those who turn to Allah in repentance are superior and will enjoy a better outcome (Q38:49–50) than those who turn off the straight path (cf. Q38:14–15). The example of Dawud, and particularly the favor shown to him, is invoked as one of the *ʾayat*, "signs" (or "verses") (Q38:29) brought by the Qurʾānic Messenger.[16]

---

13. A *hadith* found in the collections of Bukhari and Muslim reports Dawud's devotion in prayer and fasting: the theme is further developed in the commentaries: see Wheeler, *Prophets in the Qurʾān*, 260–61.

14. El-Badawi, *Qurʾān and the Aramaic Gospel*, 117, has pointed out that in Syriac Christianity David was "an archetype of prophecy as well as of repentance."

15. For example, Ibn Kathir (born ca. 1300, d. 1373) writes, "In discussing this passage, the scholars of *Tafsir* mention a story which is mostly based upon *Israʾiliyat* narrations. Nothing has been reported about this from the Infallible Prophet that we could accept as true. But Ibn Abi Hatim narrated a *Hadith* whose chain of narration cannot be regarded as *Sahih* [reliable] because it is reported by Yazid Ar-Raqashi from Anas, may Allah be pleased with him. Although Yazid was one of the righteous, his *Hadiths* are regarded as weak by the Imams. So, it is better to speak briefly of this story and refer knowledge of it to Allah, may He be exalted. For the Qurʾān is true and what it contains is also true." (*Tafsir Ibn Kathir*, commentary on 8:321.) Ibn Kathir goes on to explain that the reference to "repentance" relates to Dawud's ritual piety in prostrating himself in prayer (Q38:24).

16. Here I refer to the Qurʾānic messenger simply as "the Messenger," which is in keeping with the Qurʾān's own preferred designation for this figure, conventionally identified as Muhammad.

Favors to the Righteous

Dawud is linked in the Qur'ān with his son Sulayman (Q38:30). The two share attributes which show Allah's favor (*faḍl*: Q34:10), including knowing the language of birds (Q27:16), wisdom, and knowledge for judgement (Q38:20, 26; 27:15; 21:78-79; 2:251). There are repeated references to Dawud singing Allah's praises together with mountains and birds (Q38:18-19; 21:79; 34:10; cf. Ps 148:9-10). He, together with Sulayman, also had a supernatural ability make coats of mail out of iron: "We made iron malleable for him" (Q34:11-13; and 21:80).[17] Dawud is also described as receiving the *zabur* (Q17:55; 4:163), identified as a written text (Q21:105), which is taken to refer to the Psalms. These references illustrate the Qur'ānic principle that Allah favors some believers and prophets over others (Q27:15; 17:55; cf. 2:253, 2:87; 5:110), by giving them particular abilities.

Validating the Qur'ānic Messenger

What is the function of these and other references to Dawud? In the Qur'ān references to past messengers serve to reinforce and validate the calling and experiences of the Qur'ānic Messenger. Examples are the so-called *punishment stories* of the Meccan period, which reinforce the Messenger's warnings of impending doom, and may be accompanied by stories of divine rescue, such as the account of Joseph in Q12. The references to Dawud, surveyed above and to Allah's favors to past messengers, both serve to validate the Messenger, by illustrating the important apologetic point that Allah does not give the same favors to all messengers.

In addition to exemplifying the general principle that Allah will show favor to those who turn to him, the listing of Dawud's unique favors in the mid to late Meccan surahs can be understood as a response to accusations being made against the Messenger around the same time. The principal accusation was that he was just an ordinary human being (Q11:27; 14:10; 23:33-34, 38; 25:20; 26:186; cf. 21:7-8) who did not show

---

17. References to Dawud (and also Sulayman) as the inventor of chain mail are already found in pre-Islamic sources (see Horovitz, *Koranische Untersuchungen*, 109), so here the Qur'ān is drawing on an oral tradition current among Arabs of the time. The reference to Dawud working with iron is an anachronism, since the Bible portrays Dawud as living in a time of transition between the bronze and iron ages: his enemies the Philistines controlled working with iron (1 Sam 13:19).

the special abilities reported of past messengers. The Messenger was being taunted to provide proof of his office and authority by performing signs like those brought by former messengers (Q6:124; cf. 20:133; 6:37; 13:7). The observation in Q2:253 that messengers have received *varied* dispensations from Allah serves as a validation of an immediately preceding assertion in Q2:252 that the Messenger is truly "one of the messengers." Since past messengers did not bring the same signs, and the Qur'ān repeatedly speaks of "varying the signs" (*nusarrifu l-'ayati*, "we cause the signs to be varied"; cf. Q6:46, 65; 7:174; 16:3–18; 17:41, 89; 18:54; 46:27) the audience is meant to understand that it would be a mistake to expect that the Qur'ānic Messenger would simply repeat the signs of others.

The intended conclusion is that no one may reject the Messenger for lack of repeating particular signs granted to past messengers. In this vein, the Qur'ān repeatedly emphasizes that believers should make "no distinction" between messengers (Q2:136, 285; 3:84; 4:150, 152), irrespective of variability in the signs associated with them. By this reasoning, the listing of distinctive favors shown to Dawud serve to validate the lack of signs attributed to the Messenger.

A major shift can be discerned in the Medinan surahs. Whereas in the Meccan surahs references to Dawud had reflected a concern with validating the Qur'ānic Messenger's lack of special signs, in the Medinan surahs there is a concern to justify enmity and the use of violence to further Allah's cause. References to Dawud no longer exemplify Allah's favor to the God-fearing; instead Q2:251 refers to Dawud as the killer of Jalut (Goliath),[18] which is but one brick in the wall of an extended defense throughout the Medinan surahs of fighting for Allah (cf. Q2:244 "so fight in the path of Allah"). A different verse refers to Dawud and 'Isa cursing the "Sons of Israel" (Q5:78), as part of a longer passage which condemns the Jews and urges believers not to take disbelievers as allies (Q5:80).[19] Both Q2:251 and Q5:78 align with and support the changed role of the Qur'ānic Messenger after the transition from Meccan to Medinan surahs.[20] In the Meccan surahs messengers functions as warners,

---

18. See Durie, *Qur'ān and Its Biblical Reflexes*, 231–39 on fighting prophets in the Qur'ān.

19. Exegetes connect this cursing with the transformation of Jews into apes of Q5:78. This juxtaposition of Dawud and 'Isa appears to be a trace of Jesus' David lineage in the gospel traditions (El-Badawi, *Qur'ān and the Aramaic Gospel*, 117).

20. See discussion of changes in the role of messengers in Durie, *Qur'ān and Its Biblical Reflexes*, 64–70.

announcing to people that Allah will punish them, en masse, if they do not repent. Qur'āni apologetic statements in this period respond to attempts to invalidate the Messenger's calling as a doomsday prophet, warning of a future punishment. One of these attempts is a demand that the Messenger perform signs like those of past messengers. The implication was that he could not be bringing a genuine message from Allah if he could not prove his calling through performing signs.

In response to this demand, the example of Dawud is cited to show that Allah varies the signs brought by messengers. Later, in the Medinan period, the focus of apologetics shifts away from validating the Messenger as a warner, to justifying enmity and violence towards disbelievers.

Conclusion

To which people was Dawud sent? Although it is not made explicit, this can only have been the people of Israel. There are three pieces of evidence for this: 1) the title *nabī*, "prophet," used of Dawud, only appears in the Qur'ān in the context of Israel;[21] 2) Dawud is included in a litany of biblical messengers (Q6:84); and in a list of messengers in a long passage addressed to Jewish "People of the Book" (Q4:163);[22] and 3) there is a reference to Dawud cursing the children of Israel along with 'Isa (Q5:78), who is repeatedly identified in the Qur'ān as also having been sent to the Jews (Q3:49; 5:72, 110; 61:6, 14). The reported enmity between Dawud and his people, the children of Israel, serves to justify the Qur'ānic Messenger's antipathy towards disbelievers among his own people and to validate his warnings to his followers not to make friends among the unbelievers.

Compared to some other biblical figures, Dawud receives comparatively little attention in the Qur'ān. There is, for example, no vestige of the messianic theology of the crucially, he is not afforded the biblical title of messiah' (*al-masih*), which in the Qur'ān is reserved solely for 'Isa. Instead the figure of Dawud is pressed into service, first in the Meccan surahs as an example of a righteous prophet who receives Allah's (miraculous) favors, in the form of special abilities which include wisdom and knowledge, understanding the language of birds, and a supernatural ability to make coats of

---

21. See Durie, *Qur'ān and Its Biblical Reflexes*, 132–33 for a discussion of the difference between 'messenger' and 'prophet' in the Qur'ān.

22. Cf. the context provided by Q4:153–73, and the references to "Jews" in Q4:160.

mail from iron. Later, in the Medinan surahs, he is presented as a fighting, cursing prophet whose enmity is directed against his own people.

This repurposing of the biblical David draws on oral narratives and traditions about Dawud current when the Qur'ān was being produced (cf. Q38:21 "Has the story of the dispute come to you?"). In coopting these materials to serve its own agendas, the Qur'ān inherits little if anything of the biblical theology associated with David.

Bibliography

Droge, A. J. *The Qur'ān: A New Annotated Translation*. Corrected ed. Sheffield: Equinox, 2014.

Durie, Mark. *The Qur'ān and Its Biblical Reflexes: Investigations into the Genesis of a Religion*. Lanham, MD: Lexington, 2018.

———. "A Stylistic, Non-Biographical Chronological Ordering of the Surahs of the Qur'ān." https://www.academia.edu/38068699/A_Stylistic_non_Biographical_Chronological_Ordering_of_the_Surahs_of_the_Qur'ān/.

El-Badawi, Emran Iqbal. *The Qur'ān and the Aramaic Gospel Traditions*. Oxford: Routledge, 2014.

Horovitz, Josef. *Koranische UntersuchunGen*. Berlin: Walter de Gruyter, 1926.

Ibn Kathir. *Tafsir Ibn Kathir (Abridged)*. Riyadh: Darussalam, 2003.

Kister, M. J. "Legends in *tafsir and hadith* Literature: The Creation of Adam and Related Stories." In *Approaches to the History of the Interpretation of the Qur'ān*, edited by Andrew Rippin, 82–114. Oxford: Oxford University Press, 1988.

Nöldeke, Theodor, and Friedrich Schwally. *Über den Ursprung des Qorans*. 2nd ed. Geschichte des Qorans 1. Leipzig: Dieterich'sche Verlagsbuchhandlung, 1909.

Puin, Gerd-R. "Vowel Letters and Ortho-Epic Writing in the Qur'ān." In *New Perspectives on the Qur'ān: The Qur'ān in its Historical Context 2*, edited by Gabriel Said Reynolds, 147–90. Oxford: Routledge, 2011.

Ta-Shma, Israel Moses. "David: in the Aggadah." In *Encyclopaedia Judaica*, edited by Fred Skolnik and Michael Berenbaum, 5:451–53. Detroit, MI: Macmillan Reference USA, 2007.

Tottoli, Roberto. *Biblical Prophets in the Qur'ān and Muslim Literature*. Translated by Michael Robertson. London: Routledge, 2002.

Wheeler, Brannon M. *Prophets in the Qur'ān: An Introduction to the Qur'ān and Muslim Exegesis*. London: Continuum, 2002.

8

The Prophet Ezekiel

Constancy and Patience

David W. Shenk

THIS ESSAY IS ABOUT Ezekiel. Yet there are no assurances that there is anything authoritative written about Ezekiel, either in the Qur'ān or in the Traditions. We need to turn to biblical sources for documented descriptions of Ezekiel's niche in Middle East history. Or we can peruse folklore.[1] However, I will lean heavily upon the biblical accounts which I believe are trustworthy.

Nevertheless, all sources are united in their proclamation that Ezekiel lived and prophesied in exceedingly troubled times. There is much within our modern tumultuous times that is akin to the tragedies of Ezekiel's era in biblical times. We have much to learn from the experiences of Ezekiel and his times and his quest for God. The most significant convergence is the reality of nations being overwhelmed with refugees. The United Nations proclaims that at this time seventy million people have become migrants. This massive movement of people is unprecedented. The fabric of global cooperation is tearing international networks into shreds.[2] Ezekiel's experience in the sixth century BC is akin to our experience at present.

1. Al-Tha'labi and Qur'ān (2:243).
2. Rev 6.

Tumultuous Times

In 599 BC the biblical prophet Ezekiel had been thrust from his homeland in Israel. Ruthless nations had occupied the Middle East. Refugees were everywhere. The plague was destroying entire villages. Injustice prevailed. Ezekiel was himself a refugee living in a resettlement area in Babylonia. The songs of the people were mixed with tears along the rivers of Babylon

I am writing this essay on Easter weekend, 2019, with Sri Lanka in mourning as suicide bombers have killed a couple hundred Christian worshippers on a Sunday morning. Others in different locations were also killed. As the biblical Ezekiel recalled the pilgrimage of Israel and the nations in the past, it had been mostly tragic. In his contemporary situation as well as past generations Ezekiel and his people have known suffering. For a thousand years and more Babylon had been the crossroads of nations and civilizations. Ezekiel had lived in the regions of Babylon. He became a refugee. The litany of disasters goes on and on.

It was within this troubled world that Ezekiel appeared among the Babylonian refugees.

In the Muslim sources and the biblical source there is deep dismay in the ways the shepherds abandon the sheep.[3] The shepherds pay no attention to the need of the sheep. Instead of feeding the flocks, the shepherds beat and wound the sheep.[4] Ezekiel also was beaten and imprisoned. Calamity was revealed in the many faces of the refugees. There was a plague raging. Death stalked the migrants in every direction. There were the raiders who took provisions from the migrants. The unkept land produced miniscule crops.[5]

It was within that kind of context that the prophet of Islam had a word of advice: "I heard the Messenger of Allāh saying: 'If you hear about it [an outbreak of plague] in a land, do not go to it, but if the plague appears in a land where you are staying, do not flee away from it.'"[6] It is within this seemingly hopeless situation that an associate protected a hundred prophets who were threatened with death by an ungodly king. That action of a just man gave hope for all other righteous men.[7] Was this

---

3. Ezek 3.
4. Yusuf Ali, 841.
5. Yusuf Ali, 841.
6. al-Tha'labi, *Kisas al-Anbia'* (*Tales of the Prophets*).
7. Dhu l-K.

righteous man Ezekiel or an associate of Ezekiel? We do not know. Yet it was in this context Ezekiel commenced preaching. His home seems to have been in a small village on the outskirts of Babylon. In later years surely his shrine attracted both Muslim and Christian pilgrims.

Ezekiel Heard the Call

It is in this tragic situation that the migrants placed their tents. It was in this tragedy that Ezekiel heard the word of the Lord. In the biblical account Ezekiel wrote, "In the thirtieth year, in the fourth month on the fifth day while I was among the exiles by the Kebar River, the heavens were opened, and I saw visions of God. On the fifth of the month—it was the fifth year of the exile of King Jehoiachin—the word of the Lord came to Ezekiel the priest, the son of Buzi, by the Kebar River in the land of the Babylonians. There the hand of the Lord was upon him."[8]

Ezekiel saw a wind storm coming out of the north—an immense cloud with flashing lightening and surrounded by brilliant light. Ezekiel's vision reminds us of the inaugural visions of revelation that the prophet of Islam proclaimed whose visions commenced in the night of power as he prayed within the environs of Mecca.[9]

Ezekiel was encouraged by the revelation he received.[10] The revelations included two nick names. The new names were *constancy* and *patience*.[11] These names were a description of Ezekiel's qualities. The challenges of helping within the massive migration of peoples was overwhelming. God blessed Ezekiel who needed a special anointing for the task before him. This is the Muslim understanding as comes to us through folklore. God blessed Ezekiel with special mercies as revealed in these two names.

The support for Ezekiel included the commissioning of other prophets as well, including Idras, Elisha, and Ishmael. An enigmatic figure (Dhu l-Kifl), is considered a comfort for the refugees for he was the one whose nickname seems to mean enfolding for comfort. He would seem

---

8. Ezek 1:1–2

9. Q97:1–3

10. Dhu l-Kifi (Qur'ān) Although scholars are not certain as to which of these various teachers or prophets are Ezekiel, I will assume throughout this essay that Ezekiel is Zul-kifl.

11. Yusuf Ali, 841.

to be the blanket-giver for the refugees. The Muslim engagement seems to suggest that all these persons became a team working with Ezekiel within extraordinary challenges, a team who were especially tested by the widening sweep of death. In this circumstance God initiated forming a team who worked with Ezekiel. Each person in this small circle communicated hope and comedy.

The team, however, do not work together in physical encounter. These are individual prophets or teachers who are proclaiming the same revelation with other messengers of God. The region under the authority of God was expanding. This was true regardless of where the message is proclaimed. This is the Muslim approach. The absence of reliable accounts is to say that what I have described in regard to Ezekiel is mostly conjecture. Our only reliable resource is Ezekiel as described in the Bible. Consequently, this essay is based mostly on the biblical accounts. Trustworthy Muslim accounts are not to be found.

Comedy within Tragedy

The biblical material revealed Ezekiel as an extraordinary comedian. His warnings of judgment were interwoven with comedy. Ezekiel acted out his prophetic proclamations. For example, when he proclaimed that Israel would be in captivity for 440 days, Ezekiel was to fuel his cook stove with cow's dung while the people tied him up with ropes for 440 days while he slept on his right side and then his left side while facing the city walls. Then he was to shave his head with a sword and take a few strands of the hair and start a fire as a warning that Jerusalem would be destructed by out of control fire. His entire prophetic mission was interspersed with these kinds of seemingly crazy metaphors. Imagine the dinnertime conversation as families chatted about Ezekiel's latest antics along the walls of Jerusalem.

The Glory Departed

God, in the writing of biblical Ezekiel, was also quite dramatic. Ezekiel was taken to the temple where he proclaimed the judgement of God upon Israel and in fact all nations. Then God began to exit from the temple in a variety of chariots and wheels and cherubim. Some wheels were large and others small and these sparkling wheels interposed with one another.

When the wheels finally left the temple, they traveled across the plains, paused, and then they ascended and took off. Alas! The glory of God had departed from the temple and the plains. The refugees had encountered the ultimate calamity. God had left them.[12]

The Glory of God will Return

Oh! No! Ezekiel from his perch beyond the plains proclaimed God would return! In fact, God would extend his love throughout the whole world. This promise filled Israel with hope. The promise of a mission to all peoples filled Israel with hope and expectation. For two thousand years and more Israel is still waiting the fulfillment of Ezekiel's promise! God will never forget his people. In the biblical vision the God of hope would return.

In the Muslim witness God sends down his blessing upon those who surrender to his will. The quest for blessing is especially pertinent within the Muslim *sufi* quest to acquire the blessings of God (*Baraka*). I experienced this hope when invited to Iran to address a gathering of some two thousand clergy on the theme of messianic hope in the Abrahamic faiths. In two days I heard twenty-one sermons on hope! I spoke on Jesus as the fulfillment of the kingdom of God. The moderator summarized my proclamation saying that Muslims have not been aware of the mission of Jesus. All participants should further investigate the eschatological mission of Jesus. That mission is grounded in power and the uncompromising sovereignty of God.

Hope in God empowered Ezekiel's confidence that the glory of the Lord would return! In this confluence of hope surrounding Ezekiel's mission in the exile we experience remarkable expectations. Especially significant is the resurrection of the dry bones.[13] Ezekiel saw a vast plain of dead bones who resurrected as Ezekiel prophesied upon them.

The Muslim *Sufis*

The sufi Muslim miracle workers would be very impressed with Ezekiel's visions! There are themes within the Ezekiel vision that in some ways are analogous to Sufism. Ezekiel spoke within a distinctive spirituality. Ezekiel as a displaced refugee of the diaspora lived within a system that

---

12. Ezek 12.
13. Ezek 37

was distinctive of a diaspora world view. Likewise, the Babylonians were formed in distinctive ways within the context of the "rivers of Babylon." These different streams of spirituality form Ezekiel within his biblical world view. Especially we listen with Ezekiel to the stirring and hopeful messages from God. This essay is an attempt to hear and believe as Ezekiel was hearing and believing.

It is quite amazing that twice in the revelations that God sent down to Ezekiel, he met God through wheels and brilliant light and cherubim. A man appeared within this holy contraption who was like the Son of Man. Dead bones came back to life. Ezekiel is prophesying within a world view that has been developing for several centuries. Receiving the unfolding of Ezekiel's revelation of Ezekiel is like sitting within the unfolding of revelation.

The Miraj for Muslims

How might a Muslim view what has happened?[14] Why is the *miraj* so important for Muslims. Muslims would likely view the nighttime journey of Muhammad from Mecca to Jerusalem as opening the door to new forums for mysticism. The nighttime transport of Muhammad into the seventh heaven opened the possibility of fresh visions of God that transcended earthly bound realities. While the Prophet was asleep in his Meccan home the horse named Al Buraq swooped down and took Muhammed to the site of the Al Aqsa mosque at the Templ Mount in Jerusalem. The horse then rose upward through the seven heavens. There he received instructions as to the required prayers for Muslims. The five times daily for prayer was negotiated with the prophet of Islam; even Moses got into the negotiations even though he had died many years earlier. That is the Muslim witness. That is what they believe.

This midnight vision has significantly formed the *sufi* quest to receive the blessing of God.[15] Orthodox Sunni Islam submits to the will of the compassionate Allāh who is unknown and unknowable. However, the *miraj* dispenses the blessing of God! This is the essence of the *Sufi* quest. Sufi Islam does not seek to know God; that quest is impossible. However, the Sufi seeks to acquire the blessing of God.

14. Q2:243
15. Q2:243

Biblical revelation takes us further.[16] The biblical and Muslim world views are so divergent that comparing the Muslim and biblical understandings does not adequately seek satisfactory comparisons. For example, in the Ezekiel scriptures God resurrects an entire army. In Islam there is little or no discussion about the resurrection but much about final judgment. Comparing these different themes does not do justice to any of these theologies. So in this essay I mostly restrict my comments to Ezekiel as described in the biblical book of Ezekiel.

How are the soldiers resurrected? It is through the word of God! How was Adam given life when he was created? We read in the beginning "God spoke." The universe is created and sustained by the word of God. In this vision we meet the One who is the Son of Man / the Word. Here is the incarnation. The Word becomes flesh. The Word becomes Son of Man. The consequence of the Son of Man proclaiming the word is resurrection! Here we meet the hope of the resurrection in fullness. In Ezekiel's vision the door is opened to meet the One who is the *Kalimatulah* (the Word of God).

The apostle John declares: "In the beginning was the Word, and the Word was with God, and the Word was God. The Word became flesh and made his dwelling among us. We have seen his glory, the glory of the one and only Son, who meeting the Word of the Gospel came from the Father, full of grace and truth" (John 1:1, 14).

The Word in Islam

Within Islam Jesus is created through the Word. This is much like Adam. God spoke and Adam was created. In Islam the Word is called: *kalimatullah*. That means "the Word of God." Can the *kalimatulah* of Islam meet the Jesus of the gospel in these scriptures? Is the Son of Man of Ezekiel also the Son of God of the Gospel? Here we meet the Word of the Qu'ran[17] meeting the Word of the Gospel.

Are they the same? The Qur'ān is clear. *Kalimatullah* means that Jesus was created through the Word of God just as Adam was created and is sustained through the Word of God. Islam is clear in the objection to Jesus as the eternal Word of God.[18] He is only a creation through

---

16. Ezek 37:1–13.
17. Q3:59.
18. Q3:59.

the Word of God. So *kalimatulah* means creation. *Kalimatulah* does not mean incarnation. This means that in the Qur'ān Jesus as *Kalimatullah* is divergent from the gospel. We therefore invite Muslims to consider the New Testament revelation of the Christ. Simply stated, we bear witness that in Jesus we meet the One who is the fullness of God.

The Hope to Know God

God in his glory returned to Jerusalem. Just as God left Jerusalem, he has now returned in all his splendid glory. The Ezekiel vision is that of God's grand plan for an Israel who repents and therefore becomes a people of witness and blessing to all nations. The pen of Ezekiel has new revelations of God's return.

The resurrection of the armies and the hope for a door open to receive the blessing of God is a beacon of hope for all peoples. One sign of this hope is the multifarious streams of water that exit from the temple bringing life to those who congregate around the temple until the surrounding deserts are recipients of life-giving water. The hope of receiving blessing from the God we cannot know has never departed from the *sufi* hope to receive the blessing of God. Muhammad was successful in finding the mystery of receiving the blessing of God. Alas, the secret for breaking through to receive the blessing of God is obscured. The blessing of God remains a mystery even when confessing belief in Allāh. The *miraj* has given hope, but the Muslim saints remain in possession of the secret paths. The persistent *sufi* will seek various *sufi* ways to receive the blessing of God. Only the truly spiritual will prevail. That is the never-ending quest.

Choosing Different Sufi Paths (Tariqa)

In the sermons in Tehran there was great emphasis on following the true paths into the mystery of God. The preachers said that when Iran puts all aspects of life under the authority of the will of God, then the savior *Mahdhi* will come and establish Islam throughout the world. They felt they were nearly at the finish line. The academics and clerics were united in believing they were on the right path for a miraculous establishment of Islam worldwide.

There are several dimensions to getting the world ready for the coming universal rule of Islam. First is to find an intercessor who seems near to God. Although the Qur'ān says there is no need for an intercessor, the Qur'ān also says "unless God has appointed the intercessor." So the quest goes forward seeking for the saint whom God has appointed. Second, God might be experienced through the repetition of God's names. That quest takes the seeker down the path of repeating God's name over and over. Third, the quest will remember that Abraham was a friend of God. In that case we can practice friendship with God by doing good deeds. Fourth, the quest can lead us to join a *sufi* community where righteous people can lead disciples in the *sufi* path that best fits the persona of a disciple. These practices are typical of *sufi* communities around the world. During our six years in Kenya we chose as a family to become neighbors to a sufi community.

Yearning to Know God

The *sufi* communities were on a quest for a spirituality Christ and the church were especially equipped to offer. The most obvious quest is the search to meet God! Now we look at the nature of the Ezekiel mission as a quest fulfilled in Christ. The forthright quest for Ezekiel and his community was to be ready to receive the coming glory of God occupying the temple. In a letter from the President of Iran, Mahmoud Ahmadinadad, to the American President, George W. Bush, he asked pointedly whether the US President was ready to meet the appointed messenger of God when he arrives. He urged that both presidents search their hearts.

The Glory of God Returns

This Jewish quest for God within Israel persisted as it was communicated generation by generation in the metaphorical language of Ezekiel. He saw a stream of water up to the ankles trickling around the feet as it meandered along the southern and eastern side of the temple. He saw the river becoming deeper as it flowed toward the salt sea, first up to the knees, then the waist, and then too deep for swimming. Trees for the healing of the nations and with fruit for all seasons of the year were bountifully present. Fish and other business thrived all along the banks of the river. Fishnets assured bountiful ingathering of fish for eating.

The vision was clear! God was on the way back to the temple! The whole region awaited the day when God would fulfill Ezekiel's vision. When Ezekiel first arrived at the river there was only desert. Later he returned to the river and there were trees all along the banks of the river. Obviously God was communicating the need for patience. Nevertheless, Israel of the diaspora yearned for the day when Ezekiel's prophecy would be fulfilled.

That yearning became a ritual of expectation during the annual eight-day Feast of Tabernacles. During the Feast the participants lived in booths to remember the tents they had lived in during their journeys into the promised land. In the evenings, parents told their children the stories of their migration. Then on the last day of the Feast the throngs surrounded the temple area as they sang a song from Ezekiel's repertoire of songs. The throngs commenced their walk from the pool of Shalom upward into the city toward the temple. They sang from Ezekiel's hymns:

"Ho! with joy we draw water from the wells of salvation."

The priest carried water in an ern on his shoulder as the throngs moved slowly up toward the altar in the temple center. All Jerusalem flowed forward singing in joyous song and expectation. Year by year the pilgrims sang in hope that God in his glory would return. Then one day at that very moment on the last day of the feast as the priest poured water over the altar a man stepped to the front of the line and with a very loud voice he cried out, "If anyone is thirsty let him come to me and drink. Whoever believes in me as the Scripture has said, streams of living water will flow from within him!"[19]

The throngs were astounded. Suddenly the meaning of Ezekiel's promise was becoming clear. The fulfillment was complete in Jesus! The water flowing from the altar was the Holy Spirit who would be poured out upon the disciples. The altar was Jesus, the Lamb of God who was crucified upon the cross. The dead soldiers who resurrected were the general resurrection of the dead at the eschaton. The experience of God was the gift of God's grace bringing believers into the fellowship of the church

In the concluding message of Ezekiel we read, "The name of the city from that time on will be, 'The Lord is There.'" In Ezekiel believers are invited to enter the city God is creating. In the very center of the city is the sacrificial Lamb. The resurrection is grounded in the cross. The sufi quest is seeking glory through ascending into the seventh heaven. This is

---

19. John 7:37–39.

a secret journey. Only a special few can penetrate those secrets. Hopefully the prophet of Islam is privy to these secrets. His disciples worship seeking to absorb those secrets.

When we lived in Eastleigh in Nairobi the sufis would meet every Thursday evening in the mosque across the street from our home. They would chant the names of their saints and the name of the Prophet of Islam. They paused from time to time to chew a euphoria-enhancing weed with tea. Then the chants would continue until late in the evening. When they left for home, eyes were glazed. The euphoria in time caused dementia. They believed they were experiencing God within their euphoria. But the euphoria they were imbibing was destructive.

Our witness was that God is most experienced in good deeds! Not in the repetition of the ninety-nine names for God. Caring for the lost sheep was Ezekiel's burden. God is concerned for all the lost sheep of all nations. When the glory of God returns to the temple, all nations will be participants in the returning glory. All God's people will join hands as a community of God's people reaching out to the nations. All are welcome to the table.

Creating Communities of Grace

Our family decision to move into the *sufi* neighborhood was appreciated. I met the imam occasionally. We were an intercultural Christian community. The emerging church was a sign of the kingdom of God right within the Muslim community. When the imam became ill, I would visit with him and pray for him. We occasionally invited Muslim leaders to our home for food and conversation. We introduced Bible studies based on those scriptures the Qur'ān declares to be sent down from heaven: the Torah, the Psalms, the Gospel, and then other holy writings as well. We explained that the Qur'ān commands Christians to make their scriptures available. We were People of the Book!

Our mission was to worship God while doing good. We asked community leaders how we could serve the community. The answer was the need for a study room for high school students. After receiving a large grant, we developed a reading room and a multi ministry community center. Our theology was Ezekiel: the name of the city was the Lord is there. We were recognized as disciples of Jesus within the Muslim community.

When the mosque acquired a large grant from Arabia for community development, the Muslims built Arabic and Qur'ānic centers throughout the region. When the churches acquired a grant, they developed a community center in the densely populated city and animal husbandry in the hinterlands. The Muslims were far more religious than were the Christians. At four in the morning our street became a gentle shuffle as the men went quickly to the mosque for prayers. I kept sleeping!

However, when the imam needed funds for high school for his three daughters, the mosque came to us for educational financial assistance. The Muslim development money went to teaching Arabic. The Christians helped the daughters of the Imam get a secular education.

On one occasion Muslim friends took me on the pilgrimage to the grave of their saint. They believed that their saint had acquired secret mystical insights into the spirit of Muhammad. It was a two-day journey. In the evening dancers played and people prayed. The nearby bushes were filled with petitions on paper imploring God. When we returned home, I asked my host to explain. He said they were sinful so God did not hear their prayers. They needed their patron saint to get through.

I asked, "Is this good Islam?"

"No this is very bad. The Qur'ān is clear that there is no intercessor unless God had appointed him."

I responded that God has appointed an intercessor. He is the Messiah. God chose the Messiah because he is without sin, he understands our situation perfectly for he has lived among us, He is the atoning sacrifice for our sins, he arose from the dead, he lives eternally and intercedes for us continually.

"Amazing," was the response of the Somali Muslims who were introducing me to the delights of their Somali culture. The book of Hebrews is excellent for sufi Muslims. It speaks into the world of sufism winsomely.

An Earthy Salvation

What we are describing is not philosophical conjecture. It is a description of earthy reality. Let us ponder the powers that converged at the altar when Jesus shouted with a "very loud" voice urging all within the throngs that day to come to him. First, we see the water being poured out at the altar. This water is a metaphor of the Holy Spirit who would shortly be poured out at Pentecost where "every nation under heaven" would hear the Gospel.

The Cross

We also see the altar. That was where sacrifices were made daily. The altar is the cross where Jesus with stretched-out arms invites all to receive his forgiveness and reconciliation. Muslims tell me that the cross is impossible because Jesus the Messiah is the incarnation of the power of God. The prophet of Islam finds it impossible to suggest that the cross is healing for the nations. In Islam there is no place for God who suffers for us and because of us. Several years ago I was invited to speak to a congregation of a hundred who were widows and orphans from the wars in Darfur, Sudan. I said that Jesus fully understands what they have experienced. Their children were born beneath the branches of acacia shrubs, like Jesus. They had become refugees in a foreign land. Their men had worked in a carpenter shop, just as Jesus learned carpentry. They saw their friends beaten. They saw their men killed and their bodies hung on trees just like Jesus was treated. They saw Jesus crying out in forgiveness for those who had beaten him. I proclaimed that Jesus forgave, and in his forgiveness empowers us likewise to forgive as Jesus forgives. In his resurrection he empowers us to forgive so that we are freed from death and bitterness.

When I concluded the sermon, those women and children went into the courtyard of their church and sang and danced as they repeated the name of Jesus over and over again. Their joy was twofold. They were receiving and expressing the forgiveness of Jesus for those who had done great evil to the widows of Darfur. Second, they were singing because Jesus had suffered. with them. In every way they had experienced the same destructive hatred that Jesus had experienced. Jesus forgave and in his forgiveness he empowered his disciples to forgive as he forgave.

In Ezekiel's vision everything converged around the altar. Where does the water flow? From the altar. Where does the glory of God go? From the altar and then returning to the altar. What happened to the dead solders? They died and then resurrected. Death and resurrection are altar-centered developments.

Your Kingdom Come

This is the nature of the Gospel. It is a cross- and resurrection- and incarnation-centered movement. It is centered in Jesus in whom we are forgiven and reconciled. Glory bursts forth from the Lamb slain from the foundation of the world (Rev 13:8).

I have mentioned the invitation to speak to Iranian Shi'ite clergy on Messianic hope. I concluded my message with these clerics with excepts from the prayer that Jesus the Messiah taught his disciples.

> Our Father in Heaven,
> Hallowed be your name,
> > Your kingdom come,
> Your will be done on earth as it is in heaven.
> Give us this day our daily bread. The
> > Forgive us our sins as we forgive those who sin against us.
> And lead us not into temptation,
> > But deliver us from evil.
> For yours is the kingdom, the power and the glory forever.

I then explained that the kingdom of God is the mission of the church for God's grand plan is that his kingdom extends to every people. When God's kingdom comes, even the cows are happy!

Streams in the Desert

It is significant that the deserts in Ezekiel's vision never go away. However, the banks of the river provide bountiful blessing. The trees and prospering businesses are nurtured through the life-giving water from the altar. This is a metaphor of the Holy Spirit within the desert. God's plan is for the church to minister as communities of grace within every desert.

We are invited to all the bountiful goodness we see in Ezekiel's vision as the glory of the Lord returns to the temple. Ezekiel's role in all this is his ministry of *constancy and patience*. The glory of God is returning! And the name of God's Mountain is "The Lord is There."[20]

I concluded my message to the Iranian clerics saying this is the mission of the church, to be a community that is flourishing in every way, and whose life comes from Jesus crucified. In our very broken world Jesus is the life from whom God in his glory comes again and again to bring forth new life as we repent daily of our sins that we might truly be healing leaves for the nations and nurturing fruitfulness for every season of the year. Ezekiel peers forward looking into the future when God's people will become one people with one Savior and King whose rule will extend

---

20. Ezek 48:35.

to the ends of the earth. The One who is the Son of Man will extend his peace to every nation under heaven![21]

Summary and Intention of this Essay

Ezekiel lived in a time of mass migrations with enormous local and international upheavals. In their extremity Israel was taken into captivity and the glory of God himself departed. In this calamity God promised he would return bringing restoration. Within Islam the *sufi* mystics yearn for a way to renew the blessing of God. There are analogies within Israel, the Muslim community, and the church that give renewed hope of the earth becoming filled with the blessing of God. Muslims are also impressed that God asserts that Ezekiel is a prophet of hope who is gifted with constancy and patience. These are gifts of character that are essential to new beginnings in troubled times.

The primary sources are Ezekiel in the Bible and the few references to Ezekiel in the Qur'ān. Ezekiel is a favorite preaching text and this presentation is mostly formed from my delight in preaching from this amazing book.

21. Ezek 37:1–28.

9

A Comparative Study of Zakariya/Zachariah and Yahya/John the Baptist in the Islamic and the Biblical Narratives

WONJOO HWANG

JOHN THE BAPTIST APPEARS as forerunner of Jesus Christ in the Bible and plays an indispensable role in the Christological narrative. For instance, John the Baptist testifies that Jesus is the Christ, "the Lamb of God who takes away the sin of the world" (John 1:29) and baptizes Jesus before his public ministry (Mark 1:9–11). His death, as the result of injustice, foreshadows Jesus's death on the cross (Mark 6:14–29). Zachariah's role, on the other hand, seems minor in comparison to John's as he appears in the backdrop of John's birth account. Zachariah appears to be related only indirectly to Jesus through the annunciation account of Mary.

What does the Qurʾān say about these two figures? How do they appear in the Islamic theological narratives? Since the Qurʾān rejects the Christological stance of the Bible, how do these two figures appear in the Qurʾān and what are their specific roles in the Islamic narratives? In order to answer these questions, this chapter examines the relevant Qurʾānic texts, various traditions (hadiths), and a selection of Muslim commentaries. This investigation will shed further light on how the Qur'ān uses biblical figures within its own theological framework.

Observations from the Historical-Literary Contexts of Two Surahs (Q19 and Q 3)

The Zakariya and Yahya pericope appears in two surahs (Q19 and Q3) of the Qur'ān while two other surahs (Q6 and Q21) only mention their names in a list. Before evaluating the detailed contents of the Qur'ānic witness, it is worthwhile to examine how Muslim scholarship has understood the historical context and the literary structural meaning of the two substantive surahs.[1] While the historical occasion (*asbab an-nujul*) of each surah is not easy to verify, it is noteworthy to see how Muslims traditionally have understood each surah and how the pericope of interest carries significant meaning.

Surah 19 (Maryam)

In regard to the historical occasion of surah Maryam (Q19), which is widely accepted as a Meccan surah, Muslims pinpoint the occasion to be when the early Muslim believers emigrated from Mecca to Habash, Ethiopia, due to the harsh persecution by the Meccan Quraish people.[2] Expecting to encounter Christian challenges against this early Muslim community, Muslim scholars contend that this surah prepared these early Muslims to counter Christians and stand firm in Islamic belief, especially in monotheism (*tawhid*). If this historical context is accurate, the Zakariya-Yahya pericope can be understood in two distinctive aspects: didactic and polemic. It is didactic because this surah is supposed to have encouraged the early Muslims to follow devout prophets such as Zakariya, Yahya, Maryam, 'Isa, Ibrahim, and finally Muhammad so that they could receive Allah's reward and avoid the eternal punishment. It is also polemic against Christians because this pericope strongly denies the deity of Jesus claimed by Christians.

---

1. Taking the historical context and thematic literary structure into consideration while interpreting Qur'ānic verses is a reasonable and widely accepted method among Qur'ānic scholars. See Sinai, *Qur'ān*, 161–214; Kuschel, *Christmas and the Qur'ān*.

2. Several sources can be mentioned. Ibn Kathir, "Surah 3"; Maududi, "Surah Mariam"; Muzammil, "Thematic Introduction."

This polemical nature of the Zakariya-Yahya pericope becomes more apparent in the analysis of the thematic structure of the entire surah. Surah Maryam can be clearly divided into two sections: narrative (vv. 2–58) and polemical (vv. 59–98).[3] The Zakariay-Yahya pericope appears in the narrative section as a basis for the latter section of the surah where the polemical portion contains warnings against idol-worshiping Meccans and unbelievers like Christians who do not accept Islamic teachings about *tawhid*. Thus one can observe polemical warnings presumably against Christians: "polemical criticism of having gods other than Allah (81–87) and polemical criticism of claim that God has a son (88–95)."[4] This polemical framework of the entire surah sheds important light on how to understand the Zakariya-Yahya pericope in the Qur'ān.

Surah 3 (Al-'Imran)

The historical occasion of surah al-'Imran, accepted as a Medinan surah, seems more complex, but Ibn Kathir (1300–1373), a prominent Sunni commentator, states that it is the ninth year (AD 632) when the deputation from the Christians of Najran visited the Muslim community in Medina.[5] While verifying its historicity with certainty seems impossible, it is important to see how Muslim scholars connect this surah to the context of encountering Christians in a polemical context. Thus, it is reasonable to say that Muslim scholars view the Zakariya-Yahya pericope within the polemical context against Christians.

The task of outlining the thematic flow of surah al-'Imran seems implausible due to its length, but it is still useful to observe the surrounding literary context to shed light on the Zakariya-Yahya pericope in this surah. The section before the Zakariya-Yahya pericope contains various

---

3. Gokkir, "Form and Structure," 7–8; Sinai, *Qur'ān*, 81–86; Kuschel, *Christmas and the Qur'ān*, 57–60.

4. Gokkir, "Form and Structure," 7.

5. Al-Wahidi, *Asbab al-Nuzul*, 32; Ibn Kathir, "Surah 3"; Maududi, "Surah Al-'Imran." Maududi's summary on Q3:33–63 is worth mentioning here: "This discourse is particularly addressed to the Christians and invites them to accept Islam. It clears Jesus and his mother not only from the stigma maliciously set upon them by the Jews, but also refutes the erroneous Christian creed of the Divinity of Jesus which had been formulated because of his miraculous birth. For this purpose, the instances of John the Baptist to a barren woman and an extremely aged man and that of Adam without father and mother have been cited to show that there is nothing in the birth of Jesus without a father to entitle him to Divinity."

strong assertions on the Qur'ān as Allah's revealed book (Q3:2–9), the fate of believers and disbelievers (vv. 10–17), Islam the religion (Q3:18–20), warnings against the Jews (Q3:10–17, 21–27), and warning against alliance with disbelievers (vv. 28–32).[6] The immediately preceding verse 32 states: "Say, 'Obey God [Allah] and the messenger.' If they turn away—surely God [Allah] does not love the disbelievers."[7]

The narrative of Zakariya-Yahya begins with Allah's choice of Islamic prophets one of which is the house of 'Imran (3:33). Maryam is born from this chosen house of 'Imran. Then Zakariya appears in the narrative as a guardian for Maryam in the temple. After the Zakariya-Yahya pericope (Q3:33–41), the narrative continues with the announcement of 'Isa's birth (vv. 42–47), the mission and miracles of Jesus (vv. 48–58), 'Isa's being human, not divine (vv. 59–63), various challenges against the people of the scripture (vv. 64–85), and warnings against apostasy (vv. 86–91).[8]

Within the larger narrative in Q3:33–63, the main character is 'Isa while Zakariya and Yahya appear only at the backdrop of the overall Qur'ānic argument about 'Isa. Even within a larger literary context of Q3:1–91, there are strong warnings for those who reject the prophet Muhammad and his message and especially against Christians who believe the deity of 'Isa contrary to Islamic teaching. This polemical tone existing in the thematic flow of the first half of surah al-'Imran determines the primary role of the Zakariya-Yahya pericope.

Zakariya in the Islamic Narratives

Zakariya in the Qur'ān

Surah 19:2–11

Surah Maryam begins with the story of Zakariya who petitioned to Allah in secret for an heir in spite of his nearly impossible physical condition due to his old age (2–3). His main concern was to have an heir who would continue his priestly ministry at the temple (5–6). Allah answers his prayer and sends good news of a son with the name, Yahya (7). In response to his surprise to

---

6. Droge, *Qur'ān*, 32–33.

7. Droge, *Qur'ān*, 33. Also the translation of the Qur'ān is from Droge throughout this chapter.

8. Droge, *Qur'ān*, 34–38.

such unbelievable news, Allah mentions his power of creation, even creating Zakariya out of non-existence (9). Then Zakariya asks for a sign, so Allah gives a sign that Zakariya will not speak to people for three nights (10). When Zakariya comes out of the chamber, he tells people by signs (gestures) to praise and worship Allah in the morning and in the evening (11). Then comes the narrative of Maryam and 'Isa.

Surah 3:37–41

The immediately preceding account deals with the family of 'Imran and the birth and consecration of Maryam by the wife of 'Imran (30–36). Zakariya is introduced as a guardian for Maryam in the sanctuary (37a). While looking after Maryam, Zakariya finds her with provision of food and asks her where they came from. She replies that Allah provided all the food without measure (37b). After having observed the miraculous provision of Allah for her, Zakariya petitions for a good offspring (38). The angel gives good news of a son named Yahya whose role is to confirm a word from Allah (39). Astounded, Zakariya asks for a sign and the angel replies that he will not speak to man except by signs for three days (41). Then follows the narrative of Maryam and 'Isa (42–63).

Surah 6:85

This verse lists Zakariya among four names that are set forth as the righteous people: Zakariya, Yahya, 'Isa, and Ilias (85). The immediate context reveals that Allah chose these righteous people and guided them. Zakariya is mentioned as one example.

Surah 21:89–90

These verses appear in the context of Allah's deliverance for the righteous people from their distresses. A series of Islamic prophets are mentioned in verses 48–94.[9] When Zakariya cries

---

9. The list of Islamic prophets in this section includes Musa and Harun (48), Ibrahim (51), Lut (71), Nuh (76), Davud and Suleyman (78), Ayub (83), Dhulnun or Yunus (87), Zakariya and Yahya (89–90), and finally Maryam and 'Isa (91).

out to Allah for an offspring (89), Allah responds to him by giving Yahya while Allah cures (the barrenness of) his wife (90a). The verse goes on to state their goodness and faithfulness (presumably the three people mentioned in the immediate context: Zakariya, his wife, and Yahya) (90b).

Zakariya in the Hadiths and Commentaries

One interesting component outside of the Qur'ān is the biographical information of Zakariya. Ibn al-'Arabi (1165–1240) provides the family tree of "Jesus and John the Baptist" in which he identifies the father of Zakariya as Barachia.[10] Strangely, the same pair of names appear in Zach 1:1 (the prophet Zachariah the son of Berechiah) and in Matt 23:35 (Zachariah the son of Barachiah) where he is introduced as a righteous martyr. John's father, Zakariya, cannot be the OT prophet Zachariah because there is more than a 500-year gap between the two. Then who is Zachariah in Matt 23:35? Could it be the father of John the Baptist? One cannot affirm this from biblical data because there is no clear evidence.[11]

Nevertheless, one possible connection can be made if one considers the martyrdom account of Zachariah, John's father, in *The Protoevangelium of James* (*Protoevangelium* hereafter).[12] While the name of his father is not mentioned in this source, his martyrdom account might have made Ibn 'Arabi suppose Zachariah in Matt 23:35 referred to John's father. While this source is not an authoritative canonical source for Christianity, it has been widely accepted by the Qur'ān and Muslim commentators. This case demonstrates that Muslim traditions or commentaries freely relied on extra-biblical sources for additional details or missing information in establishing the Islamic narratives.

The most important role of Zakariya in the Qur'ān is his role as a devout guardian of Maryam (Q3:37). The commentary of Jalalayn records the account of how Zakariya was chosen among twenty-nine competing candidates for her guardianship by using quills in the Jordan river. It

---

10. Gloton, *Jesus Son of Mary*, 93.

11. NT scholar Craig Blomberg seems to prefer to take this Zachariah to be the OT prophet in Zach 1:1. He states: "Although there is no independent pre-Christian tradition of the martyrdom of the prophet Zachariah, the son of Barachiah, certain post-Christian Rabbinic texts seem to hint it." See Blomberg, *Matthew*, 349.

12. This apocryphal book, also called *The Infancy Gospel of James*, is dated to around AD 145 and is not part of the Christian Canon. Mattison, "Infancy Gospel."

also records that Zakariya kept Maryam in "a gallery-room with a ladder in the temple" and provided food for her.[13] At-Tabari (839–923) more specifically mentions that the food provided from Allah was "the fruit of summer in winter, and the fruits of winter in summer," which emphasizes the supernatural dimension of this incident.[14]

According to Q3:37–38, this miraculous provision of food by Allah for Maryam seems to have encouraged Zakariya to have faith in Allah and make a petition for an heir for his priestly service.[15] When Allah answered his petition, Zakariya responded with another question: "How shall I have a son?" Commentators do not consider this to be a doubting response of Zakariya in contrast to the biblical account (Luke 1:18–20), but only a natural response due to the surprising news.[16] This way of interpretation is noteworthy because Sunni theology teaches that all the prophets of Allah are sinless in respect to major sins.

While the Qur'ānic text provides highly commendable characteristics of Zakariya as a prophet of Allah (Q6:85 and 21:89), there are several interesting accounts in the hadiths that seem contradictory. For example, according one tradition, Zakariya became afraid when he learned that Maryam was pregnant while she was under his guardianship in the temple.[17] In regard to his death narratives, Zakariya, being fearful, fled into a tree but was sawn in two by the persecutors who cut the tree in half.[18]

Yahya in the Islamic Narratives

Yahya in the Qur'ān

Surah 19:7 and 12–15

Yahya's name first appears in Allah's announcement to Zakariya (7). This verse specifically mentions that this name had not been

---

13. Jalalayn, *Sura al-'Imran*.
14. At-Tabari, *Sura al-'Imran*.
15. At-Tabari, *Sura al-'Imran*; Ibn Kathir, *Al-'Imran*.
16. Ahmadiyyah scholar Muhammad Ali says: "There is no disbelief on the part of Zacharias. It is simply an expression of wonder as to how a son can be born to him, for he had already reached a very old age." See Ali, *Holy Qur'ān*, 140.
17. Al-Majlisi, *Hayatul Qulub*, 619–31.
18. Brannon M. Wheeler quotes Wahb b. Munabbih for two traditions about his death. Wheeler, *Prophets in the Qur'ān*, 292. Also see Parrinder, *Jesus in the Qur'ān*, 55.

assigned to anybody before.[19] At the end of Zakariya's account, Allah commands Yahya to take hold of the Book with might (12a). The following verses (12b–14) describe the exemplary characteristics of Yahya due to Allah's favor upon him. Allah mentions his secure protection for Yahya on three special occasions of his life (15).[20]

Surah 3:39

Yahya is simply mentioned as the angels made an announcement to Zakariya about the birth of his son. The role and the commendable qualities of Yahya are described in detail. It is interesting to see that Yahya does not appear as an active player, but as Allah's favorable answer to Zakariya's prayer.

Surah 6:85

The explanation of this verse is provided above.

Surah 21:90

Yahya appears simply to be a gift of Allah to Zakariya for his petition. It seems reasonable to accept that the personal pronoun of the "implicit" subject (they) in the last sentence includes Yahya. So one may conclude that Yahya has the commendable personal qualities that are described in this verse.

Yahya in the Hadiths and Commentaries

Yahya is mentioned more in extra-Qur'ānic accounts than the Qur'ān primarily because of his connection to 'Isa. Overall, while Yahya is highly esteemed, some of these stories seem legendary and others are

---

19. Several different explanations exist about the meaning of this verse. One would say that this name, Yahya, had not been used for others in the past. Ibn Kathir and Jalalayn hold this view. According to the Bible, however, the name John was not used within the circle of Zachariah's relatives (Luke 1:61).

20. A nearly verbatim statement of Q19:15 appears in 19:33 for 'Isa with a different subject.

contradictory to historical facts. By taking the Arabic name, Yahya, to mean "he shall live," Ahmadiyyah commentator Ali (1874–1951) contends that "he would not die in sin like other relations."[21] This notion that Yahya was sinless is also shared by fifteenth-century Sunni commentators, Jalalayn: "He [Yahya] was pure and sinless and never disobeyed God. In fact, what is said of one prophet is equally true of all. They are all pure from birth, and never disobeyed God."[22]

Yahya's relationship with 'Isa appears more explicitly in the hadiths and commentaries. Mostly, Yahya is considered to be the first who believed in 'Isa and confirmed him as the prophet of Allah. In the commentary of Jalalayn on Q3:39, "a word from Allah" which Yahya confirms (*musaddiqan*) is taken to mean 'Isa.[23] One hadith mentions that Yahya recognized 'Isa and greeted him in the womb of his mother.[24] However, one must beware that this confirmation of Yahya is not the same Christological confirmation by John the Baptist in the Bible as will be argued later.

Yahya's prestigious status in Islam is further illustrated in the account of the night journey of Muhammad recorded in an authoritative hadith, Sahih Muslim Book 1:47.[25] There Muhammad is said to have seen 'Isa and Yahya together in the second heaven during his visit to the seven heavens, and the two are introduced as cousins on the maternal side. At the same time, there exist several strange stories of Yahya in the traditions. One hadith records the dialogue between Yahya and 'Isa: "John and Jesus met and John said, 'Ask God's forgiveness for me, for you are better than me.' Jesus replied: 'You are better than me. I pronounced peace upon myself, whereas God pronounced peace upon you.' God recognized the

21. Ali, *Holy Qur'ān*, 140.

22. Ali, *Holy Qur'ān*, 596. Jalalayn agrees when he says in his commentary on verse 3:39, "it is said that he never sinned and never so intended." Gordon Nickel, however, rightly criticizes this aspect of Islamic theological hermeneutics in *Qur'ānic and Islamic Interpretation*, 174. He critically states the problematic notion as follows: "The Muslim doctrine of prophetic sinlessness took root even though the Qur'ān, too, provides examples of the sins of prophets and of them asking God for forgiveness (including David, at Q38:24f.)."

23. Al-Jalalayn, *Sura al-'Imran*; Ibn Kathir, *Al-'Imran*. Maududi also agrees on this view when he identifies "a word of Allah" to be Jesus Christ. Maududi, "Sura Al-'Imran."

24. Al-Majlisi, *Hayatul Qulub*, 624–25. This story seems to allude the biblical account in Luke 1:41, 44. However, not all commentators take this view because one can take "a word from Allah" to mean the divine prophecy of the birth of the son to Zakariya. See Ali, *Holy Qur'ān*, 140.

25. Sahih Muslim, Book 1:74, "Chapter on Night Journey."

merit of them both."[26] The pronouncements of blessing here probably refer to the similar statements in two verses (Q19:15 and 19:33) where only the subjects are different; Allah in 19:15 and 'Isa himself in 19:33.[27] Nevertheless, it is certainly strange from the biblical perspective to portray John the Baptist as more superior or more important than Jesus Christ.

The most perplexing aspect in reviewing the traditions on Yahya is finding multiple versions of his death account. While most of them contain the motif of martyrdom, "the unjust death by evil persons," their details vary wildly and differ from the biblical account (Luke 6:14–29). Some versions contain clearly false historical data while others seem to be legendary. For example, the death of Yahya is connected to the vengeful punishment of Allah upon the persecutors through the destruction of Jerusalem by Babylonian king Nebuchadnezzar.[28] According to historical records, Nebuchadnezzar who destroyed Jerusalem lived almost six hundred years before John the Baptist. This demonstrates an apparent chronological error in these traditions. Yet in another source according to Ibn Kathir, Yahya's death took place when he stood against Herod Antipas who desired to marry "Salome, his brother's daughter."[29] This caused Salome to get furious and want to kill Yahya. She devised a plot to seduce king Herod Antipas and the king eventually killed Yahya and brought his head to Salome after having been "bewitched by her charm."[30] It is not always easy to know how to make sense of all these ahistorical contents in the traditions and the commentaries that depend on various hadiths.

---

26. This account is attributed to Ibn Hanbal. Requoted from Kuschel, *Christmas and the Qur'ān*, 56.

27. One may see this episode as an allusion to biblical accounts in Matt 3:13–14; or vv. 11–12.

28. Wheeler collected several traditions by at-Tabari, Suyuti, Ibn Abbas, and Ibn Masud concerning the death of Yahya. See Wheeler, *Prophets in the Qur'ān*, 292–96.

29. Ibn Kathir, "Story of Prophet." There are clearly conflicting historical details in this account. The Bible states that Herodias divorced her husband Philip in order to marry King Herod Antipas who was a half-brother of Philip. John the Baptist stood against this marriage because it was a violation of the Mosaic law (Lev 18:16). It was not the daughter of his brother as in the account of Ibn Kathir, but the wife of his half-brother. The name, Salome, appears as one of the women who came to the tomb of Jesus in the biblical account (Mark 15:40; 16:1).

30. Ibn Kathir, "Story of Prophet."

Comparative Observations from the Biblical Narratives

When the Islamic narratives on Zakariya and Yahya are compared with the biblical accounts, one may find not only similar elements but also many significant differences that engender crucial theological breaches between the Qur'ān and the Bible.[31] This section highlights some of the key differences between the Qur'ān and the Bible in regard to the two figures so that these observations may lead to a better understanding of their roles in the respective theological narratives, Qur'ānic and biblical.

First, the Qur'ān describes that Maryam grew up in the temple under the guardianship of Zakariya (Q3:37). This is not supported by the Bible and it seems rather strange to imagine a girl "growing and living in the temple" in the first-century Judaism context.[32] One wonders why the Qur'ān emphatically stresses this upbringing of Maryam. The answer to this question is that the family of 'Imran is highly favored by Allah above all people as Allah brings 'Isa through Maryam into this world as his prophet (Q3:33).

The miraculous provision of food for Maryam in the temple is completely foreign to the Bible. Moreover, the Qur'ān implies that this supernatural provision of Allah for Maryam emboldens the faith of Zakariya that he makes a petition for an heir (Q3:38). The Bible mentions the prayer of Zachariah in Luke 1:13, but it is not so explicit whether he asked for his heir at that moment of temple service. R. H. Stein does not think that his prayer was specifically for a son at that moment because he was in the midst of public service in the temple and because Luke 1:7 describes the barrenness of his wife and their old age. Therefore, it is more likely that the prayer the angel referred to in Luke 1:13 is "his prayer that

---

31. Some critiques of the Qur'ān have debated over the genealogical information that is clearly wrong in the Qur'ān. For example, Maryam is identified as a daughter of 'Imran in Q19:35 and a "sister of Aaron" in Q19:28, which is certainly unsupported by the Bible's testimony. In the Bible, 'Imran is the father of Aaron, Moses, and Mariam so the Qur'ānic biographical data seem anachronistic. To resolve this problem, Suleiman A. Mourad presents the case that the Qur'ānic presentation of Mary takes this ancestry to denote a spiritual heritage. See Mourad, "Mary in the Qur'ān," 163–66.

32. The Arabic term that refers to the place of Maryam in the temple is *al-mihrab* (Q19:11, 3:37). This term refers to a "private quarters" or "prayer niche" of a mosque in the post-Islamic period. It can also refer to "temple or sanctuary" in general. See Badawi and Haleem, *Dictionary*, 197. However, it seems strange to use this term to refer to a special place for keeping a young girl like Mary inside the first-century Jewish temple. One may see it as an anachronistic error.

was made in the past"³³ for a child. What is more significant in the biblical narrative is not just that this child is born as the fulfillment of God's answer to the prayer, but also that this child becomes the forerunner for the coming Messiah, Jesus Christ.

Another significant difference appears in the nature of the sign after the announcement of Yahya in the Qur'ān. Zakariya was surprised by the news about his son, so he asked for a sign himself (Q19:10; 3:41). The Bible, however, shows that Zachariah became doubtful about this news, so a sign was given as a punishment for his unbelief in the promise of God (Luke 1:20).³⁴ Moreover, the duration of his speechless condition lasted until the eighth day after John was born according to the Bible (Luke 1:57–64) whereas it was only three days (nights) in the Qur'ān (Q19:10; 3:41).

The Bible plainly admits the shortcoming of Zachariah in his failure to believe this news from an angel. The Bible does not attempt to portray any biblical figure as a "sinless or faultless" man of God. On the contrary, the Qur'ān and its commentators cannot acknowledge any human fallibility like Zakariya's unbelief because the Islamic theology emphasizes the sinless quality of every prophet of Allah. Zakariya's response in the Qur'ān is considered acceptable before Allah and his request for a sign is positively answered. As much as Zakariya and other prophets are elevated as the prophets of Allah, the state of 'Isa becomes relativized and consequently the Christological emphasis of the Bible is subtly but surely rejected.

Yahya's accounts in the Qur'ān are fairly brief although more data are available in the hadiths. Nevertheless, the significance of John the Baptist in the Bible cannot even be compared to that of Yahya in the Islamic narrative. The importance is not so much in how highly the Islamic narrative speaks of him or the different accounts it has, but what is omitted

---

33. Stein, *Luke*, 75. He comments on Luke 1:13: "Verses 13b–17 speak more of John the Baptist as forerunner than to the Messiah's coming. It appears in light of 1:7 and the latter part of this verse that Luke expected his readers to assume the content of this prayer involves the birth of a child. This prayer will be answered but in a richer sense than Zechariah and Elizabeth ever dreamed. No doubt Zechariah and Elizabeth, as devout Israelites, also prayed for the coming of the redemption of Israel. Both these prayers were to be answered in the same event because their son would prepare the way for the Messiah."

34. Stein comments on this point: Zechariah was graciously given a sign as an aid to faith even though the sign was also a rebuke for lack of faith. The sign was a punitive miracle but contained the promise "until the day this happens." Muteness is a sign in Ezek 3:26; 24:27 and a judgment in 2 Macc 3:29. Stein, *Luke*, 77.

from the ample biblical data on John the Baptist with its rich theological meaning and emphases. The significant role of John the Baptist in biblical history can be summarized as follows:

> John the Baptist is a forerunner of the Messiah as he fulfilled various OT prophecies (Isa 40:3; Mal 3:1–4; 4:1). He lived with Elijah-like lifestyle (Matt 3:4) and did the ministry of turning the people of Israel to God through the baptism of repentance (Matt 3:5—6; 11). His primary role was to witness to Jesus Christ as the One who would baptize people with fire and the Spirit (Matt 13–17). His death was the result of injustice while he challenged the king and the leaders, and it can be understood as a precursor of the death of Jesus Christ.[35]

From the Qur'ānic testimony about Yahya, he appears to be Allah's gracious gift to Zakariya as a reward for his faithful devotion to Allah. Strangely, there is no record of Yahya's active actions, but instead he is described to be a prophet of Allah who has excellent qualities. Even in describing the most explicit role of Yahya in relation to 'Isa in Q3:39, there is no clear Christological confirmation as in the biblical narrative. In other words, since the most crucial role of John in the biblical narrative is his Christological connection with Jesus, the Islamic narrative deprived this completely and only emphasizes Yahya as a Muslim prophet who would introduce the two key following prophets, 'Isa and Muhammad. In the end, one must acknowledge that Yahya in the Islamic narrative appears to be substantively different from John the Baptist in the biblical narrative.

Intertextual Observations with Apocryphal Sources

One interesting question that deserves discussion is: Where do the Qur'ān and hadiths find various details of the narratives on Zakariya and Yahya which the Bible remains silent on? Some examples include the biological information (names of Zakariya's parents), Maryam's life in the sanctuary, Zakariya's guardianship of Maryam, and the various death accounts of Zakariya and Yahya. Since it is a well-attested fact that the Qur'ān shares common stories with the NT apocryphal sources,[36] it

---

35. This summary is the writer's from Baker and Beitzel, *John the Baptist*, 1200.
36. Tisdall, *Original Sources*.

is worthwhile to investigate which sources provided the details for the Islamic narratives of Zakariya and Yahya.[37]

Several components of the Qurʾānic description on Maryam and Zakariya are attested primarily to two NT apocryphal sources, *Protoevangelium* and *The Gospel of the Birth of Mary* (*GBM* hereafter).[38] Using the chapter divisions of *GBM*, for example, the birth and consecration of Maryam by her mother (Anna) and father (Joachim) are recorded in chapters 4–5, Mary's life in the temple and miraculous feeding by angels in chapter 7, and Zachariah's care for Mary in chapter 8. All these extra-canonical details are too similar to be ignored. One of the most persuasive explanation for these related contents is that this apocryphal source was widely known in the world of Arabia at the time of Muhammad or the first Muslim communities because in some cases it was even "publicly read as canonical in the eastern churches."[39]

The death account of Zachariah, although it appears only in hadiths, is another interesting story that finds its connection to apocryphal sources. *Protevangelium* (chapter 14) records the innocent death of Zachariah by Herod when he sent his servants to search for his son, John the Baptist. When they intimidated Zachariah, he replied, "I am martyr of God, and if I shed my blood, the Lord will receive my soul. Besides know that ye shed innocent blood." Later Zachariah "was murdered in the entrance of the temple and altar, and about the partition."[40]

This early church tradition from this apocryphal source was widely circulated and thus became well-known among Christians in the Arabian Peninsula.[41] In turn, it might have influenced the Islamic narratives on Zakariya. As it was shown above, the death of Zakariya in the hadiths is also described as an innocent martyrdom while some details significantly digress from the apocryphal source. Nevertheless, the martyrdom motif

---

37. Mourad provides a useful chart comparing the five sources (the Gospel of Luke in the Bible, *Protoevangelium of James*, the *Infant Story of Thomas*, and *Gospel of Pseudo-Matthew*, and the Qurʾān) regarding Mary and Jesus in the Annunciation story. Although his focus in on Mary and Jesus, his article contains significant material involving Zachariah and John the Baptist as well. See Mourad, *Mary and Jesus*, 13–24.

38. Hone, *Apocryphal New Testament*, 24. *GBM* is also referred as *The Gospel of Pseudo-Matthew*.

39. Hone, *Apocryphal New Testament*, 24.

40. Hone, *Apocryphal New Testament*, 36.

41. Mourad thinks that "these close similarities are proof that the Qurʾān is borrowing canonical and extracanonical material that was used by mainstream Christians." See his essay, "Mary in the Qurʾān," 166.

in the hadith might have served the polemical purpose against unbelievers and persecutors as well as the didactic purpose for encouraging the Muslim community to endure under persecution.

Theological Evaluations

One key point in this chapter is to understand the theological significance of the Zakariya-Yahya pericope in the Islamic narratives and to evaluate it with respect to the biblical theological framework. A naïve assumption would lead one to conclude that these two figures are common in both Scriptures and play the same roles in both Islamic and Christian narratives. This simplistic idea is clearly rejected by the investigation of this study.

First, one has to notice that the two surahs (al-'Imran and Maryam) contain a significant amount of polemics against the Jews and Christians as much as didactic content for the early Muslim community according to most Muslim scholars. This overarching literary context must be considered in interpreting the narratives of Zakariya and Yahya. Several points can be mentioned how these two figures play their roles in this literary context.

Both Zakariya and Yahya are identified to be exemplary prophets in Islam. Zakariya's solemn devotion to Allah is emphasized by his priestly role in the sanctuary and his guardianship over Maryam. Allah answers his petition for a son based on his righteousness. Yahya is born out of this godly heritage and lives with commendable character because of Allah's favorable blessing. Both figures also introduce the narrative of Maryam and 'Isa as a family of 'Imran who is identified as a righteous person in the Q 3:33. From a didactic perspective, they all become moral guides for Muslim communities to imitate. A straightforward lesson is that Allah rewards the righteous as he did to all these righteous people in the Qur'ān.

Moreover, the idea of Allah rewarding the righteous seems to be closely connected to miraculous births on several occasions in the Qur'ān. The birth of Maryam from her pious parents (Anna and 'Imran), the birth of Yahya from Zakariya, and the birth of 'Isa from Maryam together strongly corroborate this principle. This didactic purpose is well demonstrated by the narratives of Zakariya and Yahya.

In addition, the Islamic narrative recounts that Zakariya and Yahya died an innocent death and thus became "Muslim" martyrs for the sake of righteousness. This aspect is especially significant considering the context of the hardships and persecutions that the early Muslim communities were facing. The clear implication for these Muslim communities was to endure to the end by following the examples of these two Muslim martyrs without compromising their faith. The narratives of Zakariya and Yahya certainly serve such a didactic purpose.

On the other hand, one needs to notice the polemical purpose of the two figures in the Islamic narrative. One implicit argument of the Qur'ānic narrative of Zakariya-Yahya and Maryam-'Isa is that both birth accounts jointly deny Christianity's claim of the deity of Jesus. As much as Yahya is a miraculous gift from Allah to Zakariya as a reward for his righteousness, 'Isa is also born of the virgin birth of Maryam by Allah's miraculous intervention. It is argued, however, that the virgin birth of 'Isa does not demonstrate his deity as much as Yahya is not taken to be divine in spite of Allah's miraculous intervention in his birth. This polemical tone in the birth narratives of Yahya/Zakariya and 'Isa/Maryam implicitly flows in the Islamic narrative, and the divine sonship of 'Isa is strongly rejected and condemned in the same surahs, Q3:59–63 and 19:88–96.[42] In this sense, the narrative of Zakariya and Yahya in the Islamic narrative should be taken as a counter-biblical or anti-Christological assertion.

Comparatively speaking, Yahya appears to be less significant than Zakariya in the Qur'ān. Moreover, the Qur'ān supposes that Yahya would become a successor of Zakariya's priestly role after him, but he later turns into an Islamic prophet. This is another subtle, yet very significant, polemical point. Kuschel takes this aspect to be an important theological purpose of surah al-'Imran which is an anti-Jewish polemic when he places this surah within the specific historical occasion in which the Jews in Medina rejected the message of Muhammad.[43] By changing the Jewish priest into an Islamic prophet, this surah might have invited the Jews to accept Islam and the prophethood of Muhammad.

The martyrdom accounts of Zakariya and Yahya also contain a strong polemic nuance against the persecutors of that time, the unbelieving Meccan tribes and the Jews in Medina. The hadiths in narrating the deaths of the two contain a strong emphasis on vengeance for innocent blood.[44] Allah's judgment against the persecutors of Muslims is explicitly mentioned in the latter section of surah al-'Imran (Q3:66–98).

42. Say Maududi, *Introduction to Sura 3*.

43. Kuschel, *Christmas and the Qur'ān*, 67

44. One Hadith vividly records the boiling blood of Yahya until vengeance is

One crucial question in this chapter is whether Zakariya and Yahya in the Islamic narratives carry the same Christological significance as in the biblical-theological framework. At a glance, one may be surprised to find that Yahya's connection to 'Isa is as the one who confirms "a word from Allah" in Q3:37, especially when "a Word of Allah" is taken to mean 'Isa.[45] Some Christians have even tried to identify such designations to 'Isa as "Word" (Q3:39, 45) and "Spirit" (Q21:91; 5:110; 2:253) to validate the deity of 'Isa al-Masih in the Qur'ān in the Christological sense and use this point in their endeavor to present the gospel to Muslims.[46]

However, Muslim scholars do not recognize such a Christological connection between Yahya and 'Isa in the Qur'ān. Although 'Isa is called as "a Word from Allah" in the English translation, the meaning of this phrase is completely different from the Christological term in the Bible, "the Word [*Logos*] of God" (John 1:1–5). Jalalayn's commentary, for example, explains that "a Word of Allah" means 'Isa "being created by a Word of Allah" or 'Isa "the one who brought the Word of Allah to people."[47] Therefore, it must be acknowledged that there is no Christological connection between Yahya and 'Isa in the Qur'ān and within the Islamic narrative. This explains why Yahya appears to be less significant than Zakariya in the Qur'ān. There is no Christological emphasis in the Islamic theology whereas Christology occupies an absolutely importance place in the biblical theology.

---

fulfilled against the people of Israel by a new king named Nebuchadnezzar. See Al-Majlisi, *Hayatul Qulub*, 630.

45. Yusuf Ali indicates that "a Word of Allah" is Jesus Christ in his translation of 3:37 and 3:45. One has to notice two details. First, he does not call 'Isa "the Word of God" so this Word is not the divine Being as in the Bible. Second, the translator uses a capitalized "Word" to distinguish it from the general term, "word." Consequently, this Word becomes a person, but not a divine being. Even in this way, the deity of 'Isa is rejected.

46. For example, Fouad Accad proposes this approach in *Seven Muslim-Christian Principles*. This way of using the Qur'ān for Christian witness to Muslims cannot be validated for the reasons listed in this chapter. Mark Durie argues against this approach: "It is ironic that some well-meaning missionaries take these terms, designed to deny the deity of Christ by pointing to Jesus' ordinariness as a creature, and mistakenly find in them some kind of special honor afforded to Christ by the Qur'ān. Nothing could be further from the truth. These are not marks of distinction, but marks of being common, everyday and ordinary. This is anti-Christian rhetoric. For missionaries tempted to read New Testament categories into the Qur'ānic text where they don't belong, my advice is: don't take the bait." See Durie, "Jesus in the Qur'ān."

47. The Jalalayn commentary on Q 3:39 states that "'Isa is referred to as God's 'Word' because he was created through the word kun 'Be.'" Jalalayn, *Sura al-'Imran*.

In the end, due to the lack of biblical Christology in the Qur'ān, the accounts of Zakariya and Yahya remain solely theocentric in the Islamic narrative.[48] Kuschel summarizes this point well: "The Christologically based 'history of salvation' (the New Testament) is systematically replaced by a theocentric history."[49] His evaluation is correct, and the absence of a Christological lens in the Qur'ān influences how to evaluate all the other biblical figures in the Qur'ān.[50] Therefore, in evaluating biblical figures in the Qur'ān one must remember that the Qur'ān views them only through the theocentric lens at the cost of Christocentric or Christological lens. It may be fair to state, therefore, that biblical figures in the Islamic narratives are introduced primarily for a polemical purpose against the Jews and Christians by reinterpreting their biblical stories.[51]

Concluding Remarks

Understanding biblical figures in the Qur'ān is more complex than it appears. A simple comparison of the two accounts, the Qur'ān and the Bible, based on the assumption that both scriptures talk about the same figures, can cause more misunderstanding than clarification in interactions between the two religious groups. As this study demonstrates, it is imperative to evaluate each biblical figure within its own religious discourse or theological narrative. Using the Christian lens in evaluating biblical figures in the Qur'ān cannot be accepted as a valid approach because the Qur'ān uses these figures and their stories for Islamic theological purposes whether didactic or polemical. Gordon Nickel provides a good snapshot of the Qur'ānic use of the biblical figures, which is worthwhile to quote in this conclusion:

> In the Qur'ān we find a kind of interpretation of Bible stories without any certain awareness of the Bible's contents. Stories

---

48. The theocentric emphasis is supported by the repeated emphasis on Allah's free choice in Q3:6, 33, 40, and 47.

49. Kuschel, *Christmas and the Qur'ān*, 68.

50. One important theological corollary is that the Islamic understanding of a prophet of Allah is completely different from the biblical definition of prophets because of the absence of this Christological perspective in Islam. See Durie, "Rasūlology," essay in this volume..

51. Gordon Nickel and Andrew Rippin note the polemical use of biblical figures in the Qur'ān in their book, *The Islamic World*, 145–56. Mark Durie identifies the Qur'ān's characteristic use of biblical figures as "repurposing." See Durie, *Biblical Reflexes*.

involving biblical characters are told not as if they came from the Bible or could be found in the Bible. The Qur'ān seems to show no actual familiarity with the text of the Bible. The stories are told as if overheard. The stories are often presented in a kind of homiletic fashion, using selected details and differing versions evidently for the teller's own purposes. Some of the details of the Qur'ānic stories are also found in the Bible. Other details are extra-biblical and familiar from rabbinic or apocryphal sources, and some details match no known source.[52]

Bibliography

Accad, Fouad. *Have You Read the Seven Muslim-Christian Principles?* Limassol, Cyprus: Al-Rabitah, 1978.
Al-Jalalayn. *Tafsir Al-Jalalayn.* https://www.altafsir.com/Al-Jalalayn.asp.
Al-Majlisi, Allamah Muhammad Baqir. *Hayatul Qulub.* Vol. 1, *Stories of the Prophets.* Translated by Sayyid Athar Husayn S. H. Rizvi. Qum, Iran: Ansariyan, 2012.
Al-Wahidi, Ali ibn Ahmad. *Asbab al-Nuzul.* Translated by Mokrane Guezzou. Royal Aal al-Bayt Institute for Islamic Thought. Amman, Jordan: Royal Aal al-Bayt Institute for Islamic Thought, 2008.
Ali, Abdullah Yusuf. *The Meaning of the Holy Qur'ān: Complete Translation with Selected Notes.* Leicestershire, UK: The Islamic Foundation, 2015.
Ali, Maulana Muhammad. *The Holy Qur'ān: Arabic Text, English Translation and Commentary.* Rev. ed. Ahmadiyyah Anjuman Isha'at Islam. Lahore, Pakistan: Ahmadiyyah Anjuman Isha'at Islam, 1973.
Badawi, Elsaid M., and Muhammad Abdel Haleem. *Arabic-English Dictionary of Qur'ānic Usage.* Boston, Brill, 2008.
Baker, Elwell W. A., and B. J. Beitzel. "John the Baptist." In *Baker Encyclopedia of the Bible*, 2:1200–1203. Grand Rapids, MI: Baker, 1998.
Blomberg, Craig. *Matthew.* New American Commentary 22. Nashville: Broadman & Holman, 1992.
Droge, A. J. *The Qur'ān: A New Annotated Translation.* Sheffield, UK: Equinox, 2012.
Durie, Mark. "Jesus in the Qur'ān: 'Word' and 'Spirit'?" https://biblicalmissiology.org/2020/10/13/jesus-in-the-Qur'ān-word-and-spirit/.
———. *The Qur'ān and Its Biblical Reflexes: Investigations into the Genesis of a Religion.* Lanham, MD: Lexington, 2018.
Gloton, Maurice. *Jesus Son of Mary in the Qur'ān and According to the Teachings of Ibn Arabi.* Translated by Edin Q. Lohja. Louisville, KY: Fons Vitae, 2016.
Gokkir, Bilal. "Form and Structure of Sura Maryam: A Study from Unity of Sura Perspective." *Review of the Faculty of Divinity, University of Suleyman Demirel* 16 (2006) 7–8.
Hone, William. ed. *The Apocryphal New Testament: Being All the Gospels, Epistles, and Other Pieces Now Extant.* London: William Hone, 1820. Logos Software Program.

---

52. Nickel, "Qur'ānic and Islamic Interpretation," 168–69.

Ibn Kathir. "Surah 3. Al-i'Imran . Ayah 149." https://www.alim.org/quran/tafsir/ibn-kathir/surah/3/149/.

———. "Story of Prophet Zakariyah/Zechariah and Yahya/John." https://www.islamawareness.net/Prophets/zakariyah.html.

———. "Tafsir of Ibn Kathir—Surah 19. Maryam." http://www.alim.org/library/Qur'ān/AlQur'ān-tafsir/TIK/19/0.

Kuschel, Karl-Josef. *Christmas and the Qur'ān*. London: Ginko, 2017.

Mattison, Mark. M. "The Infancy Gospel of James: A Public Domain Translation." https://www.academia.edu/37472926/The_Infancy_Gospel_of_James_A_Public_Domain_Translation.

Maududi, Sayyid Abul Ala. "The Meaning of the Qur'ān: Surah Al-'Imran." https://www.englishtafsir.com/Qur'ān/3/index.html#sdfootnote39anc.

———. "The Meaning of the Qur'ān: Surah Mariam." http://www.englishtafsir.com/Qur'ān/19/index.html;.

Mourad, Suleiman A. "Mary in the Qur'ān: A Reexamination of Her Presentation." In *The Qur'ān in Its Historical Context*, edited by Gabriel Said Reynolds, 163–74. New York: Routledge, 2008.

———. "On the Qur'ānic Stories about Mary and Jesus." *Bulletin of the Royal Institute for Inter-Faith Studies* 1 (1999) 13–24.

Muzammil, H. Siddiqi. "A Thematic Introduction to the Suras of the Qur'ān." https://www.soundvision.com/article/a-thematic-introduction-to-the-surahs-of-the-qur-an#19.

Nickel, Gordon, and Andrew Rippin. *The Islamic World*. New York: Routledge, 2008.

Nickel, Gordon. "Jesus." In *The Wiley Blackwell Companion to the Qur'ān*, edited by Andrew Rippin and Jawid Mojaddedi, 288–302. 2nd ed. Chichester, UK: Wiley, 2017.

———. "Qur'ānic and Islamic Interpretation of the Bible." In *The Oxford Encyclopedia of Biblical Interpretation*, edited by Steven L. McKenzie, 2:167–76. London: Oxford University Press, 2013.

Parrinder, Geoffrey. *Jesus in the Qur'ān*. New York: Barnes & Noble, 1965.

Sahih Muslim. *The Book of Faith*. https://sunnah.com/muslim/1.

Sinai, Nicolai. *The Qur'ān: A Historical-Critical Introduction*. Edinburgh: Edinburgh University Press, 2017.

Stein, R. H. *Luke*. New American Commentary 24. Nashville: Broadman & Holman, 1992.

Tisdall, W. St. Clair. *The Original Sources of the Qur'ān*. London: SPCK, 1905.

Wheeler, Brannon M. *Prophets in the Qur'ān: An Introduction to the Qur'ān and Muslim Exegesis*. New York: Continuum, 2002.

10

Mary/Maryam as a Prophet in the Islamic and Christian Traditions[1]

JACQUELINE HOOVER

MARY/MARYAM[2] IS IMPORTANT IN both Christianity and Islam. But do these religions see her as a prophet? What are the grounds on which they might decide whether she is a prophet? And what implications might follow if she were accepted as a prophet, for example, for the role of women and interfaith relations? In this chapter I want to explore these questions and how they have been addressed historically and in contemporary discussions. In doing so I acknowledge that her role in these two religions is not quite the same, and that the concept of prophecy is not quite the same in them either. But prophecy is important in both religions and, in my view, there is enough common ground to justify such a joint exploration.

---

1. I would like to thank Bill Janzen for his editorial assistance.

2. Mary is the English translation of the Latin Maria. The Arabic name Maryam is a translation of the Hebrew Miriam, rendered in Greek as Mariam.

Maryam as a Prophet in the Islamic Tradition

The question of whether Maryam should be seen as a prophet has long been discussed by Muslim theologians. A key scholar who believed that she was a prophet is Ibn Hazm (d. 1064) from Muslim Spain. He accepted the reference in the Qur'ān, in Surat Al 'Imran (3:45), about Maryam receiving a word from God, as proof that she was a prophet. In his view receiving God's revelations was key but he also looked carefully at what inspiration (*wahy*) consisted of. Not all *wahy* would meet the criteria for prophethood.[3]

For Ibn Hazm, the fact that Maryam was a woman did not disqualify her. He notes that God gave revelations to some women through an angel. On this basis he identifies four women prophets in the Qur'ān, namely, the mothers of Isaac and Moses, Pharaoh's wife, and Maryam.[4] In a modern feminist discussion of the issue, Abboud draws on Ibn Hazm to argue that accepting Maryam as a prophet would empower women to claim leadership roles and give them more confidence.[5]

These views, however, do not reflect majority Muslim opinion, which is that a woman cannot be a prophet. This position is defended by Ibrahim. For him, to receive a revelation from God via an angel is not enough to make one a prophet. He holds that there has to be a message with content including a caution for a particular people;[6] also, the prophet must recognize himself as a prophet and identify himself in public as such.[7] This is difficult for women because of veiling and segregation.[8]

Kaltner and Mirza, who appear to support the view that Maryam was a prophet, argue that she shares characteristics with other prophets. They explain that she was rejected by her people like other prophets when she brought them God's word.[9] Mourad explains that Maryam was given a child and not a message, but he points out that the Qur'ān, in 3:45

---

3. Ibrahim, "Ibn Hazm's Theory of Prophecy," 81, 87; Schleifer, *Mary, the Blessed Virgin*, 83.

4. Ibrahim, "Ibn Hazm's Theory of Prophecy," 82, 89; Schleifer, *Mary, the Blessed Virgin*, 84.

5. Abboud, *Mary in the Qur'ān*, 130–31.

6. Ibrahim, "Ibn Hazm's Theory of Prophecy," 89.

7. Ibrahim, "Ibn Hazm's Theory of Prophecy," 90.

8. Haddad and Smith, "Virgin Mary in Islamic Tradition," 179.

9. Kaltner and Mirza, *Bible and the Qur'ān*, 115.

and 4:171, identifies Jesus as "the word of God."[10] Is that not a message with content? Admittedly, this phrase does not mean sharing an essence with God, as Christians understand it. But there is no doubt that in Islam Jesus is understood as a prophet, in line with other prophets who predict the coming of Muhammad (Q61:6). I would argue that this is a message, that this "word" received by Maryam does have content and that it was given to a people.

One verse in Surat Yusuf (12:109) long used to argue that no woman can be a prophet says: "We did not send forth before you except men."[11] And the word for men here is *rijal*, an Arabic word that excludes women. Ibn Hazm, however, holds that this verse refers only to messengers and not to prophets. He says that the verse was revealed in response to some people who doubted that Muhammad had been sent by God. The doubters had claimed that if God had wanted to communicate with human beings, he would have sent an angel. Ibn Hazm held that this Qur'ānic verse affirmed that God sent human beings, thus supporting the view that Muhammad was a messenger from God.

Even though Ibn Hazm held that the Qur'ān does not exclude the possibility of a woman being a prophet,[12] he, like the majority of Muslim scholars, including Abboud, distinguishes between prophets and messengers. A messenger (*rasūl*) is one who brings a divine law or book, whereas a prophet (*nabī*) is one who warns, repeating what others have already preached. Ibn Hazm then argues that while women can be prophets, they cannot be messengers. Ibrahim, mentioned above, holds that the Qur'ān does not distinguish between prophets and messengers and that women are precluded from both roles.[13]

Another argument that Ibn Hazm uses in favor of seeing Maryam as a prophet is that she received *rizq* (provision) in the *mihrab* (sanctuary). The *mihrab* is the special room where she was taken as a child (see below). To receive *rizq* would be a miracle. Muslims generally distinguish between "miracles" attributed to prophets (*mu'jizat*) and "wonders" attributed to saints (*karamat al-awliya'*). In claiming this miracle for

---

10. Apart from referring to Jesus, Mourad suggests it might also refer to the cause of Maryam's pregnancy: Mourad, "On the Qur'anic Stories," 13–24.

11. Majid Fakhry's (2002) translation of the Qur'ān is used throughout this book chapter for Qur'ānic quotes.

12. Ibrahim, "Ibn Hazm's Theory of Prophecy," 83; Abboud, *Mary in the Qur'ān*, 142; Kaltner, "Muslim Mary," 176; Schleifer, *Mary, the Blessed Virgin*, 75.

13. Ibrahim, "Ibn Hazm's Theory of Prophecy," 82, 85.

Maryam, Ibn Hazm argued that she was not only a saint (*waliyya*) but also a prophet.[14] In contrast to Ibn Hazm, al-Hakim al-Tirmidhi (d. 869) categorized *rizq* as a wonder.[15]

Ibn Hazm also uses the claim that prophets are perfect to support his view that Maryam was a prophet. He quotes the Hadith, "There are many perfect men, but none among women except Maryam, the daughter of 'Imran, and Asiya.'"[16] For Ibn Hazm, this Hadith means that the Prophet intended to say that these two women, Maryam and Asiya, are prophets.[17] In Surat al-Ma'idah (Q5:75), Maryam is referred to as a godly woman (*siddiqa*), as is Asiya. However, Ibrahim again remains unpersuaded. According to him, perfection, or their description as the best for all believers in Surat at-Tahrim (Q66:11–12) does not prove prophecy. For that they would have to be named as prophets in the Qur'ān.

Ibn Hajar al-'Asqalani (d. 1449) also drew on the Hadith, stating that Maryam and Asiya are perfect (*kamal*), and claimed that it expressed something about Maryam and Asiya that went beyond sainthood, that the two must be counted as prophets because they were the only women described as perfect. He added,

> The most perfect type of human beings are prophets, followed by the *awliya'* and then the *siddiqun* [righteous] and the *shuhada'* [martyrs]. And if they [Mary and Asiya] are not to be considered prophetesses, then there is no reason to consider that there exists among women a single saint [*waliyya*], or a righteous one [*siddiqa*], or a martyr [*shahida*]. Yet the reality is that these characteristics are frequently met with amongst women.[18]

Abboud recognizes in Maryam "an important link in a genealogically determined chain of prophets." She sees Jesus' matrilineal name ('Isa, son of Maryam) as proof of her prophethood[19] and identifies prophetic signs (*alamat nubuwwat Maryam*) in her life.[20] Lybarger goes further. He notes that Maryam and Jesus "appear to form a single continuous

---

14. Schleifer, *Mary, the Blessed Virgin*, 74.
15. Winter, "*Pulchra ut Luna*," 452.
16. Ibrahim, "Ibn Hazm's Theory of Prophecy," 95; Schleifer, *Mary, the Blessed Virgin*, 79–80.
17. Schleifer, *Mary, the Blessed Virgin*, 86.
18. Schleifer, *Mary, the Blessed Virgin*, 82.
19. Abboud, *Mary in the Qur'ān*, 134.
20. Abboud, *Mary in the Qur'ān*, 143.

representation" and constitute a "broad, transgendered conception of divine messengership in the Qur'ān."[21] Abboud also identifies "Miriamic" traits of prophecy in Maryam.[22] This refers to Miriam who, in the Hebrew Bible, is the sister of Aaron and Moses and the first named woman prophet (Exodus 15: 20–21), and in the Qur'ān (19:28) as the sister of Harun.

The question of whether Maryam and women more generally can lead others in prayer also enters the discussion. In Surat Al 'Imran (3:43) Maryam is told to, "prostrate yourself and bow down with those who bow down." Muhammad Jamal al-Din al-Qasimi (d. 1914) holds that this means that Maryam can lead others in prayer. He cites the late medieval theologian al-Suyuti (d. 1505) to the effect that "because of Mary, women are qualified to lead prayer."[23] It appears, however, that al-Qasimi believes that this role cannot be opened for women generally. He writes that "women are unfit for continued service in a place of worship because of menstruation and other female conditions."[24] Thanks to Maryam's perfection, however, she could rise above the status of ordinary women and be counted among men.[25]

Obviously, such an interpretation is problematic. If Maryam is presented as an honorary man, she cannot be a role model for contemporary feminists seeking leadership roles in mosques. But the view of Maryam as an honorary male has deep roots. The famous Persian poet al-'Attar (d. 1221 or 1230) even stated, "When a woman becomes a man in the path of God, she is a man and one can no longer call her a woman." Concerning Maryam, al-'Attar noted that "the first *man* to enter paradise would be Mary, the mother of Jesus."[26] Her perfection has allowed her to reach the exalted status of manhood.

In a recent survey on women's leadership within mosques, Maryam is used as a precedent to argue for the permissibility of female prayer leadership. The survey report refers to Ibn 'Arabi (d. 1240) who connected

---

21. Al-Qurtubi (d. 1273) already described Maryam as a sort of hermaphrodite for her to be able to conceive through an angel. Haddad and Smith, "Virgin Mary in Islamic Tradition," 167; Lybarger, "Gender and Prophetic Authority," 249–50, 265. Kecia Ali takes this further and offers a queer reading of Maryam. Ali, "Destabilizing Gender, Reproducing Maternity," 89.

22. Abboud, *Mary in the Qur'ān*, 134.

23. Haddad and Smith, "Virgin Mary in Islamic Tradition," 173.

24. Haddad and Smith, "Virgin Mary in Islamic Tradition," 164.

25. Haddad and Smith, "Virgin Mary in Islamic Tradition," 173.

26. Shaikh, *Sufi Narratives of Intimacy*, 53.

the prophecy of women with such leadership. For Ibn Arabi, the Prophet Muhammad's recognition of perfection in Maryam qualified her as a prophet. According to him, "This perfection is in reference to prophecy, and prophecy is leadership (*imama*), thus a woman's leadership [in prayer] is sound."[27]

Finding historical precedents is important for contemporary Muslim women desiring to see women leaders in mosques. Without precedents, women's leadership will be rejected as innovation (*bid'a*) and as creating a new ritual practice. Yusuf al-Qaradawi (b. 1926), for example, considers Amina Wadud's leading a mixed congregation in prayer in New York in 2006 as an innovation, without precedent, and therefore unacceptable.[28]

Given Ibn Hazm's ideas on the prophethood of women and Maryam in particular, it has been asked whether he was influenced by his context in Muslim Spain and the views of the Zahiri law school which was prevalent there. The Zahiri school gave women a more active role than other law schools. Ibn Hazm, a Zahiri, argued that women should pray in mosques whereas most other schools encouraged women to pray at home.[29]

Was this greater openness on the part of the Zahiris due to their context in Muslim Spain, on the western edge of the Muslim world? It is widely believed that women there had a higher status than in the Muslim east.[30] Ibrahim and Abboud argue this is the reason for more openness to women being prophets in the west. Abboud also argues that the more restrictive context in the east probably influenced Muslim scholars there against Maryam's prophethood.[31] Fierro claims that the status of women in Spain was not higher than elsewhere and that the discussions about the prophethood of women were controversial within the Muslim community in Spain.[32] Instead she wonders whether these discussions helped conversions to Islam in a context where Mary was much valued.[33]

The debate as to whether Maryam was a prophet continues today. Schleifer summarizes aptly, "[Maryam] had the attributes and the

---

27. Elewa and Silvers, "I Am One of the People," 158.
28. Elewa and Silvers, "I Am One of the People," 167–68.
29. Adang, "Reading the Qur'ān," 76–77, 90, 96.
30. Adang, "Reading the Qur'ān," 97.
31. Ibrahim, "Ibn Hazm's Theory of Prophecy," 97; Abboud, *Mary in the Qur'ān*, 134, 138.
32. Fierro, "Women as Prophets in Islam," 184.
33. Fierro, "Women as Prophets in Islam," 193–94.

experiences of prophets, and there is no satisfactory argument against . . . [Maryam's prophecy], [thus] she should be logically classified a prophetess, although this should not be regarded as proven beyond dispute."[34]

Maryam and the Birth of Jesus in the Qur'ān and the Islamic Tradition

Also important for understanding Muslim views of Maryam are the birth narratives in the Qur'ān. Like the New Testament, the Qur'ān has two annunciation accounts. In the first narrative, in Surat Al 'Imran (Q3:35–47), Maryam is described as belonging to the house of 'Imran. When the wife of 'Imran gets pregnant, she consecrates her unborn child (Maryam) to God and asks God to protect the child. A well-known Hadith relates the answer to her request: "Every child that is born, is touched by Satan, and this touch makes it cry, except Maryam and her son." This Hadith has been used to form the later Islamic doctrine of impeccability (*'isma*—immunity from error or sin) of Maryam, Jesus, and prophets in general.[35]

According to this narrative, Maryam, while still a small child is placed in a special room in the sanctuary (*mihrab*). Only Zachariah has access to her, and he takes care of her. He is surprised to find her with provisions (*rizq*). In verse 42, Maryam is described as chosen, purified and preferred over womankind. Some medieval scholars assumed the purity referred to Maryam's total devotion to God. Others applied it to physical purity (*tahara*) and to an absence of menstrual blood and postpartum bleeding.[36] Scholars also discussed if the preference was meant for her time only or for all times. Verse 43 enjoins Maryam to prostrate and bow down. Interpreted as a reference to prayer, this underlines her ritual purity since menstruating women do not pray.[37]

34. Schleifer, *Mary, the Blessed Virgin*, 94.

35. The Islamic notion of sinlessness is less precise, and sin is perceived differently, than in Christianity. Haddad and Smith, "Virgin Mary in Islamic Tradition," 172.

36. Maryam's spiritual and physical purity is also linked to Fatima, the Prophet's daughter, and the two are often compared. McAuliffe, "Chosen of All Women," 27; Pierce, *Twelve Infallible Men*, 117–20; Sered, "Rachel, Mary, and Fatima," 136–37. Fatima is named Maryam al-Kubra (the Greater Maryam). Haddad and Smith, "Virgin Mary in Islamic Tradition," 180. Fatima is especially important for Twelver Shiites because she links the Prophet with the Imamate. Pierce, *Twelve Infallible Men*, 120. An Iranian film made in 2000 celebrates Maryam's life from a Muslim respective, *Saint Mary: Maryam al-Muqaddassah* by Shahriar Bahrani. See Speelman, "Iranian Religious Films."

37. Kaltner, *Ishmael Instructs Isaac*, 215.

In verse 45, an angel announces a word to Maryam and tells her that she will have a son and that he will be prominent. She responds by questioning how she can have a child when she has not been touched by any man? Her response is similar to her response in the New Testament.[38] The Qur'ān states, in verse 47, that God does whatever he pleases: "He simply says to it 'Be', and it comes to be." Jesus is created by the word of God. This is similar to the creation of Adam.

The second annunciation narrative is in Surat Maryam (19:16–29). Here, Maryam withdraws to an eastern place and screens herself. While some exegetes as Ibn Kathir (d. 1373) interpret this as her totally dedicating herself to God, others interpret it as Maryam putting on a veil (*hijab*) or even a face-veil (*niqab*).[39] When all alone the spirit of God appears to her in the form of a well-shaped human and announces to her "a boy most pure." Just like in Surat Al 'Imran, she responds, "Shall I have a boy, when no man has touched me and I have not been an unchaste woman?"

Upon hearing this news, she, according to this second narrative, withdraws to a distant place where she delivers the child under a palm tree. In pain she cries out and wishes to die. A miraculous voice then tells her to shake the palm tree and eat the dates that fall down. This unidentified voice is interpreted to refer either to Jesus or to Muhammad.[40] Then she is told to take a vow of silence.[41] After returning to her people who address her as sister of Aaron, she is accused of being unchaste, but the newborn Jesus speaks up to defend her.

Mary as a Prophet in the Christian Tradition

In Christianity the discussion about Mary has not focused as much on whether she is a prophet. What stands out is a deep veneration and devotion toward her. This appeared in the early years of the faith and has continued into the modern era, at least among Catholic and Orthodox

---

38. Kaltner and Mirza, *Bible and the Qur'ān*, 113.
39. Haddad and Smith, "Virgin Mary in Islamic Tradition," 166.
40. Kaltner and Mirza, *Bible and the Qur'ān*, 114–15.
41. Maryam's submission and great devotion to God shown in her retreat east away from her people and her vow to a fast of silence inspired Muslim mystics. Lamrabet, *Women in the Qur'ān*, 87; Cornell, *Rabi'a from Narrative to Myth*, 154. The famous Sufi woman saint Rabi'a al-'Adawiyya (d. 801) was compared to Maryam on account of her chastity, her divine election, and her complete trust in God. Cornell, *Rabi'a from Narrative to Myth*, 293.

Christians. This is evident in statues, shrines, pilgrimage sites, icons, feast days, artwork, hymns, music, and in innumerable churches and other institutions with names such as Notre Dame . . . or "Our Lady of . . ." One illustration of this is "Our Lady of Guadeloupe," who has long had a central role in the culture of Mexico.

There are biblical grounds for this veneration of Mary. One such ground comes from the way Mary responded positively when the angel Gabriel told her that she was pregnant by the Holy Spirit and would bear the Savior (Luke 1:26–38). By her willingness, it is said, she became the primary participant in the incarnation of God and in the process of human redemption. Another basis comes from her role in having Jesus perform his first miracle, at the wedding at Cana, where he turned water into wine (John 2). The third and strongest basis for the devotion to her comes from the scene at the crucifixion of Jesus where he asks Mary to accept a "disciple whom he loved" as her son, and also asks that disciple to accept Mary as his mother (John 19:26). The implication of this, as interpreted by Catholic and Orthodox Christians, is that Jesus was asking Mary to care for all Christians, and also asking Christians to look to her for care and protection. A fourth biblical ground is in the Acts of the Apostles (1:14), where Mary is seen to be praying with a group of believers.

The Catholic and Orthodox churches have developed significant doctrines in support of the devotion to Mary.[42] The four most commonly cited doctrines are her immaculate conception, her description as the Mother of God, her perpetual virginity, and her bodily assumption into heaven. Critics have argued that these go beyond what the Bible teaches, that they owe more to the non-canonical Protevangelium of James, written late in the second century.[43] Protestantism, which emerged in the sixteenth century, tended to argue that the focus on Mary detracted from the more central person of Jesus and rejected it as unbiblical.[44] The Second Vatican Council in the mid-1960s also reduced Marian devotion among Catholics in the global north. But elsewhere it continues.

This discussion of Mary's large and important role in the Christian world does not yet address the question of whether she is a prophet. For that we need to look elsewhere. One important ground for claiming that

---

42. For differences between Orthodox and Catholic beliefs on Mary see Cunningham, *Gateway of Life*, 176–87.

43. Elliott, "Christian Apocrypha," 2–3.

44. Radford, *Feminine Face of the Church*, 1.

she is a prophet appears in the Magnificat (Latin for Mary's Song) in the Gospel of Luke 1:46–55, part of which reads:

> He has shown strength with his arm,
> he has scattered the proud in the imagination of their hearts,
> he has put down the mighty from their thrones,
> and exalted those of low degree;
> he has filled the hungry with good things,
> and the rich he has sent empty away.

Here, Mary, while she is pregnant with Jesus, sings a prophetic song with a strong social justice emphasis that connects with the Hebrew Bible. Mary could not have sung this way if she had not known her people's scriptures and their history. Also noteworthy is that in Luke's Gospel, first written in Greek, her name was Miriam.[45] This connects her to her ancestor, Miriam, the sister of Aaron, who had a prophetic role of her own (see Exod 20–21).

But why did Luke then not refer to Mary as a prophet explicitly? Even the account of her annunciation is similar to the annunciation accounts of ancient Hebrew prophets. Croy and Conner argue that Luke refrained from calling her a prophet because of her virginity.[46] The Greek-Roman world in which Luke wrote connected prophecy and virginity with "ecstatic possession." Because this possession could have "sexual connotations"[47] Luke wanted to make sure that Mary's conception by the Holy Spirit was not misunderstood as sexual or as a situation where she was overpowered against her will.[48] It is also possible that Luke refrained because in early Christianity prophecy was perceived as a divine gift that could be given by the Holy Spirit to anyone. It was not to be seen as only for elite people serving at sacred sites.[49]

Sometime later, when paganism was in decline and the issue of "ecstatic possession" had lost its sensitivity, many of the early church fathers did describe Mary as a prophet and a virgin. Eusebius (d. 339/340), for example, called her a prophet and identified her with the prophetess in Isa 7:14 or 8:3.[50] For Luke, "Mary is a virgin (explicitly) and a prophet

---

45. Good, "What Does It Mean," 100–102.
46. Croy and Conner, "Mantic Mary?," 261.
47. Croy and Conner, "Mantic Mary?," 265.
48. Croy and Conner, "Mantic Mary?," 260, 271.
49. Croy and Conner, "Mantic Mary?," 266.
50. Croy and Conner, "Mantic Mary?," 270–71.

(implicitly), but she does not seem to be a virgin *because* she is a prophet, nor vice versa." Even though Luke does not name Mary as a prophet, he describes her as carrying "prophetic speech."[51]

These ideas in favor of seeing Mary as a prophet are welcomed by feminist Catholic theologians who have long argued against the exclusive emphasis on her as a devout virgin and mother.[52] Now they can emphasize her prophetic ethical voice in the Magnificat in speaking justice to power. Instead of describing Mary only as submitting to God, they see her as cooperating with God for the purpose of social justice.[53] This allows them to claim Mary in a new way.

This leads to the conclusion that in Christianity, as in Islam, there are good grounds for accepting Mary/Maryam as a prophet even though neither religion makes that affirmation in a definitive way.

Marian Spirituality as a Shared Ground and as a Point of Difference

Since Mary/Maryam is important in both religions, though not in quite the same way, it raises the question of whether there is a shared spirituality. One shared area may lie in a common source, namely the above mentioned non-canonical Protevangelium of James. It's stories about Mary's parents, her birth, her upbringing and her presentation in the sanctuary appear to be echoed in the Qur'ān, in Surat Al 'Imran.[54] But the Protevangelium of James also refers to Mary's immaculate conception and her perpetual virginity which were accepted as important particularly by the Catholic and Orthodox churches.

There are more contemporary developments that also suggest a shared spirituality. In Egypt, in April 1968, apparitions of Mary appeared above a church dome in Zeitoun, a district of Cairo. The apparitions continued periodically for two years. It was a time of national stress. It was only ten months since the Egyptian defeat in the Six-Day War with Israel. There were tensions between Christians and Muslims. But these apparitions, seen by both Christians and Muslims brought thousands of people,

---

51. Croy and Conner, "Mantic Mary?," 271.

52. See Armanios, "'Virtuous Woman,'" 125–27 for a discussion of Coptic women and their relationship with Mary.

53. Llywelyn, "Mary and Mariology," 32–33.

54. Mourad, "On the Qur'ānic Stories," 13,17; Elliott, "Christian Apocrypha," 2–3.

from both faiths, together. Mary was welcomed as a caring mother giving hope, peace, and unity, even though each community appropriated her in their own way.[55]

For the Christians of Egypt these apparitions confirmed an historic relationship of Mary with their homeland.[56] After the birth of Jesus, the Holy Family fled to Egypt (Matt 2:13–15). According to tradition, the family stayed for several years, traveling through the country and blessing many places. One such place is in Matariyya, close to Zeitoun, where an old sycamore tree, known as "Maryam's Tree," is thought to have sheltered the Holy Family from the sun. The site attracts many visitors, especially barren Muslim and Christian women.[57] Mary is seen as a symbol of fertility in popular Muslim piety. Surat Maryam is recited by women struggling to conceive. It is also recited during pregnancy, childbirth and for blessing a mother and her new-born baby.[58]

Another kind of common ground between the two religions appeared in Lebanon, in 2010 when the government made the feast of the annunciation on March 25th a national holiday. For the inauguration of this holiday the Lebanese singer Tania Kassis sang the Ave Maria accompanied by the Adhan (Muslim call to prayer).[59] Much loved, her "Islamo-Christian Ave Maria" brought many Muslims and Christians together and was used to promote national unity in Lebanon. Also in Lebanon, but at a different level, a judge in February 2018, ordered three young Muslim men to memorize verses about Maryam and Jesus from Surat Al 'Imran because they had insulted Christianity. The judge saw Maryam as a bridge and thought this would teach them to become more tolerant and more appreciative of Christianity.[60]

---

55. Nelson, "Virgin of Zeitoun," 9–11; Hearden, "Lessons from Zeitoun," 416–18. More recent apparitions in Assiut and Warraq have not brought Muslims and Christians together as in Zeitoun. Hassan, "Egypt." The 2011 film *La Vierge, les Coptes et moi* ("the Virgin, the Copts and Me"), part comedy, part documentary, directed by the French-Egyptian Namir Abdel Messeeh, investigates Marian apparitions.

56. Heo explores the connection between Mary and Egypt as an Arab Holy Land. Heo, *Political Lives of Saints*, 82.

57. Nelson, "Virgin of Zeitoun," 9.

58. Demiri, "Mary in the Qur'an," May 2, 2017.

59. "Islamo-Christian Ave Maria," http://teachmideast.org/articles/ave-maria-performance-accompanied-by-the-islamic-call-to-prayer/. This is from the 2012 performance in Paris.

60. See "Lebanese Judge Orders."

In addition, there are instances where Christians have sought to use Mary to their advantage in relations with Muslims. After the reconquest of Spain was completed in 1492, many mosques were converted into churches and dedicated to Mary because her body was seen as a bridge for converting sacred space.[61] Also, for many centuries, Mary was invoked to support Christians who were captured by Muslim armies and forced into slavery, to help them resist conversion to Islam.[62] She has been invoked in missions in efforts to persuade Muslims to convert to Christianity. The famous *Cantigas de Santa Maria*, a late thirteenth century collection of poems, tells the story (Cantiga 46) of a Muslim who promises to consider converting to Christianity if he would witness a miracle. As he looks at an icon of Mary with her child, she starts to lactate. In response, he converts immediately.[63] In the nineteenth century, Catholic missionaries in the Middle East believed that their devotion to Mary provided a common ground that might help draw Muslims to their faith. In contrast Protestants saw it as a hindrance and thought that they were closer to Muslims on account of their rejection of icons and focus on the Scriptures alone. This applied especially to Presbyterians.[64]

It can also be noted that in the eleventh and twelfth centuries when Christians and Muslims were fighting in Spain, the Christians sometimes invoked Mary as a protector in battle. At times they even claimed to see her participating actively in the fighting on their side. This view of Mary coming to the aid of Christians in war goes back at least to the fifth century when Byzantine Christians invoked Mary for military victory against enemies.[65] It has also resurfaced in recent years as some websites and blogs appear to encourage Catholics to pray to "Our Lady of Victory" and recite the rosary in order to defeat Islamic terrorism.[66]

---

61. Remensnyder, "Colonization of Sacred Architecture," 193–99.
62. Remensnyder, "Christian Captives, Muslim Maidens," 656.
63. Holt, "Cantigas de Santa María," 223–24; George-Tvrtković, *Christians, Muslims, and Mary*, 98–99.
64. George-Tvrtković, *Christians, Muslims, and Mary*, 148–49.
65. George-Tvrtković, *Christians, Muslims, and Mary*, 19–26.
66. George-Tvrtković, *Christians, Muslims, and Mary*, 72.

Conclusion

It must be noted that even though Mary/Maryam has a substantial role in both Christianity and Islam and even though there are good grounds in both religions for accepting her as a prophet, in neither faith is she the central figure. She is secondary in Christianity to Jesus, and in Islam she is eclipsed by the Muslim women of the early Islamic community who fit the Islamic model of womanhood to a greater degree.[67] A Hadith notes, "The women of Quraish are the best of those who ride camels, . . . and Mary never rode a camel."[68] While Muslims scholars interpreted this in various ways, it does point out that Maryam lived in a different time and place. But instead of this being a negative factor, it may make interreligious dialogue focused on her more productive and less divisive than if it is focused on the central figures. So, what might interreligious dialogue focused on Mary lead to?

First, a focus on Mary the prophet can bring Muslims and Christians together to talk about a deeply honored woman we share in our scriptures. A focus on her prophecy can broaden and deepen these discussions to include contemporary concerns relevant to all, Muslims and Christians.

Second, Mary the prophet has an ethical voice and a message for the world. This ethical voice challenges Christians and Muslims to submit to God and work for social justice to empower the poor. For Christians, a focus on Mary the prophet with an ethical voice can bring Christians from all denominations together. A focus on Mary the prophet reduces a focus on the doctrinal beliefs which separate Christians, and the Christian witness can become more unified.

Third, a focus on Mary the prophet challenges the image of Mary as the embodiment of a perfectly submissive woman. Catholic and Orthodox Christians and Muslim women often have difficulty taking Mary as a model inasmuch as her perfection and purity place her beyond the lives of ordinary woman. Mary the prophet circumvents this to some degree. It also challenges Protestant Christians to take her more seriously.

Fourth, Mary the prophet has great potential to bring Muslim and Christian women together by inspiring them to lead active lives in the faith, opening the door for leadership roles within the mosque and the church.

---

67. Additionally, Takács compares Mary in Christianity to the Prophet Muhammad as bearers of God's Word in his article. Takács, "Mary and Muhammad."

68. Schleifer, *Mary, the Blessed Virgin*, 75.

Fifth, Mary the prophet challenges Muslim and Christian men to listen to her ethical voice. Mary the prophet deepens belief in God who is beyond human understanding and uses all people to point to his love for the world and humankind.

Bibliography

Abboud, Hosn. *Mary in the Qur'ān: A Literary Reading.* London: Routledge, 2013.
Adang, Camilla. "Reading the Qur'ān with Ibn Ḥazm: The Question of the Sinlessness of the Prophets." In *Controverses sur les Écritures canoniques de l'Islam*, edited by Daniel De Smet and Mohammed Ali Amir-Moezzi, 269–95. Paris: Les Éditions du Cerf, 2014.
Ali, Kecia. "Destabilizing Gender, Reproducing Maternity: Mary in the Qur'ān." *Journal of International Qur'ānic Studies Association* 2 (2017) 89–109.
Armanios, Febe. "The 'Virtuous Woman': Images of Gender in Modern Coptic Society." *Middle East Studies* 38.1 (2002) 110–30.
Cornell, Rkia Elaroui. *Rabi'a from Narrative to Myth: The Many Faces of Islam's Most Famous Woman Saint, Rabi'a al-'Adawiyya.* London: Oneworld Academic, 2019.
Croy, Clayton N., and Alice E. Conner. "Mantic Mary? The Virgin Mother as Prophet in Luke 1.26–56 and the Early Church." *Journal for the Study of the New Testament* 34.3 (2011) 254–76.
Cunningham, Mary B. *Gateway of Life: Orthodox Thinking on the Mother of God.* Yonkers, NY: St Vladimir's Seminary Press, 2015.
Demiri, Lejla. "Mary in the Qur'ān." *L'Osservatore Romano*, July 20, 2018.
Elewa, Ahmed, and Laury Silvers. "I Am One of the People: A Survey and Analysis of Legal Arguments on Women-Led Prayer in Islam." *Journal of Law and Religion* 26.1 (2010–11) 141–71.
Elliott, J. K. "Christian Apocrypha and the Developing Role of Mary." *The Oxford Handbook of Early Christian Apocrypha*, edited by Andrew Gregory et al., 1–23. Oxford Handbooks in Religion and Theology. Oxford: Oxford University Press, 2015. DOI: 10.1093/oxfordhb/9780199644117.013.38.
Fakhry, Majid, trans. *An Interpretation of the Qur'ān: English Translation of the Meaning, a Bilingual Edition.* 2000. Reprint, Reading, Berkshire: Garnet, 2002.
Fierro, Maribel. "Women as Prophets in Islam." In *Writing the Feminine: Women in Arab Sources*, edited by Manuela Marin and Randi Deguilhen, 183–98. London: Tauris, 2002.
George-Tvrtković, Rita. *Christians, Muslims, and Mary: A History.* New York: Paulist, 2018.
Good, Deirdre. "What Does It Mean to Call Mary Mariam?" In *A Feminist Companion to Mariology*, edited by Amy-Jill Levine with Maria Mayo Robbins, 99–106. London: T. & T. Clark International, 2005.
Haddad, Yvonne Y., and Jane I. Smith. "The Virgin Mary in Islamic Tradition and Commentary." *The Muslim World* 29.3–4 (1989) 161–87.
Hassan, Amro. "Egypt: Is It the Virgin Mary or Just a Curious Flash of Light?" *Los Angeles Times*, December 15, 2009. https://latimesblogs.latimes.com/

babylonbeyond/2009/12/egypt-people-turn-to-holy-phenomenon-in-times-of-crisis-.html.

Hearden, Maura. "Lessons from Zeitoun: A Marian Proposal for Christian-Muslim Dialogue." *Journal of Ecumenical Studies* 47.3 (2012) 409–26.

Heo, Angie. *The Political Lives of Saints: Christian-Muslim Mediation in Egypt*. Oakland: University of California Press, 2018.

Holt, Edward Lawrence. "Cantigas de Santa María, Cantigas de Cruzada: Reflections of Crusading Spirituality in Alfonso X's Cantigas de Santa Maria." *Al-Masaq: Journal of the Medieval Mediterranean* 27.3 (2015) 207–24.

Ibrahim, Zakyi M. "Ibn Hazm's Theory of Prophecy of Women: Literalism, Logic and Perfection." *Intellectual Discourse* 23.1 (2015) 75–100.

Kaltner, John. *Ishmael Instructs Isaac: An Introduction to the Qur'ān for Bible Readers*. Collegeville, MN: Liturgical, 1999.

———. "The Muslim Mary." In *New Perspectives on the Nativity*, edited by Jeremy Corley, 165–79. London: Bloomsbury, 2009.

Kaltner, John, and Younus Y. Mirza. *The Bible and the Qur'ān: Biblical Figures in the Islamic Tradition*. London: Bloomsbury, 2018.

Lamrabet, Asma. *Women in the Qur'ān: An Emancipatory Reading*. Markfield, UK: Square View, 2016.

"Lebanese Judge Orders 3 Muslims to Memorize Qur'an Verses Hailing Mary, Jesus." *Al Arabiya English*, February 11, 2018. https://english.alarabiya.net/en/variety/2018/02/11/Lebanese-judge-orders-3-Muslims-to-memorize-Qur'an-verses-hailing-Mary-Jesus.html.

Llywelyn, Dorian. "Mary and Mariology." In *Oxford Handbooks Online*. N.p.: n.p., 2016. DOI: 10.1093/oxfordhb/9780199935420.013.62

Lybarger, Loren D. "Gender and Prophetic Authority in the Qur'ānic Story of Maryam: A Literary Approach." *The Journal of Religion* 80.2 (2000) 240–70.

McAuliffe, Jane. "Chosen of All Women: Mary and Fatima in Qur'ānic Exegesis." *Islamochristiana* 7 (1981) 19–28.

Mourad, Suleiman A. "On the Qur'ānic Stories about Mary and Jesus." *Bulletin of the Royal Institute for Inter-Faith Studies* 1.2 (1999) 13–24.

Nelson, Cynthia. "The Virgin of Zeitoun." *Worldview* (1973) 5–11.

Pierce, Matthew. *Twelve Infallible Men: The Imams and the Making of Shi'ism*. Cambridge, MA: Harvard University Press, 2016.

Radford Ruether, Rosemary. *The Feminine Face of the Church*. London: SCM, 1979.

Remensnyder, Amy G. "Christian Captives, Muslim Maidens, and Mary." *Speculum* 82.3 (2007) 642–77.

———. "The Colonization of Sacred Architecture: The Virgin Mary, Mosques, and Temples in medieval Spain and Early Sixteenth-Century Mexico." In *Monks & Nuns, Saints & Outcasts: Religion in Medieval Society*, edited by Sharon Farmer and Barbara H. Rosenwein, 189–219. Ithaca, NY: Cornell University Press, 2000.

Schleifer, Aliah. *Mary, the Blessed Virgin of Islam*. 3rd ed. Louisville, KY: Fons Vitae, 2008.

Sered, Rachel. "Rachel, Mary, and Fatima." *Cultural Anthropology* 6.2 (1991) 131–46.

Shaikh, Sa'diyya. *Sufi Narratives of Intimacy: Ibn 'Arabi, Gender, and Sexuality*. Chapel Hill: The University of North Carolina Press, 2012.

Speelman, M. Gé. "Iranian Religious Films and Inter-Religious Understanding." *Exchange* 41 (2012) 165–98.

Stowasser, Barbara Freyer. *Women in the Qur'an, Traditions, and Interpretations.* Oxford: Oxford University Press, 1994.

Takács, Axel. "Mary and Muhammad: Bearers of the Word—Their Roles in Divine Revelation." *Journal of Ecumenical Studies* 48.2 (2013) 220–43.

Winter, Tim. "*Pulchra ut Luna*: Some Reflections on the Marian Theme in Muslim-Catholic Dialogue." *Journal od Ecumenical Studies* 36.3–4 (1999) 439–69.

www.ingramcontent.com/pod-product-compliance
Lightning Source LLC
Chambersburg PA
CBHW051738230426
43670CB00012B/2067